Walk Carefully
Around
the Dead

WALK CAREFULLY
AROUND
THE DEAD

PAIGE COTHREN

Walk Carefully Around the Dead

Copyright 1998 by Paige Cothren

Cothren, Paige
     Walk Carefully Around the Dead

ISBN 0-9667072-0-6

Second Printing

Published by Paige Cothren
Owned by The University of Mississippi Alumni Association,
M-Club Alumni Chapter.

Playing football for the Ole Miss Rebels

from Nineteen Forty-Seven until the mid Nineteen-

Sixties manifested an antithesis in its purest form:

On one hand, a dormitory filled with healthy,

virile, testosterone-laden, extremely energetic young

men -- and on the other hand --

WOBBLE DAVIDSON,

whose calling summoned him to challenge, to control,

and to funnel all these attributes into the classroom

and on to the playing field. For the players, this con-

trast was like driving a high-powered race car, one foot

on the accelerator, one on the brake pedal,

and both on the floorboard!

~ Paige Cothren

"FRESHMEN --

Do what I tell you to do.

Put your trust in no man.

And walk carefully around the dead ...

and you might make it here

at Ole Miss!"

~ Wobble Davidson
To every freshman team he coached

CONTENTS

PREFACE

WHAT IS IT ABOUT Y'ALL?

In August, Nineteen Ninety-Five, about thirty ex- Ole Miss football players were eating lunch, following the annual M-Club Golf Tournament, around three tables under the big oak trees behind the University Golf Course Club House. We were waiting for the M-Club meeting to begin. All of us had slaved (or so we thought then) for Coach John Vaught and his staff. Wobble Davidson had been our Freshman Coach. Like verbal paint cast against an abstract canvas, the stories were flying and our laughter was deep. It must have been easy to tell how attached to one another we are after all the years, how much we esteem each other still, how much we enjoyed our years at Ole Miss. A preponderance of the tales were "Wobbleisms", a name genesised from innumerable recitings of Wobble's humorous statements and exploits.

About fifty other M-Club athletes were in attendance, most of whom seemed to be conscious of the story telling and subsequent laughter, although we were notoriously unconscious of their consciousness.

A huge, and much younger, former Ole Miss tackle walked over to our table and listened to a few of the tales. Then, with a somber expression on his face he asked, "Paige, what is it about all you guys who played here in the Fifties and early Sixties? After all these years you still seem to be so close to one another. What causes that? My teammates don't seem to be close at all compared to you. When we do get together, like this weekend, we don't have nearly as much fun as y'all do."

Several fellows in our group ventured an answer. I hope the following pages will confer the answer to you. The men who played football for the Ole Miss Rebels from Nineteen Forty-Seven until the mid Nineteen Sixties were special. But we were made special, not for whom we were or are, but by whom we were coached.

WARNING — IT'S A LITTLE RISQUE

Please be advised that many of the tales contain risque language. These stories lose their humor when truth becomes distorted, for whatever reason. At the time, none of us labeled the language of the coaches nor of the players bawdy, but even so, the events herein recorded never occurred in the presence of women. In fact, in researching the material for this book, I was astounded to discover that Sara Davidson had never even heard the stories about her husband which contained lascivious language, Wobble having shielded her from the knowledge all these years. Other wives of Vaught's staff members have expressed the same thing, one being my own precious Aunt, Anna Poole who, at this writing, passed away only four months ago. Once when I inadvertently stated that her husband, my Uncle Buster, had sought to modify my behavior with a few words of profanity, she challenged me. It appeared that she knew nothing about it, so I elected not to debate the issue with her. In plainer yet more intelligent words, I dropped the subject in a hurry.

WHERE THE TESTOSTERONE FREELY FLOWED

Football in the afore-mentioned years was a very masculine sport. It still is —, but I think it was a little more rugged back then. (The following information will elucidate that statement). Football players prided themselves on BEING tough and to some degree, in TALKING tough. Such was the athletic culture in which we lived. Though most of the players had probably never heard of testosterone, football and its coaching provided an arena upon which it was certainly allowed to freely flow, and it's reflected in the language which, in order to preserve truth, has been herein recorded, though coded.

Many of the words, therefore, which refer to different members and/or functions of the human body have been abbreviated simply by stating the first and last letters and substituting dashes (—-) for all the letters in between. If in doing that I failed to alleviate the offense, please forgive me. If, in so doing, I camouflaged the actual word beyond recognition, your children or grandchildren can probably decipher it for you.

I hope, in spite of possible offense, you will treasure this work, certainly not because of the author, but due rather to the content—and its purpose — an attempt, however feeble, to preserve a long-past athletic culture, and to honor the coaches and players, who with these events and thousands more, built a foundation upon which that honor might, in glory, rest.

INTRODUCTION

W hen my son Jay, who at this writing is thirty-six years of age, was a student at Liberty University, he exclaimed one day, "Dad, the Fifties must have been a great time to be in college." I enthusiastically agreed.

I was a student at Ole Miss from Nineteen Fifty-Three to Nineteen Fifty-Seven, as were many others whose memories are recorded in this book. (Some who contributed narratives attended Ole Miss in the late Nineteen Forties. A few graduated in the mid Sixties.) All of us played football at Ole Miss. All of us spent our first year under J.W. "Wobble" Davidson and graduated to Coach John Vaught's staff, comprised of Buster Poole, my beloved uncle; Bruiser Kinard; Junie Hovious; John Cain; trainer Doc Knight; Head scout Tom Swaze; Ray Poole, another beloved uncle who joined the staff in Nineteen Fifty-Five; and Country Graham, who assisted Wobble with the freshman. Billy "Nub" Sanders, loved by all of us, served as equipment manager. Tad Smith was our Director of Athletics.

Before Coach Vaught and his staff got us however, Wobble had to finish with us. Or to put it another way, we had to go through Wobble to get to Coach Vaught and his staff, and at the time that wasn't all that easy. In retrospect though, it was hilarious.

It was hilarious in part because of the culture in Southern America after World War II, a society which had never existed before and will probably never exist again, for several reasons. And it was hilarious in part because of the coaches for whom we played, beginning with Wobble. Wobble and the coaches will be examined later, the culture now.

A NEW WORLD

World War II ended in Nineteen Forty-Five and this nation mutated into a *Neos Kosmos*, a New World, of celebration and ecstasy. Fear acquiesced to joy, and love of life, which many doubted they would ever experience again, suddenly erupted. The negativism produced by more than four years of war yielded to positivism, a belief that life would get better. With the G.I. Bill and other Federal Aid programs, higher education became a possibility for many young Americans and college became a center for the positivism. "Bring on the good times," we all expected. "I'm a lover not a fighter," became as much a by-word in peace as "Kilroy was here," had been in war. Parties and dancing replaced the battleground. Nowhere was this seen more clearly than in the big dances which focalized college life in those years, featuring big bands and "on stage" singers.

Each fall the night before registration for classes, Ole Miss sponsored a street dance on the square in Oxford featuring one of those big bands stationed on a platform stage immediately south of the Courthouse. All the students came. On the platform with the band sat three men, each of whom reported on his respective area of responsibility: Chancellor John Williams welcomed the student-body back to Ole Miss and Oxford; Coach Vaught expounded on the football team; And Blind Jim Ivey spoke to the newcomers.

Blind Jim, as he was lovingly called, declared himself to be "Dean of the Freshman." He was black and he was blind, and he was a very special part of our University when few blacks were...! The crowd hushed when, with the aid of his walking cane and led by a freshman, he shuffled to the microphone. "Freshman, I am Blind Jim. I am Dean of the Freshman Class an' I be'n to ever' Ole Miss football game since Nineteen-o-One and I ain't ne'er SEEN the Rebels get beat." With that proclamation of compulsory truth, the students roared, the band played, dancing commenced, and school officially began. Bleary eyes greeted the professors the following morning at the registration tables.

College life from Nineteen Forty-Six until the mid-Sixties was an exciting yet simple life. Almost all the students lived on the campus in dormitories or fraternity/sorority houses. Almost all of us knew each other if not by name, at least by sight. Campus crime was almost non-existent and social problems were few, so students' pranks, it seemed, were expected as part of college life, and unless serious property damage resulted, faculty leadership endured them. Panty raids, for example, drew snickers from almost everyone on or off campus, and the same was true at other colleges too, even Mississippi State.

In Nineteen Fifty-Seven several carloads of students traveled to State to see the Bulldog/Ole Miss basketball game. I was among them. When we came out of the gym after the game we discovered one of our cars missing. Somebody looked up and found it. State students, apparently, had confiscated a large crane and deposited the automobile on top of a one-story flat-top building nearby. Obligingly, Campus Security retrieved it for us and we all went merrily back to Oxford, after a quick detour by the "Crossroads" for a few beers. Everyone from Ole Miss and State, including the State Campus Police thought the dastardly deed was funny. Today someone would probably be arrested and lawsuits filed. Then, it was viewed as an innocent and not unexpected prank. "Mark one up for the Rednecks!," someone from Ole Miss exclaimed, "We'll get 'em back." And we did, a few years later when some Ole Miss students stole Bully, the State bulldog mascot, an account to be reviewed later in this work.

College society in those years, from Nineteen Forty-Six until the mid-sixties was as I mentioned, simple. Life at Ole Miss consisted of classes, parties, football games, parties, basketball games, parties, baseball games, and parties at Sardis Lake. Oxford offered very little nefarious activity, and other than an occasional dance or concert at Fulton Chapel neither did the University. Television had yet to assault the South and escape routes to Memphis roller-coastered up and down and around and around, discouraging all but the most venturous from a weeknight challenge, if not a weekend one. Few students owned cars anyway. Many young ladies were sent to school at Ole Miss in part because there was no Crossroads, that infamous juke-joint positioned between Starkville and what was then M.S.C.W.

College life in those days was simple for another reason too. Its purpose was clearly discernable. The college campus was a place to receive an education, to enjoy life, and to learn to establish independence. Now, most students achieve independence at some point in high school, but in those years it usually occurred at college. Independence meant that the little bird was pushed out of the nest and must learn to fly all on its own. However, college life assumed new purposes in the late Nineteen Sixties, for better or worse. College lost its innocence and college campuses became platforms for propagating political and social change, confusing its historical purpose. Some social change, especially concerning the role of Blacks in society, needed to occur, of course. But many other changes transpired too, affecting the relationship between students and faculty. Faculty, assuming a less important role, relinquished to the student body a more prominent function in running the campus. Across the nation, students began to rebel against social and cultural leadership.

In the period of time with which we are concerned here, however, the Chain of Command was alive and well and every student at Ole Miss in those days knew his or her place perfectly in relation to faculty; in the athletes' case, in relation to coaches and faculty.

KING FOOTBALL

At Ole Miss in those days football was "King". Oxford nightlife was non-existent so for many students, football games seized center stage. During the war, people living in measured fear had little interest in sports, nor means by which they could attend athletic events. Gas was rationed, roads undeveloped, automobiles almost impossible to buy. But after the war rationing ended. And the boys came home. Two of those boys were Charlie Conerly and Barney Poole, another of my beloved uncles. Charlie came back to Ole Miss from the South Pacific and Barney came back from West Point. Johnny Vaught moved into the Head Coach's office, assembled his staff and Ole Miss football was, in Nineteen Forty-Seven, poised to explode, and it did. Ole Miss won the SEC Championship and defeated TCU in the first and only Delta Bowl in Old Crump Stadium in Memphis. Both Charlie and Barney were consensus All-Americans and both set national records that year, Charlie passing, and Barney pass receiving.

WE LEARNED

World War II taught us many things. We learned to pull together as a people and a nation. We learned how to fight when forced...! We learned how to exist on fewer "things" than we thought we could! And to the dismay of all the football players who would play at Ole Miss for the next twenty years, our coaches, all of whom had served in the military, had learned submission to authority, and discipline. And boy, were they "chomping at the bit" to implement what they had learned.

Enter Wobble! Hired to coach the freshmen, his responsibilities expanded far beyond simply coaching. His was the task of turning young, mama-dependent boys into tough young men who could win football games for the Rebels and after graduation, master life for themselves. In order to do that, Wobble and his new bride Sara became dorm parents. They lived on the first floor of Garland and later Miller Hall, where the Coach ruled our lives with more than a firm fist. He was a "ghost" in the dorm. We couldn't "get by" with anything. At the first sound of horseplay he would appear, out of nowhere. Long before Ali, he could float like a butterfly and sting like a bee. Unlike the heavyweight, his "sting" consisted of laps in the stadium, not around but up and down, among other things.

Have you ever walked up all the steps in Vaught-Hemingway Stadium from the field to the press box? It's a long way, sixty-six steps. When Wobble caught us misbehaving, he made us run, not walk, to the top of the stadium and down from ten to fifty times depending upon the degree of our crime.

The first time I was given the "privilege" of running the stadium came as a result of a little event which occurred in the dorm one night about 11:00 o'clock (There would be others.) I roomed with Jerry McKaskel, a half-back who, like me, was from Natchez, where we played high school football together. Next door to us roomed a freshman halfback, Dallas Whitfield, from Picayune. Dallas had a habit of coming into my room after I was asleep, waking me up, and giving me a big "good night" hug. (No evil thoughts, please. We both had girlfriends.) He prided himself, rightly so, on being my "irritant". One night in retaliation, I carefully placed a water-filled condom between his sheets knowing he would come in, sit on his bed to remove his shoes and burst the booby-trap, which is exactly what he did. I knew it had worked when I heard him bellow a few choice expletives. Several minutes later a subdued Dallas eased into my room in his dry pajamas and went through his usual vexatious ritual. As he was leaving, he stopped at my door and almost apologetically inquired, "Oh, Paige, by the way, somebody put a rubber filled with water in my bed tonight. Would you know who did it?"

"Yep, Dallas, but I'm not gonna rat on him."

"Please tell me!," over and over he pleaded.

Finally, with mocked shame, I relented. "Only if you promise not to tell I told."

"I promise!"

"It was Johnny."

Quarterback Johnny Carson was a very nice guy, a tall, good-looking young gentleman-type, who had grown up on a plantation just south of Columbus, Mississippi. He would never have placed a water-filled condom in someone's bed. Johnny would have perished even the thought.

But revenge-saturated minds dismantle common sense so Dallas never considered the possibility that Johnny wouldn't have done it. He retrieved a waist-high garbage can from the end of the hall, took it to the shower stall, filled it with water, dragged it back to Johnny's room and carefully leaned it against his door. Then he knocked. Johnny opened his door.

Some players swore later that water drained through Johnny's floor, into the room below and then into Wobble's apartment below that room. I never knew whether that was true or not, but I do know Wobble appeared instantly. Peeping out my door (This was in the days of bed-check and the waterfall occurred thirty minutes after that), I heard Wobble sentence Dallas, Johnny, and Johnny's roomate, Gordon Wakefield, to fifty laps in the stadium. Believing Johnny's denial of having placed the condom in Dallas' bed, Coach told them, "If you can find out who did it, you'll only have to run twenty-five! I'll give you until practice tomorrow."

After practice the next day, Wobble assembled the freshmen and unnecessarily (everyone knew by then) recounted the event to the team. Then he asked the condemned three if they had found the fourth criminal. When they replied they had not, Wobble said, "You will run fifty laps in the stadium UNLESS the guilty person steps forward, then the four of you will run ONLY twenty-five laps each."

It took me awhile to decide. ONLY twenty-five laps?? There was no such thing as ONLY twenty-five laps in Hemingway Stadium, especially after the second of two-a-day practices! It was almost dark.

That was the longest step I ever took. By the time we finished our laps it was so dark Coach Wobble was only a tiny white speck in the middle of a black sea of grass. We missed supper.

THE TIMES WERE DIFFERENT THEN

To really appreciate the humor in the stories to follow, one must understand the times. The war had taught people to be strong and tough and unemotional. Soldiers in combat were afraid, of course. They should have been...! But they were taught to discipline that fear, to conceal it, to suppress it so that it did not show. After the war, that characteristic endured, not upon battlefields but upon college athletic fields. As football players we were taught, yea commanded, to extirpate emotion during football games. "If you want to cheer, go be a cheerleader," we were told. We were allowed to cheer after the game but not during it. There were no high-fives in the Fifties!

As I previously mentioned, those were years of discipline and submission. We thought our coaches had rights of life or death over us. Some freshmen couldn't handle that and they lasted only a short time at Ole Miss.

Those of us who remained submitted totally to the coaches, without question. We never argued with them; we never verbalized a difference of opinion; we never even allowed a difference to reflect in the expressions on our faces nor the tones of our voices, silently confessing absolute submission.

I played fullback at Ole Miss. A fullback at Ole Miss in those days was supposed to run over tacklers, not around them. We were to "soften the defensive players up," so that by the fourth quarter they might hesitate at "sticking their heads in there," as the coaches phrased it. (I don't think it worked!) I had been more of an elusive runner in high school, but at Ole Miss, though I believed I could have gained much more yardage by trying to evade tacklers, I never did. I ran the ball through the hole, which the quarterbacks called, and I ran low, as hard as I could and in a straight line. The halfbacks evaded tacklers, the fullbacks attacked them. I never questioned that concept. The coaches said it and I did it with almost a reverential awe and in total compliance with their commands. With few exceptions the other players complied, too.

A SUMMARY

These and other cultural characteristics and attitudes formed a background against which the tug-of-war between coaches, who exercised complete authority, and players who knew it, yet who were tenacious in their efforts to effect their own kind of fun, produced countless episodes of fear and humor. Although some of the events may seem cruel by today's critique, all of them continue to be funny to the storytellers, those to whom these events occurred! No story appears in this book, therefore, save those which are humorous to the one who shared it. We hope the tales, some perhaps embellished slightly, will, for you older people, remind you of the "good 'ol" days; for you younger people teach you a little about a long ago culture; and for all of you, tickle your funny bone just a little and perhaps put a smile upon your face.

Oh, what the heck...go ahead and belly-laugh! That's what we really want!

CHAPTER I

I'M ALL YOURS, COACH

A gainst the background of a culture carved out of a World War where discipline and dedication were valued; where visible emotion was de-emphasized; where national fear ceased to exist; and where total submission was demanded; a perfect environment was established on college athletic fields and courts for humor. That environment existed after the war, probably in part because the end of the conflict generated a national "sigh of relief." It ceased to exist after the Nineteen Sixties due to factors already discussed in the Introduction.

Of the college football coaching staffs which might have been assembled, Coach Vaught's staff collectively contained all the elements necessary to engender respect from the athletes who played under them. For a statement to be funny or a command to be blindly obeyed, one must respect the person making the statement or issuing the command. Where respect ceases to exist, resentment flourishes and mirth crashes like a Jap Zero shot out of the Pacific sky. I will discover little humor in the words or actions of a person whom I resent. When a wife begins to lose respect for her husband, she seldom resorts to a state of indifference. More often than not, resentment replaces respect and she finds little jocularity in her husband's words or deeds. We both feared and respected Coach Vaught, his staff, and especially Wobble. After all, Coach Vaught's staff, to a man, had been great college football players. Two of them, Buster Poole and Bruiser Kinard, played in the National Football League, both receiving All-Pro honors. In an existential world, having "been there" demands credibility. Coach Vaught's staff had certainly been there! As coaches of football, they had earned their stripes as football players.

I WOULDN'T WANT TO THINK ABOUT IT

The boycott by seventy or so Memphis State football players in the early Nineties might send a cold chill through me if I allowed it —! The mental picture which emerges as I transpose the MSU players and what they did, to the Ole Miss football team of the Nineteen Fifties is not a pretty one!

Wow, I shudder to think what would have happened if a Vaught - coached team had boycotted practice and decided it was time for him to be fired. Of course those were the "good 'ol days" when the coach "fired" the players, rather than the reverse. In 1955, football players boycotted even the thought of confronting the coach. That was the only boycott we knew anything about or had the courage to implement.

In those days, whether rightly or wrongly, the coaches possessed full rights to a college football player's life, as previously mentioned, possibly stopping just short of the right to life or death, although the players were never absolutely certain of that. The Ole Miss coaching staff under which I played had no trouble making me believe that they inherited the right of life and death over me, and I had two uncles, Buster and Ray Poole, on the coaching staff. For years now, I have walked and talked softly around them, and I'm a father of two and grandfather of four.

One day in spring practice, Jerry Stone, a linebacker crushed my right cheekbone with a carefully planted elbow. That was before players started wearing facemasks, cages that could deflect a 105-howitzer projectile. The lick knocked me out. A couple of student managers dragged me from the practice field and transported me to the small hospital in downtown Oxford. The doctor tried to insert a special balloon through my nose into the sinus cavity in order to pump the cheekbone out, but my nose had been broken so many times he couldn't get it through my nasal passage. Finally he said, "Paige, I hate to do this but I'm going to have to pull it out." Thank goodness I didn't know what that meant or I might still be running.

With my face quickly swelling, the doctor positioned his little medical instrument about the size of large scissors and shaped like ice tongs, upon my cheek. Like a dentist hiding the needle from his patient, he kept it out of my sight until time to use it. Then he placed one point onto my cheekbone just beneath my right eye and drove it into the broken cheek bone with his fist. He located the other point just above my teeth and did the same. Placing his left hand on my forehead, with his right hand he pulled. An eternity, 30 seconds or so, later, my cheekbone popped out.

I stayed in the hospital overnight. By the time I went to sleep the swelling extended well beyond my nose. My right eye was completely closed and I could barely see through my left one, the swelling invading even the left side of my face.

No one came to check on me.

The next morning the doctor released me. The hospital was about a mile from the campus. I walked back, holding the swelling with my right hand. It kept bouncing up and down when I walked.

If you could walk you were at practice! That rule had existed at Ole Miss for as long as had football, and it was enforced. That afternoon I walked to practice, holding the swelling.

A hurt football player had to report to Coach Vaught each day and Coach made the decision whether or not the player would practice. If he decided the player should practice he would ask him THE QUESTION which all injured Ole Miss football players hated to hear.

"Can you go, son?"

I could scarcely believe my ears. Standing in front of Coach Vaught with fear and trembling yet with a degree of security, he asked me THE QUESTION.

"Can you go, son, can you go?"

"Coach," I politely asked, "do you mean practice?"

"Boy, don't get smart with me! Can you go?"

Only two acceptable answers existed to that question, "Yes" and "No." If you answered "Yes" then you practiced, full speed. If you said "No", then you probably went home for good. So even an irreligious injured player prayed that Coach Vaught wouldn't ask THE QUESTION, that Coach would see he was too hurt to practice.

I thought about that 150-acre farm I came from, about plowing a mule the rest of my life. Or maybe I could get a job at Crosby in the sawmill! Both thoughts appalled me, so with a doubtful lump in my throat I lied, "I can go, Coach."

"Go get 'em on then," he said, meaning the pads.

Doc Knight our trainer wrapped my head with an ankle wrap to help keep the swelling from bouncing when I ran. With a crushed cheekbone, no facemask, my head wrapped with an ankle wrap, and unable to see very well, I scrimmaged. I wish I had a picture of it, I must have looked hilarious. I remember running funny, a little sideways.

Fire the coach for that? Sue him? Boycott practice? Not on your life! Rather, I thank the Lord for being able to play under a coach and a staff all of whom sought to teach me discipline, how to keep going in spite of a little physical pain.

For every player, football inevitably ends, but the discipline which it teaches remains with him a lifetime. My respect for the coaching staff which demanded the utmost of me will never die until I do.

By the way, the next fall we won the Southeastern Conference Championship and beat TCU in the 1956 Cotton Bowl game.

THE MOST - - AH - - VISIBLE COACH

Of all the coaches on Coach Vaught's staff, Wobble Davidson was most visible to the players. He had access to us our freshman year both on the field and in team meetings as did Coach Vaught and the varsity staff with upper-classmen. But because he was the players' "dorm father" he superintended almost every other area of our lives, literally twenty-four hours a day. We couldn't have gotten away from him if we had tried other than by leaving school, which some did. To the players he seemed to possess the attribute of omnipresence, especially when we had violated one of his rules. Little in Garland Dorm, and later in Miller Hall escaped his attention.

No man has ever been more mentally and emotionally suited for his task of dorm parent to college football players than Wobble. His sharp mind, his quick wit, his one-liners, and his ability to quickly and impartially administer discipline with a sense of humor forced all of us to both fear and respect him. But his wit occupies "center stage" in this book. His quick, pithy one-liners came to be labeled "Wobbleisms" by the players. Even now, when ex-players congregate, they usually exchange Wobbleisms somewhere in the conversation.

Years have neither dimmed the Wobbleisms from the old football players' minds nor deprived Wobble of his quick wit. While visiting Wobble and Sara to ask their permission to include him in this book, I joked, "Coach, when this book is published you'd better get ready—the women are going to line up at your front door just to get a glimpse of you."

Instantly he retorted, "Tell only the ones with teeth to come and ask them to bring their Social Security checks."

All of the athletes who played football, first for Wobble and then for Coach Vaught and his staff left Ole Miss convinced that the coaches had been vitally interested in us and concerned about us, in spite of what may now appear to others as somewhat cruel coaching behavior. Wobble, though, possessed a unique ability to generate within the subconscious minds of most of us the notion that we were special young men. He accomplished that feat in part by assigning us nicknames, usually a magnification of a personality trait or physical characteristic. To be given another name by a person we both feared and respected engrafted into our minds the belief that we occupied a part of his, even when the nicknames may have been less than complimentary. (Note the list of nicknames at the end of this book.)

To a guard who liked to roam around at night and sleep all day, Wobble awarded the name "Possum." To a short dumpy halfback he assigned the name "Hobby-Horse." He called a very handsome blond running back who was less than aggressive, "Milk-Toast." He labeled me "Uncle Bus," for obvious reasons. (I could hardly refer to my Uncle Buster as "Coach," so I called him "Uncle Bus.")

Many of Wobble's nicknames have stuck with the ex-players throughout their lifetimes. Grandfather Richard Price is still known as Possum and Frank Halbert is still Hobby Horse. Bobby Ray Franklin answers still to "Waxy." Buddy Alliston is "Cosmetics."

By the way, Wobble assigned me a second nickname. Since I wasn't a real Poole, Wobble reasoned that I must be a "Cesspool."

GETTING TO KNOW WOBBLE

Some of my deepest pleasures in formulating the material for this book and then recording it were my visits with Wobble and Sara in their beautiful home immediately off the square in Oxford. Prior to each visit, I called and made an appointment. With customary grace and hospitality, they invited me into their home. Wobble and I would usually sit at the kitchen counter where we would look at notes, record stories and remember—! With great discipline on my part, I have learned to call Coach Wobble, "Wobble." I still want to answer "Yes sir" and "No sir," which from time to time I find myself doing.

The visits were always punctuated with funny stories from the past. Occasionally I would forget to turn on my tape recorder, totally engrossed in his narrative.

I asked Wobble, as I did my Uncle Ray Poole, to recall humorous events from their playing days and their coaching days, as well as the days in between, the War years. Both of them possessed great senses of humor then and now and both were committed practical jokers in their younger days. If

I could get a reading on their behavior before their coaching days at Ole Miss, I figured, that might help all of us understand them, particularly Wobble, better. At the very least these stories would make entertaining reading.

NEED A LIGHT?

"Coach, to start with, all my life I've heard Ray tell a story about you pouring lighter fluid on someone in a hospital room who had undergone surgery. Is there any truth in that?," I asked.

"Oh, that was Charles Day from McComb," Wobble immediately answered. "My best friend! We were in the Marine Corps together. Fortunately but unfortunately we served together. He was in a different unit but we would get together on weekends, and he was a pretty wild person. He had played football at Ole Miss too, before the war. Some of his habits and mannerisms were uninhibited, to say the least."

"We'd be playing cards," Wobble continued, "or shooting dice, as most soldiers did, and we wore these narrow military caps which we called P—s cutters. Day would never throw a lighted cigarette butt away. He would catch me, and other men too, not noticing and he would drop it on top of our p—s cutters or in the cuff of our pants and just let the d—n thing burn. We'd finally smell smoke and look around to see who was on fire. Sometimes the cigarette butt would burn all the way through the hat onto our heads. He would even squirt lighter fluid up and down your back and set your shirt on fire."

Wobble continued talking, I continued laughing.

"We were in Honolulu and Day had to have a hemorrhoid operation during an R and R period, so several of us went to visit him in the hospital, as compassionate friends will—-! We carried two cans of lighter fluid with us. 'Look Charles, we brought you something,' we announced to him. His eyes bugged out and he yanked the sheet up over his head yelling 'Corpsman, Corpsman,' referring of course to the medical assistants in the hospital. We squirted the lighter fluid all over his sheets and threw a match onto his bed. Up the flames went and out of the bed bounded the marine, sore a-s and all. The sheets were still burning when the corpsman arrived. We thought we were going to get court marshaled, had to appear before the captain in what was called 'Captain's hour.' Day had torn the stitches loose in his a-s when he jumped out of the bed. We didn't get court marshaled, but

Charles never set us on fire again either."

"I didn't have a shirt nor a pair of pants, nor a hat that wasn't scorched," Coach concluded.

By the time Wobble had finished telling the story, my sides were aching, and I was gasping for air. It also helped me decide to cancel that operation.

I had heard the story all my life, but to hear it from the mouth of the participant intensified the humor. I thought, as he concluded, no wonder he understood the levity of football players in a dormitory, though discipline of course, demanded recompense. He must have been smiling as he watched the guilty satisfy the demands of their sins on the steps of Hemingway stadium. At least I would like to think so. I never got around to asking him.

"You were the freshman coach for many years here at Ole Miss; do you remember much about your freshman year at Ole Miss?" I prompted Wobble.

"Yes! We lived in a dorm right across from what once was the old Grill but they were just building it when I was a freshman. We made ourselves slingshots. We didn't have much of anything else to do. We'd go down to the railroad tracks on Sunday and shoot birds and those little glass insulators on light poles. The varsity would haze us constantly. They were bored so they constantly spanked us. We would jump out the windows of the dorm and hide in a mule barn right behind Vardaman where the health center is now - h—l, we came to know the mules better than we did our professors — spent more time with them. We slept with them every other night."

"During the winter," Wobble continued, "the dorms, especially the bathrooms were really cold and the varsity made the freshmen warm the toilet seats. 'Come here freshman,' they would call; 'I need to s—t. Put your warm a-s on this commode, — NOW!' "You never saw such scurrying around in your life as the frosh, trying to avoid a butt-whipping, hustled to warm the toilet seats."

"Bullet White was our freshman coach. He was a transfer to Ole Miss and HE wasn't supposed to haze us but he did. I was his freshman responsible for warming his toilet seat. I got smart. I started taking the toilet seat loose and putting it on my steam-heat radiator to keep it warm. One day Bullet yelled, 'Freshman, I'm ready to take a s—t. Get my commode ready.'

I didn't realize that I had gotten the seat almost red-hot. Blistered Bullet's butt, not the smartest thing a freshman even did to an upper classman."

WOBBLE AND UNCLE RAY

Ray Poole was not one of a kind. He had an uncle, Uncle Boss as he was called, from whom he must have learned some of his mischievous ways. (Uncle Boss, Ray and the Pooles will be discussed in another part of this undertaking.) Ray and Uncle Boss together were two of a kind. No prank lay beyond either of their imaginations or their willingness to execute. I spent a good part of my younger life hanging by my over-all suspenders from the deer antlers mounted in the hallway of the Poole home in South Mississippi, having been deposited there by my Uncle Ray. My earliest revelation of fear occurred between the Brushy Creek bridge and the Brushy Creek, at about the age of four. A favorite Poole pastime on a hot summer afternoon was, for Ray, Buster, Barney, Philip, Fleming, Jackie, Oliver, and Les, throwing me off the bridge and seeing who could dive in and get me. Their assurances that someone would pull me out before I drowned did little to assuage my fears. I learned to swim early in life but I always hated diving.

Wobble roomed with Ray when they were students at Ole Miss.

"He was terrible," Wobble declared. "I slept in the bunk above him and I knew that at some point every night he was gonna kick me out of bed. He got a piece of wood shaped like a drumstick and he finally punched a hole all the way through my mattress. When he wasn't kicking me out of bed, he was punching me through the hole. He would worry the h—l out of me. There was never a time when he wasn't up to something."

I certainly understood that! I grew up with him. As all of his nieces and nephews would testify under oath, Ray was a relentless antagonist.

THE DAY WOBBLE DE-WIRED THE DORM

In the mid-Fifties, Wobble ruled that no player could install a telephone in his room. But after the war, some players came back to Ole Miss who had served in army communication units and knew how to wire buildings for telephones. Unbeknowing to Wobble they had wired Garland with South Central Bell's approval.

Lea Pasley, a halfback from Sardis, had capitalized on the Veteran's knowledge and had plugged a telephone into the line. Wobble found out about the secret line, chopped a hole in one of the walls and started pulling the wires.

"Pulled the d—n phone right out of Lea's hands" confessed Wobble, "Lea was talking to Big Band representatives about coming to Ole Miss to play for a dance. By the time he finished the conversation, his head was banging on the wall."

The Chancellor and South Central Bell both called him on the carpet for that one. "For awhile, I thought I was going to get fired," Wobble concluded.

Years after his retirement, an alumni group in Jackson roasted Wobble. At the end of the program, the "Roasters" presented Wobble with the Ma Bell Award for being the only person in recent history to de-wire a building not intended by the phone company to be de-wired. Chancellor-to-be Robert Khayat tendered the plaque.

"Still have the d—n thing hanging on my wall," Wobble concluded.

THE PREACHER

"What was one of your most memorable game experiences when you were a player," I asked Wobble.

He thought for a minute. Like cards shuffling in the hands of a gambler, I could see the shuffling of experiences in his mind, trying to determine which one he wanted to deal upon the table of memory. I waited expectantly.

Suddenly Wobble exclaimed "Stuart Smith! Stuart played end; good defense but he couldn't play offense. He was muscle-bound, a weight lifter from Meridian. His dad was the Bishop of the Church in Mississippi I think, so we always liked being around Stuart, thinking he was gonna study for the ministry—- Divine protection you know. We called him Preacher."

Ole Miss was, according to Wobble, playing in Memphis in old Crump Stadium; Harry Mehre was coach. First play or two, Preacher took a forearm across his nose. Those were the days before facemasks and his nose was broken and laid over on his right cheekbone. "Coach brought him out of the game and straightened his nose with the sticks," continued Wobble. (Two sticks were inserted into the nostrils of a broken nose in order to re-align it.) "Then he sent Preacher back into the game. A few plays later someone pushed Preacher's nose over onto his left cheekbone."

"Preacher left the game again and the same sticks were re-inserted into his nose and it was re-set a second time."

"Preacher," Mehre yelled. "Get back in," meaning into the game.

Players accessed the field in Crump Stadium via a tunnel. The tunnel led from both teams dressing room, under the northside stadium out to the field behind the visiting team's bench.

"Get back in there," Mehre yelled again.

"But Preacher couldn't get back in. He had disappeared. When coach yelled for him to go back in the second time, he went back in all right, he went back into the dressing room through the tunnel."

"Where the h—l is that Preacher," Mehre screamed again.

"The next time we saw Preacher," Wobble exclaimed, " He had his street clothes on and that was well before the game ended. The Preacher had deserted the pulpit."

So much for Divine protection!

STOP THIS MOTEL AND LET ME OFF!

Most of this work focuses upon tales emanating from life at Ole Miss. A few stories, however, too humorous to ignore thus demanding to be included, occurred later and elsewhere. Such is the case in the episode from the life of Wobble given enthusiastically to me by none other than our esteemed and beloved Chancellor, Dr. Robert Khayat.

When Robert came back to Law School at Ole Miss, he was also scouting for the New Orleans Saints. Wobble was scouting for the Dallas Cowboys. They both happened to be in Nashville viewing both a Vanderbilt game and an Austin Peay game. Robert had gotten a room at the Holiday Inn Capitol.

At the time they ran into one another, Wobble had not yet gotten a place to stay so Robert invited him to share the room at the Holiday Inn.

"The Holiday Inn Capitol in Nashville was right down by the railroad tracks," explained Robert, "the switching yard. They were banging trains. Everytime they would bang the trains together it would shake the entire building, almost shake us out of bed. And they banged together every few minutes, all night long."

The scouts were each lying in their beds, unable to sleep because of the obstreperous vibrations just outside their windows.

"Sometime in the middle of the night," Robert mused, "Wobble picked up the telephone and called the desk.

"Ma'am, would you tell me when this d—n motel is gonna' get to Chicago?"

Robert and I were having lunch together in a restaurant in Oxford when he related that story. If I had had a mouth full of food at that precise moment, I'm certain I would have sprinkled the adjoining tables. What other person, I wonder, could have germinated that concept, could have formulated that salient question from that particular situation?

No one, I suspect.

THE SERIOUS PART

Numerous other places in this book reveal former football player's opinions of Coach Wobble, and in fact, the entire Vaught coaching staff. Wobble is loved, respected, and appreciated by the overwhelming preponderance of them, if not all. I could, if I so desired, propel this book down a demure trail and fill uncountable pages. I promised you a humorous book though, and I think I have kept that promise. But some sobriety must be met, some seriousness explored. For had it not been for a deep commitment by Wobble to the Almighty in a dark hour of this Nation's history and an enigmatical moment of his own, he might not now be billeted in the hearts of Ole Miss Alumni.

The time was War, the place was the South Pacific, the setting was Hell, and when Wobble's close friend and former teammate at Ole Miss, Billy Sam, was killed, the future Rebel coach was driven to evaluate the rest of his life, if indeed an extended one should be granted him.

It was — and he spent his life fulfilling his vow, that given the opportunity, he would make men out of boys, that he would, if God let him live through the perils of South Pacific purgatory, dedicate his life to young men and women. Those of us who toiled, and sweated, and feared, and laughed under him, believe his vow was completed, his commitment was consummated.

The greatest game a coach can plan
Is making a boy into the best possible man.

So formed the philosophy and trademark of the Coach.

PROFANITY

The world has changed!

"Wow!" I can almost hear you exclaim. "I might never have known that had I not read this book!"

I know, you know, everyone knows the world has changed but I need to elucidate the truth for two very important reasons: first, that you might better understand Wobble and the Ole Miss coaches of years past; and so you may not be offended when you read the profanity.

Back in the late Forties, Fifties, and early Sixties, American culture allowed cursing, without condemnation, in private settings. It was restricted, however, in public ones, like radio and television. Those two social mores have perfectly reversed. Today, the airways sag under the load of public profanity. Football fields, while not totally void of it, certainly feature less and very little is directed specifically toward the players.

The Ole Miss coaches of the aforecited years emanated from the war with a disposition of mind clearly different from the accepted standards of today, but just as clearly acceptable to the requirements of their day. Private profanity in Nineteen Fifty-Five wasn't considered profane. Very few of us, privileged to have played under the men, judged them then or now as maledictive. They were coaches and strong words were one of their whips with which they motivated us.

What they did in that day would not be welcome today. What the players did on campus and in town would not be either. But at the time, both were not only passively permitted but actively acceptable, perhaps even desirable in the same way a loving wife might put her arms around her husband's neck, look deeply into his eyes, and say, "I love you, you old b — —-d," "profanity" thereby metabolizing into a term of endearment. It spoke of intimacy.

Such was the athletic culture at Ole Miss in the days of Wobble. When words proceeded from the mouths of our coaches, including Wobble, which would today be labeled profane, they were never so identified by the players. Instead to us they were funny threads woven into the fabric of caring, demanding coaches, and they were seldom, if ever, offensive to those who had never heard the phrase "politically correct."

A MEMORY FROM G.G.

Gerald Morgan was signed by the Rebels out of Mendenhall in the mid-Fifties as a quarterback. Now a Presbyterian minister in Atlanta, what G.G., as he was called at Ole Miss, lacked in athletic ability, he made up in heart. His contribution to this book paints an explicit and different portrait of Wobble Davidson which I thought you might enjoy reading. It follows.

"Intense, focused, dedicated, tough, fierce competitor, disciplinarian, mean as a snake, quick-witted, smart"... all are descriptions which have been used to describe Wobble Davidson. I have also heard many of his players tell of his efforts to make the M-Club like a fraternity. He worked at making his athletes mold into a family.

"I was never higher than 4th string on the depth chart so I spent all my years with the red shirt team which was Coach Wobble's responsibility to equip to run the opponent's plays against the Varsity. As the QB for this group whose alumni included All-Americans like Gene Hickerson and Charlie Flowers, I got to know Coach Davidson well. I loved Ole Miss and wanted more than anything to be part of the team. Coach Davidson and all of the athletes made me feel like a significant part and not just a scrubb. I really feel that the bond of friendship we have experienced is a result of Coach Davidson's efforts to make us a family.

"When I became head coach at Drew and Archie Manning was in the 10th grade as a 130 pound quarterback, Coach Davidson came by to watch the morning practice. He stayed for lunch with my family and visited with me until late afternoon. His insights were helpful but his interest in me and my family was a tremendous encouragement. As always he had witty comments to keep the mood light.

"I was the slowest back at Ole Miss and ran sprints with the slower linemen. Coach had not forgotten my slowness, so suggested that when I coach track to 'just tell them how to do it and not try to demonstrate.'

"He also said, 'Coaching is 90% athletes, 8% luck and 2% coaching; and Gerald, you don't have any athletes.' We were weak, slow and small as a team but we did have heart and that had to carry us until weights, track, and maturity caught up.

"On my 60th birthday, Coach Wobble wrote me one of the most wonderful letters that I have ever received. His insights and tenderness were evident throughout the letter as he talked of my coaching and years spent in the Christian ministry, and the need to close strong in the last quarter of my life."

CHAPTER II

LIFE IN THE DORMITORY
A CHANGE

I've experienced many changes in my life. When I was seven years old, my Mother and Dad moved from the city to the country, from Crosby, Mississippi out to the Homochitto Community. Okay, so Crosby isn't really a city but the five hundred or so people who lived there made it look to me at age seven, like a city. Anyway, five hundred people were four hundred more than the one hundred at Homochitto, almost all of whom were relatives.

We moved in with Mama Poole. Mama Poole was the mother of my Mom, her three sisters, and her three brothers, Buster, Ray and Barney Poole. None of the three brothers were married then, but they were gone most of the year, first to play football and then to the war. It was 1942. Mama Poole needed someone to live with her, or so all her children thought. Mama Poole didn't. I'm not certain she was ever asked but the Poole family was so close it really didn't matter. She would never have gotten upset with her children, no matter what they decided to do for her. Papa Will Poole her husband, had died years before.

Becoming a "younger brother" rather than a nephew to the three Poole brothers cast upon me a major change. Some of the reasons will be discussed in the section on the Pooles. For now, however, let me just say that none of their many nieces and nephews envied me.

Several years after the war, my Dad, Mom, Sister and I moved from Homochitto to Natchez. Now that was a major change for a sixteen-year old country boy! To me Natchez was one of the biggest cities in the world. The antebellum homes, a hundred or so of them, both fascinated me and intimidated me, all at the same time.

Natchez was a semi-closed society, although at the time I didn't know it. After living there for awhile, I heard people say, "If you weren't born here you would never be accepted."

But I was—! The people in Natchez welcomed me with open arms and I just kept doing what I had done at Crosby High: play football; date girls; play basketball; date girls; play baseball; date girls; and study. I studied because my mother said "Study" and I didn't know how to rebel against her. My own children taught me how to do that.

After I graduated from Ole Miss, I got married; played pro football for the L.A. Rams and the Philadelphia Eagles; owned three Piggly Wigglys: went back to school at age thirty-eight; got my Master's degree; counseled for twenty-five years; and helped develop Grand Oaks Resort in Oxford. I did most of that after becoming a Christian and all of it represented great change in my life. But none of these changes was the biggest change in my life.

THE BIGGEST CHANGE

Going to Ole Miss and living in Garland Hall was!

I regret that college athletes are now cheated out of living in an athletic dorm. I'm really sorry all college students are—! I know I'm old fashioned, and I know dormitories have followed after nylon shirts and multi-petti-coated skirts. But even a nylon shirt offered some redemptive value. A poor boy could finally acquire a twenty-dollar bill, fold it, and stick it in his semi-transparent shirt pocket for all to see and everyone thought he was rich. And a pretty coed sitting down in her multi-petti-coated skirt, pushed it straight up in the air. Looking at her from the front, you still couldn't see anything, but a girl's skirt protruding into the air so far that it blocked her view certainly activated a young man's imagination. We kept hoping someone would invent a chemical which would dissolve petti-coat material. We already had the squirt guns.

Dorm life was a change for everyone in the Fifties and early Sixties, a severe and drastic change. No longer did our Moms wake us up for school, now we must wake ourselves up. No longer did they wash and iron our clothes, nor prepare our meals, nor make us study. Dorm life forced us to grow up, to learn how to tend to our own needs, to organize our own lives, though admittedly some of us did it poorly.

Athletic dorm life welded lives together because for four years I knew with whom I would be rooming and the room in which I would be living. I knew how many hours I would be sitting in a classroom and how many I would be sweating on a football field. I knew I would get chewed out by coaches and ignored by some professors because I was a "meat-head." I knew I would be cheered and loved by most of the students and Ole Miss grads when we won football games. And I knew sports writers were going to write something nice about me or write nothing at all. Living in a dorm brought stability into our lives and permitted us to know about a lot of things before they happened.

But I didn't know about Wobble. Oh, I knew the Freshman Coach! He had played football at Ole Miss with Ray and Barney and had visited us one summer at Mama Poole's. But I didn't know about life with him as my "Dorm Parent."

Wobble and Sara and their children lived in an apartment on the northeast corner of the first floor of Garland Dorm. He was our vicarious parent, our Moms and Dads all rolled up into one. He possessed the perfect attributes for a task-master: sharp eye-sight; acute hearing; flawless sense of smell; quick mind; strong stair-climbing legs; the ability to impute fear into the toughest athlete; and a great sense of humor. Wobble would punish us severely one day and do it in such a way that we would find it humorous the next day. Like broken teeth before the day of face masks, his discipline of us metastasized into badges of courage, and his punishment formulated anecdotes which will be recited for as long as Ole Miss athletes "don the gear" on Saturday afternoons.

WHAT PRICE MID-NIGHT SNACK?

One Wobble-rule which the coach failed to enforce occasionally, due neither to an anemic effort nor inability, was the NO FOOD IN THE ROOMS rule. The appetites of young, robust, starving football players caused his periodic failure. A late night snack seemed only natural to all of us. One of my teammates often complained, "Man, as hard as they work us, you'd think they'd feed us!"

The fact is, Ole Miss did feed us and quite well but Wobble believed we should eat at mealtime and not in our rooms late at night. The on-going battle between the reconnoitering coach and the recalcitrant players raged as long as Wobble and Sara occupied an apartment in either Garland or Miller Hall. Had we players applied ourselves as intently to the pursuit of academic excellence as we did to securing a hiding place for our "after-dinner snack," the athletic Department might have released all the tutors and saved a lot of money.

Wobble, some of us believed, could hear the sound of a football player crunching a cracker at 200 paces.

Sam Owen, a lineman at Ole Miss in the early Sixties wasn't crunching a noisy cracker, though. He and his roommate were eating peanut butter and banana sandwiches at 2:30 A.M. — you'd think Wobble would have been asleep.

Sam tells the story.

"My roommate Skippy and I were going to study late so we went to the store and bought some peanut butter, bananas, bread and milk. We put the milk on the window ledge outside to keep it cold. It was 2:30 in the morning but we knew Coach Wobble had a sixth sense about breaking rules so we took great precautions to keep from being caught."

Hiding, or trying to hide from Wobble demanded creativity. Sam and Skippy yanked a blanket off one of the beds and draped it over the desk, the light, and the chairs, with the illegal peanut butter, bananas, bread and milk. It was pitch dark in the room.

"We got under the blanket," Sam continued, "and proceeded to construct our inch thick peanut butter and banana sandwiches. Just as Skippy and I took our first bites, we heard a noise that sounded like a key being inserted into the door. Looking at each other with horror, peanut butter splattered upon our faces, we froze, — didn't move a muscle, not believing what we thought we were hearing."

Very slowly the blanket lifted off the two malefactors. Towering above them, holding the edge of the blanket, stood Wobble.

"What are you two boys doing under this blanket," the Coach asked suspiciously.

"Well Coach," Sam explained, "I was helping Skippy study and we got hungry — decided we wanted a peanut butter and banana sandwich."

"Well I'm glad you're studying. Now you need to go to bed and get yourselves some rest because it's awfully late," Wobble gently implored. Then he quietly walked out of the room.

"Coach was so nice, we ate two sandwiches, joked about not being punished for our crime, finally turned the lights out and went to bed."

When Sam and Skippy arrived at the dining hall for breakfast the next morning, the "forgiving" coach had posted a notice on the bulletin board. It read, "Owen and Brinkman meet Coach Davidson at the stadium this afternoon at 2:30 in full uniform.

They reported to Wobble, fully dressed in football uniforms at 2:29.

Wobble was sitting on a first row seat in Hemingway.

"Sam," Coach quietly asked, "did you and Skippy get your assignments done?"

"Yes sir," Sam replied.

"Well that's good but you know the rules. You can't eat in the dorm. I want twenty laps in the stadium from each of you, but take your time," Wobble surprisingly stated. "I'll wait for you."

"Take your time!!?" Coach had never told offenders to take your time when running Hemingway. The two got a little suspicious.

"Yes sir," Sam responded.

By the end of the fourth lap their legs were severely aching. (I know the feeling.) Wobble stopped them.

"You boys tired?" Wobble 'graciously' asked.

"Yes sir."

"Well have a seat and rest some."

Something was desperately wrong. Wobble Davidson had never, never asked law-breakers in the midst of satisfying the demands of their crime by running Hemingway if they were tired. And he had certainly never invited them to take a seat and rest. For twenty years he had yelled "keep moving-don't slow down-keep moving."

By that time Sam and Skippy were nervously glancing at each other, their minds racing, trying to grasp the meaning of Wobble's unorthodox and unexpected compassionate behavior.

Sam optimistically leaned over and whispered to Skippy, "Mrs. Davidson must have really gotten onto Coach for being so mean to us."

About that time Wobble reached under a seat on the first row of the stadium and pulled out two large grocery sacks, the contents of which he dumped out on the landing below the first row of seats.

"Now you two B— —-ds who like peanut butter and banana sandwiches so much—-Let's see how much you're gonna like them after today," he quietly threatened.

Each bag contained twenty peanut butter and banana sandwiches. "Eat four of them right now for the first four laps and then eat one every other lap after that," the Coach commanded, "I'll be watching."

"We started running up and down that stadium eating those peanut butter and banana sandwiches," laughed Sam, "and when we got to the top, we vomited them over the back of the stadium, ran down, got another one, ran up the steps eating it, and lost it over the back of the stadium."

"You know what!" Sam concluded, "I still like peanut butter and banana sandwiches. I didn't for a while but I do now."

Makes a person wonder if Elvis ever ate his peanut butter and banana sandwiches running up a stadium. Naw, I suppose not!

"Why," you might reasonably ask," would Sam Owen find this event so humorous years later?"

Probably for three reasons. When players reverence and respect coaches as much as we did Wobble and all the other coaches on Vaught's staff, against the cultural background of total submission, almost everything they did to us evolved into humor with the passing of time, even though the discipline may hurt at the moment, "They might have killed us," we imagined.

Also, any attention from a coach in those years may have been appreciated, even when the attention involved punishment. Ole Miss, by NCAA rule, could and did sign as many players as they wished. Fierce competition between players resulted. Attention from a coach meant that he acknowledged your presence and perhaps your importance to the team.

Finally, for a coach to go to the trouble and expense of making forty peanut butter and banana sandwiches, bringing them to the football stadium and effecting their consumption as part of a discipline indicates a deeper, underlying concern than simply administering punishment. Wobble wanted to teach a lesson which not only affected the player's life in the dormitory but which might remind him to obey the rules for the rest of his life.

It worked! Sam remembers.

KING OF THE DOMINOS

Dewey Patridge found the Christmas week as boring as many other football players at Ole Miss who were required to stay on campus in preparation for a bowl game. Constantly searching for some kind of entertainment, he and several of his teammates decided to see if they could get into a locked fraternity house to watch television, all the residents having gone home for Christmas. They found an open window.

After entering, Patridge found an unlocked bedroom door. In the bedroom he discovered a long, white bathrobe which, after watching television for awhile, he confiscated.

"It was long and made out of terry-cloth," Quail explained. "Man I liked that thing. Never had owned a bathrobe before."

Dewey figured that the fraternity boy would be well pleased had he realized he contributed such an important gift to a member of the football team.

Along with his teammate Rudolph (Words) Smith, Dewey lived on the first floor of Garland, but he spent most of his spare time up on the third floor playing dominos with Joseph and Reggie Robertson. Joseph and Reggie were cousins and both were my cousins, their mothers being Pooles.

Dewey, his teammates Words Smith, so nicknamed by Wobble because he never talked, Reggie, and Joseph and others played dominos just about every night. They usually kept the noise down, or at least they tried — to keep Wobble out of the room.

They played dominos naked for a reason!

Every night, upon declaring a winner, the domino players, with great pomp and ceremony would dress the King of Dominos in the terry cloth robe, which had within a few weeks turned black with dirt. The king would then prance and strut around the room to the applause and cheers of his subjects, who bowed to His Majesty, offering themselves to do his every bidding.

Late one night the nude Dewey headed to the third floor to battle his enemies for the Crown. Reaching the top of the last stairway and turning down the hall toward the Robertson's room, he suddenly stood face to face with Wobble.

"D—n you, Indian," exclaimed the Coach, as he gazed at the naked figure in front of him, "I've never seen an Indian pervert before. Put some clothes on."

"Coach, I was fixing to, right now in a minute."

Patridge watched the coach disappear down the stairs. Quickly he turned into the "domino hall."

The contest rapidly got out of hand. The players grew loud; they argued and slammed the dominos down on the metal desk, creating a loud resonant thunder-like rumbling.

"You could probably hear the dominos hit that metal table a mile away," exaggerated the halfback.

"You could hear them arguing, laughing and slamming the dominos down on that metal desk all the way down into our apartment," mused Wobble. "I never heard such a noise in my life, so I went to break it up."

By the time the Coach reached the noisy den the King had just been "crowned." The festival ended as quickly as it had begun, the members of the royal court facing their adversary.

"The next time I hear a domino shuffle on this table, I'm going to make y'all eat every d—n one of them."

Then Wobble turned toward Dewey.

"Indian, you get your a-s back down on the first floor. I don't want to catch you back up here. If I do, I'll tell you where you're going to start living— in a d—n tee-pee outside. That's where you belong anyway—and put some clothes on. I'm tired of looking at your naked a-s."

Don't try to convince me that academia doesn't demand from it's participants maximum intellectual commitment —- three naked student domino players crowning another naked domino player "King" and dressing him a filthy terry cloth robe for his in-house parade! Had a psychiatrist observed the event, his diagnosis would produce extremely interesting reading.

The domino players probably never knew the coach exited the room quickly to prevent the royal party from hearing his deep laughter.

THE GUITAR PLAYER

Occasionally Ole Miss signed a football player sporting talents other than football. Stan Hindman was a gifted sculptor, even teaching the art in college, as well as selling his own works. Jimmy Weatherly, a musician and singer, became, in addition, a prolific songwriter, and still earns his living in Nashville with those abilities.

In the fall of Nineteen Fifty-Three, a guitar picker and singer from Corinth, Jimmy (Turkey) Hurley cast his lot with the Rebels. In the words of some of us non-professional appreciators of the art, (amateurs) he could "hum the strings."

Ordinarily, Turkey, who lived in Garland Dorm, though most freshmen roomed in Vardaman, played his guitar and sang alone and very softly with his door closed or when he knew Wobble was away from home. Once he forgot.

"I walked by Turkey's room," remembered Buddy Alliston, "heard the pickin' and went in."

Soon, other players, looking for anything to do in order to avoid studying or boredom drifted in! Before long, his room was filled with foot stomping, singing, and dancing football players. A full-scale party had erupted. They forgot about Wobble momentarily, the majesty of the musical moment dulling their senses and sensibilities, not to mention their fears.

As quickly as they had forgotten about him, they remembered him, for there he stood, almost ghostlike, in the doorway. His weight was on his left leg, his left arm reaching up the door frame like a vine growing up an oak tree. Silently, he looked at them, as one by one they ceased performing, until the singing and playing had completely stopped. The musician and his choir looked at the coach nervously and the coach returned the gaze, turning his head ever so slightly until he had looked each one of then directly in the eye. Then he turned his attention totally to the guitar picker, and for a minute, at least, or maybe it was two hours, he stared at Turkey, who glanced alternatingly up and down, waiting for the turbulence which was bound to come.

Finally, the Ghost of Garland spoke. His voice was so low and his tone so soft, the warblers had trouble hearing him.

"Turkey," he whispered, "If I ever catch you playing that d—n guitar in this dorm at night again, I'm going to stick it up your a-s, twist it, and break it off."

With that statement, Wobble turned and walked softly down the stairs, leaving behind him a fulmination of laughter. Not being assigned laps in Garland made his statement much funnier, although most of the laughter may have been caused by fear and nervousness.

Turkey wisely chose to conduct no more concerts in Garland at night. An embedded guitar, he properly reasoned, might hinder his performance on the football field.

Did you know?

OLE MISS MILESTONE VICTORIES
100th win - Sept. 25, 1925 vs. Arkansas
200th win - Sept. 20, 1947 vs. Kentucky
300th win - 1960 Sugar Bowl vs. LSU
400th win - 1973 Villanova

FOR A DROP OF COLD WATER

A lot of mischief occurred in the athletic dorm during the Christmas Holidays, as I have mentioned in other stories, because the players were bored. Football players remained on campus for sixteen straight Christmases at Ole Miss preparing for bowl games, after the other students went home. Idle hands are the devil's workshop, even when the hands are eighteen to twenty-one years old.

Bobby Ray "Waxy" Franklin, nicknamed by Wobble because of his well-manicured hair, tells a story which transpired during the week of boredom following the Nineteen Fifty-Nine season. The Rebs were polishing up to defeat LSU in the Nineteen Sixty Sugar Bowl game. As usual they found themselves alone on the Ole Miss campus, looking for something exciting to do. Waxy found it.

"Bo Ball, Warner Alford and Robert Khayat were taking a bath in the second floor shower. I passed by the bathroom and heard their commotion. That hot shower must have felt real good to them because it was really cold outside," Waxy explained.

The boredom and the temptation together formed an irresistible opportunity for Franklin.

Explaining, he said, "The water cooler was right by the shower door. I filled a large waste can full of ice cold water from the water cooler and bombarded the three bathers. You've never heard such commotion in your life. You would have thought someone had shot at 'em!"

Waxy knew Wobble would be quickly appearing in response to the noise, but he figured he had just enough time to douse the screamers one more time before the coach arrived. In his own words, "I got 'em again," and the bellowing increased but Waxy discovered that his timing was too close

"I was sprinting down the hall when I heard Wobble hustling up the stairs. By the time he got to the hall, I had slowed down to a casual walk, assuming an air of total innocence."

"What are you doing with that waste can, Waxy?", the coach demanded to know.

"Saw some trash on the floor, Coach. Just went to pick it up."

His heart racing and his legs wanting to—, doubting he had convinced Wobble, Waxy forcing himself to calmly walk, turned into the room

"Oh h—l," he thought, "my a-s is caught now!"

Water had run out of the shower stall, onto the bathroom floor and out into the hallway by the time Wobble confronted the screamers.

"Who threw this d—n water all out on the floor, Warner?"

"Coach, I don't know."

"You're a d—n liar!," Wobble countered.

"Bo, who threw this water out on the floor?"

"Coach, I don't know either."

"Khayat, do you know?"

"No, Coach," the future Chancellor lied.

"That's what I figured," the Coach asserted. "You're all lying."

Wobble asked them several more times but they collectively protected Waxy. Honor amongst "thieves" prevailed, even when faced by the progenitor of fear.

Turning from the mum men, Wobble walked down the hall to Ray Brown's room. Ray had enrolled in Law School after his first year with the Baltimore Colts and had been given the job of Dorm Supervisor. In part, his responsibility consisted of restraining noise.

"Miss Brown," Wobble quizzed, referring to his "Mothering" responsibilities, "Who threw the water on the hall floor?"

"I don't know."

"How come you don't know, you're the d—n dorm supervisor?"

"I just don't know, Coach."

"They all knew," Waxy declared, "but they wouldn't tell on me."

Wobble then trekked back into the shower room and asked again, "Warner, Bo, Robert, do you know YET who threw this water?"

"No, Coach," they answered in unison.

"Then, I'll see you in the morning at 5:00 o'clock in the stadium. Maybe that will help you remember."

"Boy they were p—sed off at me!" Waxy concluded. "But I knew they wouldn't tell, honor and all that, you know, and I sure wasn't going to-. They ran the stadium at 5:00 o'clock in the morning."

"Did Wobble know you did it?" I asked.

"Absolutely. He knew I did it. But because they wouldn't tell on me, he made them run the stadium. That morning when they finished, I laughed at them and they cursed me like I was a dog, but I never admitted doing it."

Football players who would protect a teammate even at their own discomfort and pain were the kind who would produce champions and championships. The Coach knew that!

DID YOU KNOW?

Only one person has won both the coveted Jacob's Blocking Trophy as the SEC's best blocker and the SEC Scoring Championship. Paige Cothren earned both the same year, 1955. That year, he also led the nation in field goals and kick scoring, tieing the national record for the most field goals in one season.

FE FE, FI FI, FO FO, FUM

Restlessness causes grown football players to deport themselves in unusual ways sometimes. Bobby Ray Franklin, nicknamed "Waxy", roomed with Marvin Terrell in Garland Dorm in the late Fifties. Ole Miss again was on campus during Christmas Holidays, practicing for a bowl game. Wobble had renamed Marvin, "Cosmetics," because in the words of Marvin's room-mate, he wore "Man-tan" on his face and constantly doused himself with cologne. Wobble sometimes jokingly questioned his masculinity because of his devotion to the mirror.

Two more masculine fellows never played football at Ole Miss, by the way, than Marvin and Waxy.

Marvin owned a record player, fairly rare for Ole Miss football play-ers in the late Nineteen Fifties. His favorite song went something like, "fe,fe,fi,fi,fo,fo,fum— I smell smoke in the auditorium, etc.etc."

"One night," Waxy related, "We were playing that song much too loud and dancing with each other, a sight in itself to behold."

Suddenly, Wobble threw open their door and there they were, Waxy and Cosmetics, two very muscular, masculine football players dancing with each other to a popular song whose words made absolutely no sense— fe,fe,fi,fi,fo,fo,fum—. The dancers stopped and looked at the Coach standing in the doorway his arms crossed, a look of disgust spread across his face.

"I'm going to fefe,fifi,fofo,fum your a-ses! What are you, d—n q—-rs?, dancing with one another?"

The Coach then stuck his head out of the dancers room and yelled, "Fellows, I want all of you to come down here and watch these q—-rs dance with one another. I bet most of you have never seen q—-rs dance together have you? Get on down here and look at this."

(Note: please don't condemn the coach for using that particular word. In the Nineteen Fifties it was used by almost everyone in America. Political incorrectness had not yet been conceived nor implemented.)

Needless to say, not only did the dancing cease, but for the next few weeks the two tough football players became even more aggressive, lest teammates should wonder.

"It wasn't long after that," Bobby Ray exclaimed, "that Wobble poked his head back into my room one afternoon and caught me asleep on my bunk. I sleep on my back with my arms crossed over my chest," he explained, "I guess somewhat like a dead person."

Waxy woke up to the sound of the coach's voice again calling the other players, and to the sound of their giggles.

"Come look at this son of a b—-h, he's dead," Wobble exclaimed. "We need to bury this son of a b—-h!, he's dead."

In the face of that assertion, life quickly flowed back into the corpse, Waxy informing them that he might look dead, but that he was very much alive. Now Wobble, proven to be wrong about the corpse, could be wrong about sexual preference, Waxy figured.

DID YOU KNOW?

SEC team records held by Ole Miss:
> Single game:
>> Pass Completions: 33 vs Alabama in 1969 (52 attempts)
>> Most Touchdowns: 14 vs West Tennessee in 1935
>> Fewest Pass Completions Permitted: 0 vs Arkansas in 1941 (0-8)
>> Lowest Pass Completions Percentage: 0.0% vs Arkansas in 1941 (0-8)
>> Fewest Plays permitted: 24 vs South Carolina in 1947
> Single Season:
>> Average Gain Punt Return: 18.8 in 1948 (36 for 676 yards)

THE MAN OF FLATULENCE

Before you read this story, please be advised that it is a little earthy-but it is funny. It's not obscene but it is coarse, and it reflects the mentality of a dormitory filled with football players in the Nineteen-Fifties. It was so hilarious to me when Bull Churchwell and Dewey Patridge told it, my laughter almost drowned out their voices on the cassette tape. Translating it from the tape to the written page proved to be difficult, too. I laughed through the entire exercise. Even now I laugh about it while driving my car, or dining in a restaurant, or sitting in church, to my shame.

I've tried to stop laughing about it. When someone asks, "What are you laughing at, Paige? Are you laughing at me?"

"Ho,Ho,Ho,Ah,Ah, No," I answer, wiping the tears from my eyes. "I'm not laughing at you, but I can't tell you -ho, ho, what- ho, ho, I'm- ho, ho-laughing at, ho, ho, ooh, ooh—!"

I've tried to figure out why it's so funny to me, and I think there are two reasons: the vividness of the incomparable picture which has been deposited in my mind and my precise knowledge of Wobble. I would have loved being there when Coach broke up that party-I long to see the expression which must have been on his face.

I ought to be mad at Bull and Dewey. The image which they superimposed upon my brain will probably linger with me always. I'm going to get in trouble laughing all the time and trying to convince people that I'm not laughing at them.

I must tell you this-the name of the main character has been changed to protect the guilty-for two very important reasons. I don't want to embarrass his family and I don't want him to kill me. I've renamed him "Brent". He was a football player at Ole Miss and apparently a bastion of grace and an elevator of culture, as you will see.

"Brent could f—t anytime, anytime," Dewey declared, stretching the final "anytime" out into four syllables.

Forming his hand in the shape of a pistol, his forefinger representing the barrel, Bull said "All you had to do is point at him like this and he would cut one. You could meet him on the sidewalk, point, and he would respond. He was so proficient, he could control his volume and tone, and do it as many consecutive times as he wanted to—!"

I'm not certain I believe he could control the volume and tone but I'm glad I wasn't there to find out first hand.

One night the two storytellers and about ten or twelve other football players were in a dorm room playing cards, using matches for chips.

"Ah, h—l, lets quit playing," one of them finally said. "Nobody's winning."

"None of us had any money anyway," Dewey confessed.

Brent, noticing the pile of matches left on the desk said, "I tell you what I'll do! I'll blow every match out for a penny apiece."

"Ah s—t, Brent, you can't do that," one of the guys disputed.

"Can too," Brent argued, and with that he stripped off his clothes and fell down onto one of the bunks.

"There he was," Dewey remembered, "lying on the bed, buck naked with his two legs sticking straight up in the air."

"Light me one, light me one," the performer demanded.

"We'd strike that son of a b—-h, hold it down about six inches from his a-shole and-'Whoooff', he'd blow it out. Just as fast as we could strike 'em, he'd blow 'em out."

By the time Bull and Dewey had related the incident to this point I was on the floor!

"You should have been there," Dewey expounded. "This was entertainment for us."

Holding my sides, I said, "Y'all didn't have television then did you?"

"H—l no, but this was better'n television," Dewey quickly replied. "Television hasn't ever been that good!"

They were laughing and cheering the continuous fifteen-minute performance of the Master of Flatulence when the door burst open, the stack of matches having dwindled by about fifty percent.

"Just about the time Coach Wobble stuck his head into the room, Brent f—ted, Whoooff-went the flame right toward him."

"It was already raunchy in there," Bull explained, "and then he f—ted a flame right toward Wobble."

Wobble, his exasperation elevating the tone of his voice, yelled, "Well I've seen everything now-got a bunch of d—n q—-rs in here. I have never seen anybody look at an a-shole like all of y'all—-Get you're a-ses down to the stadium, everyone of you-NOW!"

I'll bet that was the only time a bunch of Ole Miss football players laughed while running laps in the stadium.

DID YOU KNOW?

A former Ole Miss All-American, Parker Hall was the first person ever to complete 100 passes in one season in the NFL. He did it with 106 in 1937 for the Cleveland Rams, later to become th LA Rams, later to become the St. Louis Rams.

GO TO HELL WOBBLE!

Ed Beatty and Herb Ray Medley, in Nineteen Fifty-Two, lived in the second floor corner room of Garland immediately over Wobble's and Sara's apartment. A group of players congregated in their room one night, late; football season had ended. Wobble loosened his grip a little after football season, not a great amount but some. The players were laughing, talking, and having a good time, a good noisy time! They had slipped some beer into the room, an act either of crowning courage or supreme fatuity, or both, given Wobble's transcendent apprehension record.

In the congregation that night was a friend of Ed Beatty, a student from Memphis, who had gotten drunk and passed out. The football players, Beatty, Medley, Monte Montgomery and the others deposited the "lifeless" body out in the hallway and locked the door, a life preserving necessity when "sipping suds" in the dorm.

Suddenly, someone banged loudly on the door.

"Who is it?" Montgomery asked.

"Coach Wobble! Open this d—n door," came back the gruff reply.

Actually it was Reggie Ott, another football player wanting to enlist in the party.

Recognizing Ott's voice Montgomery screamed, "Go to hell Wobble," temporarily forgetting the proximity of Beatty's room to Wobble's.

Within seconds Wobble stood outside the door, the body on the floor momentarily capturing his attention. He looked down at the body, then he looked at the closed door, then back down at the body, nudging it with his foot. Realizing it wasn't a football player, he stepped over it, stumbling in his haste to open the door which he did.

Reggie, who had gotten into the room before Wobble arrived, jumped into the closet pulling the door shut behind him. Wobble grabbed Monte by the collar and exclaimed, "I'll see all of you in the stadium tomorrow afternoon and that includes you too, Ott." Apparently Reggie's attempt to disappear had failed.

The next afternoon the revelers found themselves running Hemingway, the Coach counting their laps and taunting them at the end of each one.

"How's that party feel to you now boys?" Wobble asked.

"Bet you think you all have gone to hell with me now, don't you, Monte?"

"Need a sip of beer fellows?"

Two changes occurred following that particular social. Beatty's room was never used again, and when a player finally worked up the courage to say "Go to hell, Wobble," he did it so quietly that no one else could hear.

DID YOU KNOW?

Two Ole Miss punters have led the Nation; Frank Lambert with a 44.1 yard average in 1964; and Jim Miller with a 45.9 yard average in 1977.

'HIT'S WAR, 'HIT'S WAR!

In the early Nineteen Sixties Ole Miss signed a boy from the Paris, Tennessee area. To label him "rural" would be an understatement. One of his teammates said he was "the ugliest, dumbest, crudest but funniest boy I have ever seen and he spoke 'rural-ese' with a high pitched nasal twang." His name was Frank and he loved to engage in shaving cream and water fights.

Wobble hated shaving cream and water fights. After one had ended, the malfeasors would try to clean up the evidence before the Coach arrived, an effort which seldom succeeded.

One night Frank, who tried to resist the temptation, could no longer. He maneuvered from the foxhole of his room into the battleground of the hallway dressed for combat in his ROTC shoes without socks, buck naked but wearing his clear plastic ROTC raincoat, his ROTC hat on his head, holding his shaving cream can with a long spout in one hand and a big pitcher of water in the other one.

Challenging everyone in his high pitched voice, the churlish one yelled, "Awe'writ, yew son's 'o b—-hes, 'hits war, by God, 'hits war! I'm gonna wet'che down an' squirt 'yer a-ses with shavin' cream- 'hits war!!"

About the time Frank concluded his challenge, the hallway door opened and suddenly before him stood Coach Wobble. Frank almost swallowed his tongue, standing in front of Wobble, naked in his transparent ROTC raincoat, with his sockless military shoes on his feet and his ROTC cap on his head, a full pitcher of water in one hand and a can of shaving cream in the other—! They were face to face and motionless, the Coach's stern gaze fixed upon the bizarre figure before him.

"Wal' lookee here," the strange looking soldier announced, "Lookee who's came up here t' visit us t'night. How yew, Coach Wobble? I'se jest a'goin' to have me a big drank o'water and shave some o' these whiskers off'en me."

With that, Frank drank the pitcher of water and headed toward the bathroom, his buns clearly flashing against the inside of the raincoat; probably needing to accomplish two "duties" now rather than one after drinking the pitcher of water.

Forty heads sticking out of twenty rooms observed in amazement as the Coach stood agape and motionless, watching the freakish figure saunter down the hallway and disappear into the bathroom.

"I'll be d—ned," one of them exclaimed. "First time I've ever seen him speechless."

Wobble shook his head in apparent disbelief, turned and walked back through the door.

Pressure brings out the best in some people and the worst in others. When Frank, in full battle array, faced Wobble, an intellect which had earned the reputation of being slow momentarily conceived the only course of action by which chastisement might be averted.

If the truth were known, I would bet Wobble "lost it" when he disappeared from the view of the forty heads protruding from the twenty rooms. No man could confront that which the Coach had faced that night without amusement, certainly not Wobble.

DID YOU KNOW?

Charley Conerly and Barney Poole both set national passing records in 1947: Charley, the most passes completed in one year; and Barney the most passes caught in one year. "Conerly to Poole" became a famous by-word in the nation.

I CAN'T BE HELD RESPONSIBLE!

Boredom during practice for bowl games afflicted all the teams throughout the years, as research for the book proved. Over and over I heard the story —- "We were practicing for the bowl, all the other students had left the campus and we were bored."

Boredom for young, testosterone laden college football players ALWAYS spells trouble—for somebody. For those of us supervised by Wobble, it usually spawned trouble for the coach, which then reverberated back to us magnified.

Such was the case for the team practicing for the Nineteen Fifty-Seven Sugar Bowl. They were alone on the campus; all the other students had left for the Christmas holidays.

"We were restless," one of the team's members told me. "Everybody was pranking around. Jackie Simpson and I think either Bull Churchwell or Possum Price were really aggravating Ray Brown our quarterback one night."

Led by Jackie, the antagonists bought some cherry bombs, highly explosive firecrackers with one-half inch long fuses, which afforded about a five-second delay from the time they were lit until they exploded.

Ray, now an attorney on the Mississippi Gulf Coast, was an excellent student. That particular night he was studying at his desk, one end of which was against his open window.

The assailants, if anything, were assiduous. Painstakingly, they measured and cut several pieces of string which were precisely as long as the distance from the window of the room above Ray's room, in which one of the attackers lived, to Ray's open window. To one end of each string they carefully tied a cherry bomb, making certain the burning fuse would not burn through the cord. Then, igniting the cherry bombs, they quickly lowered them to Ray's open window, where they exploded within three feet of him, rattling not only his head but also the entire building. Anticipating certain retribution, everyone in the dorm sprinted to his room and closed the door, my informer related. "Not a creature was stirring, not even a mouse," by the time Wobble arrived at the point of explosion.

The investigating Coach discovered a dormitory filled with totally innocent and ignorant football players. Taking his inquisition to every room, he found some players "asleep;" some were "studying;" others were quietly listening to their radios; while the most committed athletes thought it would be good for Wobble to discover them discussing the Texas Longhorns, their Sugar Bowl opponent.

"Who set off that d—n bomb?" the Coach asked every player. No one knew anything about it!

The next morning Wobble called a team meeting in the old gym where he sat the players in the bleachers. Fear, which tends to neutralize testosterone, although in Nineteen Fifty-Seven, football players at Ole Miss knew little about that, ran rampant.

The players glanced nervously at one another, saying nothing, waiting for Wobble now standing silently before them, his eyes fixed upon the floor, to speak. After several haunting minutes the Coach lifted his head and looked at the anxious football team. His voice was stern, his delivery very deliberate.

"Fellows, you know, I served in World War II. I spent a good part of the war in fox-holes. I slept very little because of rifle fire, hand grenades and incoming mortar and artillery shells and when I did occasionally doze off, the explosions all around me would wake me up. I lived in constant fear of death. Because I care for your safety, I want you to know that I came out of the war about half shell-shocked. A shell-shocked person cannot always control himself. The next time one of those cherry bombs explodes, I cannot hold myself responsible for what I might do—-they sound too much like artillery shells exploding—-SO I'M LIABLE TO KILL THE NEXT SON-OF-A-B—-H WHO LIGHTS ONE—!", his voice rising with the "anger" which all of the players had been expecting. Then he turned and walked out of the building, leaving an entire football team silently anchored to their seats, where each player remained for the next four or five minutes.

Trudging back to the dorm, one of the players turned to a teammate and asked the question pervading the minds of all of them, "Do you think that's true?"

"I don't know," the friend answered, "but I'll be d—ned if I'M gonna be the one who finds out!"

SUPERMAN

We know for certain now, driving and alcohol DO NOT mix. We've always known it physically but now we understand it legally—better not drink and drive anymore.

Football and alcohol might not mix any better.

Ole Miss signed a big, fast running back from Corinth in the early Nineteen Fifties, named Jimmy. Jimmy spent many afternoons on the practice field running over people, and he was fairly adept at it, even when he was a freshman.

Jimmy was also a member of the Air Force R.O.T.C., and one night all the members of his unit threw a huge party. Jimmy went and he participated fully in the festivities.

"For some reason," his roommate Buddy Harbin explained, "I got in before he did that night. It was after the football season and on the weekend and there was no bed-check."

In the middle of the night Jimmy staggered into the room. His Air Force tie was crooked, pulled over to one side; his round blue military hat was cocked over to the side of his head, the bill pointing sideways; his shirt tail dangled from under his dress blue coat.

"Roomie," Jimmy announced to Buddy with a slurred tongue, "I've decided I'm Superman."

"You are?", Buddy asked, a sympathetic smile on his face.

"Yep!—You see that wall 'rite thar?", pointing at the space between the lavatory and a bed. "'Wal lemme' show you how I'm gonna run through it."

He backed up to the other side of the room and ran full speed, — into the wall.

"You remember the old Roadrunner cartoons, Paige?" Buddy asked, —how the old coyote would run into a stone wall or a tree and melt down into a pile on the ground? That's exactly what Jimmy did. He hit the wall full speed, and knocked himself out, —cold as a wedge, and melted into a heap on our floor."

Buddy and another football player carried unconscious Superman to the shower where they soaked him down with cold water.

"In a few minutes Jimmy started to quiver a little, so we knew he wasn't dead," related Superman's roomie, and after a little while he partially revived. Finally, flat upon his back, he opened his eyes and looked up at me. I assured him he wasn't dead."

Of course everyone already knew that. You can't kill Superman.

All of which reminded me of the time I did the same thing, only the wall which I challenged was in Baton Rouge and named Earl Leggett, a three hundred pound All-American tackle for LSU. The result was about the same.

DID YOU KNOW?

The last Ole Miss Athlete to play three major sports was Eddie Crawford, who played football, basketball, and baseball in 1956-57.

WHAT IT WAS, WAS A WINSTON

Wobble hated cigarettes, as a fair number of Ole Miss football players discovered, about as much as he did loafing—and he could not tolerate loafing. He disliked card playing almost as much as he did cigarettes and loafing. Heaven forbid that he should encounter an Ole Miss football player guilty of all three. Heaven have mercy on one committing two out of three.

Jerry Brown and several others were playing cards one night. The door was closed and a feeble attempt was being made to keep down the noise. But as everyone who ever lived in Wobble's dorm knows, more than a feeble attempt must be made to deflect Wobble. Noise, any noise, any decibel of noise, attracted him like a moth to a flood light. Jerry was smoking a cigarette.

"I believe Coach could hear a deck of cards shuffle on an airplane flying over Oxford," one former player said to me. "And he could smell cigarette smoke at two hundred yards, against the wind."

Wobble usually only broke up the card game, scattering the players, but he put smokers in the stadium.

Suddenly the door opened, revealing the prosecutor.

"Break up the card game and go to your rooms," the Coach commanded.

Then turning toward Jerry, Wobble asked, "What's that you're smoking Mr. Brown?"

"A Winston!"

"I'll tell you what you do," Wobble responded. "You get your a-s down to the Student Union, buy a pack of Winston's, and meet me at the stadium."

Jerry Brown was a tough football player. Once in his career at Ole Miss he considered challenging the Coach to his face. But when Wobble invited him out into the hall to "see how tough you really are," discretion triumphed over valor. Jerry was also a smart football player.

Without hesitation, but with much consternation, the smoker trudged to the Student Union, bought the cigarettes and perambulated unenthusiastically to the stadium. Wobble was waiting.

"Hand me the pack, Mr. Brown," the Coach demanded.

Holding it up in front of Jerry's face, Wobble pronounced, "There are twenty cigarettes in this pack. You owe me twenty laps."

Lighting a cigarette he stuck it in Jerry's mouth. "Have it smoked by the time you get back down here," the enforcer warned.

Billy Ray Adams, Jerry's teammate and one of the card players, said, "Wobble made him smoke a cigarette every lap. He would light up a fresh one at the bottom, run to the top of the stadium puffing on the cigarette, and turn the butt into Wobble when he got back to the bottom. For the next two months when Jerry heard the word "CIGARETTE" — he gagged."

Soon after Jerry's adventure, Wobble caught four players engaged in a "no holds barred" water fight. Few water fighters ever escaped his notice. He hated water fights, especially after the players moved from Garland Dorm into Miller Hall, a new and very nice facility for the late Fifties.

Like the old Christmas song states, "the weather outside was frightful" — it was in the dead of winter, very cold outside.

The Coach surprised the four water warriors. They were standing in the hall dripping wet with water, buckets still in hand, their disconsolate eyes fixed upon Wobble as he walked up to them.

"Meet me at the stadium in thirty minutes," Coach commanded.

"The temperature had to have been in the twenties or low thirties," one observer remarked to me. "And the wind was blowing hard."

When the four arrived at the stadium, Wobble was waiting for them — with four buckets filled with water.

"You owe me ten laps to the top of the stadium and back. You like water fights so much, I want you to have one everytime you finish a lap, starting now."

Wobble then made them douse each other with water, run to the top of the stadium and back down to the ground. By the time they got back down, he had refilled the four water buckets.

When finally they finished their laps, Wobble almost pleadingly said, "Now fellows I think this was fun. The next time you gentlemen want to have a water fight, just let me know and we'll meet down here again."

"Co-Co-Coach," one of them shivered over his shoulder as he sprinted toward the warmth of the dressing room, "I don-don-don't th-think we'll ha-ha-have another wa-water fi-fight anytime so-soon."

YOU'D THINK I'D BE SAFE THERE

Not many areas in an athletic dorm provide perfect seclusion. We certainly failed to get it in our rooms, most of which were like Grand Central Station. In those isolated and rare moments when I did want to study, I went to the library. Even the Library grew a little noisy when several football players were "studying" at the same table.

The showers were certainly public and not places of separation. There were no shower doors or curtains, just an eighteen-inch high wall separating the shower area from the rest of the tiled toilet. They were community showers, large enough and with showerheads enough to bathe six large football players.

In Garland, even shaving was semi-public. Each room offered a small lavatory with an even smaller mirror above it, an indifference to some young athletes whose beards had not yet developed to the shaving stage.

About the only place that a fellow living in an athletic dorm could find a few moments of quiet and peaceful sequestration was the toilet. Ah, the toilet! It had a door, which separated a person from everything outside. Locking it from within, a user could enjoy the full fruits offered by the tiny cubicle in complete solitariness. After all, which foolish teammate would dare subject himself to the natural odorous results of invading such a privacy. Wobble, the Ghost of Garland probably couldn't even find you in the toilet.

That's precisely what Dudley Turkhurst thought one fine Spring day. Like all industrious football players, he decided to cram two endeavors into the same time frame, performing both, his daily constitutional and smoking a cigarette, in the safe confines of the toilet. (Dudley had probably taken a Time/Management course in Business School and was eager to test a theory.)

He was extremely relaxed and completely enjoying himself when suddenly two feet appeared under the cubicle door. At the same instant, the man attached to the feet banged loudly on the thin metal separation and yelled, "Open the door."

Dudley reached up and unlatched his door. "How did he know?," the caught athlete wondered. "I just lit it up."

The door swung open. Wobble looked down into the guilty face of the felon sitting upon his throne, smoke swirling around his head.

"Um Huh," Wobble grunted. "As soon as you empty that a-s out, I'll see you at the stadium."

Dudley ran laps up and down Hemingway the rest of the afternoon.

Someone remarked later, "Man if you can't hide from Wobble on the commode, there's no use trying to hide from him anywhere."

Twenty years of Ole Miss football players would heartily agree!

DID YOU KNOW?

Following the 1956 season, Paige Cothren either held or had tied all the National College field goal records: Most field goals for career; Most in one season; longest; and most points by field goals.

THE NIGHT THE LIGHTS WENT OUT

One winter night in the late Fifties, a storm roared through Oxford. The lights went out in Garland Dorm, about 6:30 P.M. The rooms were pitch black.

Bull Churchwell and his roomie George Blair wanted to go to town, but they couldn't see how to get dressed — but not to worry. Football players then may have been less than ingenious when it came to finding study time, but they were more than sagacious when figuring out how to get to the movies.

Churchwell retrieved the large metal trash can from the end of the hall into which he dropped a couple of newspapers and a match. Then, fed by one sheet of newspaper at a time, the fire created just enough light by which he could dress. Bull placed the can in the hall immediately outside his door, along with a stack of newspapers which he had confiscated from several rooms.

"You dress first, George, and I'll feed the fire," Bull exhorted.

After George dressed, Bull said, "Now George you feed it and I'll get ready, but don't put but one sheet at a time in it."

About that time Jackie Simpson and Kent Lovelace, who had groped up the stairs, spotted the firey lamp. One of them grabbed the stack of newspapers and threw all of them into the can, creating, as you might imagine a sudden raging fire. The other one threw a hand full of cherry bombs into it.

"Sounded like a war," Bull reflected. "Fire was bumping the ceiling, and the bombs blew burning newspaper all over the hall."

George frantically placed his right foot against the metal furnace and pushed.

"The can slid almost all the way down the hall," Bull continued. The cherry bombs were still exploding when the can came to rest."

Wobble hustled up the stairs. So did Bobby Ray Franklin, a quarterback, and in the darkness they bumped into each other on the stairway. Bobby Ray grabbed the dark figure next to him and excitedly said, "Come on, let's get up there and shoot some more cherry bombs."

"You little son of a b—-h, you'd better get back down those stairs or I'll shoot your cherry bomb."

By the time Wobble chased Waxy back down the stairs and arrived at the scene of the crime both Bull and George had locked their door and hidden in the closet.

"Ya'll weren't the only ones who hid in their closets," a teammate countered. "Every football player in the dorm had hidden in his closet."

Good thing Mississippi State football players didn't know about that—the night every Ole Miss player hid in his closet! What an encouraging incentive that would have been for the Bullies.

DID YOU KNOW?

For more than thirty years, Showboat Boykin held the National record for most touchdowns scored in one game, seven against State in 1951.

KNOCKING WHAT OUT?

Not many Ole Miss signees, in the late Forties, Fifties, and early Sixties brought complete wardrobes to Ole Miss. The problem wasn't that we left them at home, we didn't have them. Most of us brought all the clothes we owned — but we didn't own many.

Though I told Louie Brown a different story (see Let's Make A Deal - Game Day), I brought three pairs of blue jeans and three pairs of dress slacks with me to Ole Miss my freshman year. I rolled in luxury with six or seven shirts.

Like a few other players, though, Dewey Patridge had fewer clothes than I.

"I didn't have any clothes," Patridge admitted. "I came to Ole Miss with a pair of blue jeans and a pair of corduroy pants."

The only coat Dewey owned was his high school football jacket from Philadelphia High School, but he knew better than to wear it. Upper classmen gave freshmen who wore their high school jackets or sweaters a hard time in those days, days of freshmen hazing. Reminding the varsity that you were once a high school hero brought all of their wrath down upon you.

A great fullback from Cleveland, Mississippi, Slick McCool came to Ole Miss in Nineteen Fifty-Two wearing his high school All-American T-shirt and a wide leather belt with "Big Slick" emblazoned upon it. He learned quickly not to wear his T-shirt. The upper classmen wore his belt out on his rear-end.

"It had turned really cold," Dewey continued. "Those corduroy pants were warmer than the blue jeans. I only had a couple of shirts, one short sleeve and one long sleeve. I didn't have a sweater."

Dewey had worn his warm corduroy pants several days in a row.

"I had probably worn them at least ten or twelve straight days," explained the halfback. I came into my room after practice one day, took my pants off, flung them across a chair, and settled down for a nap."

Suddenly the door opened displaying Wobble.

"Coach!," Dewey greeted.

Wobble said nothing. He glanced around the room until his gaze focused upon Dewey's corduroy trousers. The coach reached down, gingerly grasping the pants by the belt, turned and walked outside the room into the hallway.

"Then I heard the d—nest sound," the halfback exclaimed. "I jumped up and ran out into the hall. There was Coach Wobble beating my corduroy pants against the wall."

"Coach, what are you doing to my pants?" Dewey frantically asked.

"I thought Coach Wobble was going crazy," he explained to me.

"You've worn these d—n pants every day since you've been here, Quail. I'm beating the f—ts out of them."

Then laughing, both of them went back into Dewey's room and sat down. Softly Wobble then looked at the part Indian boy and said, "You are just like I was when I got to Ole Miss, Quail. Not a pot to p—s in nor a window to throw it out."

DID YOU KNOW?

Eleven former Ole Miss football players have been selected to the National Football Hall of Fame.

THREE CHERRY BOMBS AND A SPRINT

Christmas of Nineteen Fifty-Seven, for Ole Miss football players was spent in Garland Hall preparing for the Sugar Bowl, a Lonesome Hotel for young men accustomed to the glitter and family of Christmas at home. There were no trees with presents, no candles pushing their soft, warm inviting light out of welcoming windows. Garland had no kitchen, no oven, no refrigerator, so there were no fruitcakes, no turkey and dressing, and certainly no eggnog, either with or without the nog.

Mrs. Calhoun and the athletic cafeteria staff had done all they could-placing small inexpensive decorations on most the tables, each offering six or eight football players a surrogate Christmas dinner, but that wasn't enough.

Christmas is home. Even for young, autonomous college football players, bent on toughness and independence, Christmas without family, food, laughter, and presents becomes just another day. Christmas in the South is remembering its real meaning with loved ones.

But Christmas cannot be cancelled, it is still Christmas. And with it comes automatically some frivolity. It was Christmas night in Garland Hall. All the other students except the basketball team had left the campus. The football players were left to their own devices about how to celebrate the occasion, which in itself was dangerous.

Because it was Christmas, Wobble loosened his authoritative grip slightly for one night, a compassionate gift to young men who were forced to spend the holidays away from home. Ordinarily, very little noise was allowed in the dormitory, especially at night. Though the noise limit had expanded temporarily, still there was one.

"The guys were trying to elevate themselves into a festive mood," related Jack Cavin, an end from Crosby. "A lot of noise was going on in the dorm. We knew Wobble was gonna' bound up the stairs pretty soon."

In the midst of all the laughter, tussling, and frolicking, somebody decided to intensify the celebration. He lit three cherry bombs, threw them into one of the empty metal garbage cans at the end of the hall, and slammed the metal lid back onto it.

"Once the bombs were lit and placed in the garbage can," continued Jack, "there was no reversal! The die was cast."

And the race was on—! Out of every room sprinted Ole Miss football players, intent on only one thing, putting distance between themselves and the explosion, which was bound to come.

Wobble, who was already coming up the stairs, heard the lid slam onto the garbage can and moved toward the sound.

The players headed toward the exit.

The timing couldn't have been more perfect. At precisely the same instant Wobble lifted the lid, the cherry bombs exploded.

"By the time the bombs exploded," declared Jack, "I had run two hundred yards. I ran two hundred yards in the same length of time it took the fuses of three cherry bombs to burn. And I didn't lead the pack. Some fellows passed me!"

Wobble's ears must have rung for a week. The athletes should have been, and probably were, grateful that it was Christmas and that their coach had once played football and committed similar deeds.

Beginning about an hour after the explosion, the players began to filter back into the dorm tiptoeing in sacred Holy Night silence. Yuletide celebration had ended-suddenly.

"No one ever admitted putting the cherry bombs in the trash can," Jack concluded, "though it was probably either Jackie (Rock) Simpson or Bobby Ray (Waxy) Franklin."

Common sense would wager that no one ever will.

DID YOU KNOW?

Kayo Dottley led the nation in rushing yardage with 1,312 yards in 1949.

TO CATCH A SMOKER

We now know cigarettes are bad for us, or at least we think they are. My Dad smoked for eighty years, minus the first ten of his life and never had lung cancer. Once when a blight hit the tobacco crop in this country, cigarettes tripled in price. My sister called me.

"Paige, don't you think this would be a good time for YOUR father to quit smoking?"

"I don't know-why do you ask?"

Well cigarettes have tripled in cost," she explained. "He smokes two packs a day. I thought that might be incentive for him."

"You may be right. I'll talk to him."

"Dad," I reminded him the next day, "you know cigarettes have tripled in price. Don't you think this would be a good time for you to stop smoking?"

"No," he sharply retorted.

"Why not?'

"H--l son, they're just now getting up to what they are worth."

I never mentioned stopping to him again, although I admit I wish I had inherited all the money he spent on tobacco through the years.

As much as my Dad loved cigarettes, Wobble hated them-and he implemented a clear rule against smoking for all Ole Miss football players.

Some rules, it has been said, are made to be broken. Training rules under Vaught's staff, especially Wobble, weren't—! His rules were clear, immutable and enforced. The penalty for breaking them was exacted without exception-laps in the stadium or worse.

Richard (Possum) Price, an outstanding guard at Ole Miss from Vicksburg in the late Fifties, was a life-long smoker. Wobble was a life-long catcher of smokers. With his becoming a Rebel, the stage was thereby set for a four year skirmish between the Coach and the smoker, a contest which would capture the interest and attention of every player.

"Wobble's goal was to catch me smoking," confessed Possum. "As determined as he was to catch me, I was determined that he wouldn't. As afraid of him as I was, I still couldn't give them up."

The ongoing battle between the guard and the Coach was hilarious.

All the players and some of the ex-players knew about it. Bets were placed by the observers and most of the money was on Wobble. But Price had refined the act of evasion, a skill more than necessary if one was to keep from being caught by the Ghost of Garland.

One ex-football player remarked, "Wobble didn't have to see the cigarette. He could smell the smoke at 400 yards and he'd trail the smoke to the smoker just like a hound dog trails a rabbit." (Sara later confessed to me the truthfulness of that statement.)

Possum, about as skilled in evasion as Wobble was in apprehension, studied Wobble's habits. From his room in Miller Hall, Price could see the lights in Wobble's apartment.

"When they went off," he confessed, my cigarette went out. Then I would watch Wobble slipping in the dark toward my room. Just as he prepared to look into my room, I would stick my head out of my door and say,'Hi Coach.'"

Stopping abruptly and gazing sternly at the smoker, Wobble would utter a frustrated"H–l," and briskly walk away.

"That little ritual occurred almost every night," Possum exclaimed, "and he never caught me, but he never stopped trying."

Knowing Price was smoking and realizing that all the other players knew and were watching, Wobble said to Bruiser Kinard one day, "I know he's smoking and I'm going to catch him. When I do, I'm going to run his butt off."

"H--l," Bruiser retorted, "I don't think I'd catch him then." Possum was too good a football player to lose to cigarettes, Bruiser surmised.

To a principled Coach, it was the principle of the thing.

"For years after I left Ole Miss," Possum confessed, "when I saw Wobble, I threw my cigarette down. If it was too late to throw it down I would cuff it." (Cuffing a cigarette involves folding your hand around it so it cannot be easily seen by others).

Wobble usually responded with a compliment of sorts.

"You can still cuff a d--n cigarette better than anyone I've ever seen, Possum."

WE'RE GATHERED HERE TODAY BELOVED—!

Football players at Ole Miss back in the Fifties and Sixties experienced a few certainties-death, taxes, long hard workouts, bed checks during the week by Wobble, and bed check on Friday nights before football games by either Buster Poole or Bruiser Kinard.

Buster's and Bruiser's method of conducting bed check was unique. Escorted by a manager carrying a basket of Red Delicious apples, they would open each room door and in the dim light, throw an apple at each bed. If the apple bounced off the bed onto the floor, the lights came on. If the apple was caught, they said, "Good night" and closed the door.

Wobble checked differently. He walked over to each bed and looked at the occupants.

An ordinary bed check turned out to be a extraordinary one when Wobble opened the door to Bill (Foggy) Basham's room one night.

Foggy, so named by Wobble because his mind seemed to function that way, was a guard who played at Ole Miss in the late Fifties and early Sixties. A liberal arts major, he differed from the preponderance of Ole Miss football players, most of whom studied physical education, business, or engineering. Math was anathema to Foggy as it was anathema to me.

I hated Math. I could never figure out the problems. A train leaves New Orleans on a certain set of tracks at a particular time, bound for Chicago at a certain speed. Another train leaves Chicago for New Orleans on a parallel set of tracks at a certain time at a certain speed. "Where do they meet?"

One thing about my answer, it was consistent. "Who cares?"

"Who cares?", two short little words, qualified me to take the course again.

I'm sixty-two years old at this writing. I can never remember using that information to solve any kind of problem in life or business.

Anyway, Foggy loved the Arts and was involved in theatre. He was adept in English, Literature, and Language. He was also in the right place at the right time in Houston, Texas, one night in Nineteen Sixty.

Ole Miss traveled to Houston to play the Cougars. Bill failed to make the traveling squad but he didn't fail to make the trip. He hitch-hiked to Houston, drank several beers with some friends, and went to the game. An Ole Miss student manager saw him enter the stadium.

By half time, Ole Miss was in a little trouble. Four of Ole Miss' five guards were hurt, and the game was close. The coaches were discussing what they should do, perhaps move a tackle to the guard position.

"Coach," the manager suddenly remembered, "Foggy's in the stands."

"Foggy's in the stands? Go get him."

It took the manager a while to find him, but just before halftime ended, the wayfaring guard had dressed in a uniform and with the rest of the team, ran onto the field for the second half. Foggy played a great game, beer and all, and Ole Miss won the game. He was promptly promoted to first team and played in every game the rest of the season.

Basham was different in many ways from the average athlete, not the least of which was his love for wild animals. Somehow, he caught a beaver in a nearby lake, tamed it, and taught it to come to him, by clapping his hands.

"D—nedest thing you ever saw," Wobble asserted. "Foggy would walk up to the edge of the water, clap his hands and the beaver would swim right up to him."

Following bed check that night, Wobble closed Foggy's door. Standing in the hall, the Coach thought, "Something doesn't look right in there. I believe something was in bed with Foggy." He hoped it was some-*thing*, and not some-*one*.

Opening the door again, Wobble re-entered the room. In the dim light he could see the outline of the guard in his bed-but he could see something else, something which looked like an animal's tail sticking out from under the covers.

"Foggy, What in h—l do you have in bed with you?," the Coach asked as he switched on the light.

"Coach, this is my beaver!"

"Both of you get you're a-ses out of here, in a hurry," ordered the coach. Then he looked at the other side of the room. It was covered with willow boughs and long grass. Foggy wanted to make the beaver feel at home.

The guard reluctantly took his beaver back to the lake. His teammates helped him clean up his room, disposing of the vegetation and beaver manure, which had accumulated for a few days.

But Bill grew lonesome without his beaver and several days later, unbeknowing to Wobble, he slipped the animal back into his room, willow boughs and all. This time the beaver tamer provided a few more amenities for his pet. He redesigned the large community shower to create a swimming pool.

The other players, however, weren't happy about their shower having been converted into a beaver swimming hole, so they retrieved a gallon of janitorial disinfectant from the dormitory supply closet and emptied it into the pool, figuring a clean beaver was more desirable than a dirty one.

It worked! The disinfectant cleaned beaver, but it also propelled him out into eternity. Father Foggy was devastated but not without understanding.

The football players, not fully realizing the consequence of their action, were sorry. They are, by their very natures, proud, honorable, and compassionate people (I write with tongue in cheek), so they organized a funeral for beaver.

Led by the grieving parent, the players conducted the procession complete with preaching, singing, and of course a eulogy. The team-mates, remembering his loyalty to Foggy and his extraordinary ability to adjust to dormitory life, laid Beaver to rest in his own coffin, built especially for him by the football players of Garland Dorm, all of whom tearfully attended.

A unanimous resolution was passed declaring that Garland Dorm without Beaver would never again be the same.

"D—n well better not be," declared the Coach.

QUANTRELL'S CASINO

I've always admired really good card players, their talents and abilities made famous by Hollywood; Randolph Scott, drawing to an inside straight, knowing before his three cards slithered across the table what they were. I knew too, because heroes, especially western heroes, always won card games in the Nineteen Fifties. For a western star to lose a card game would have been his extempore demise, a fall from Grace, his coup de grace, a fumbled ball going over the goal line for the winning touchdown in the Sugar Bowl.

I played some cards, Casino and Hearts, with my roommate at Ole Miss, Jerry McKaskel. We played for intellectual pride, which ought to have been gleaned from test grades, but weren't. Jerry and I kept score on the wall of our room. We closed the score out, totaled the wins and losses at the end of each school year, and continued the games the next fall. As I recall, Jerry's column of wins was infinitely longer than mine.

I tried again in pro football. Somehow I discovered that Lamar Lundy, a huge tight end from Purdue, later to become one of the Rams defensive Fearsome Foursome, liked to play hearts. I challenged him.

For two years we sat together on every plane trip and played hearts. He and McKaskel could have had a calorific contest. The only difference in playing Lamar was that we had no stationary wall on which to emblazon our score. I stayed away from the Halls of Las Vegas.

Every Ole Miss squad, I suppose, contained at least one prolific card player, a young, bright and extremely valorous football player, so described because of Wobble's dislike for cards.

The Freshman coach and dorm parent viewed cards as trouble, a potentially disruptive non-redemptive exercise. And of course, he was right, especially when the stakes are one hundred percent of a very small bank account. Wobble never expressly forbade the playing of cards but he very strongly counseled against playing poker. Those players who partook brandished a special courage, or so the rest of us thought.

Gene Paul Bardwell, nicknamed Quantrell because of his daring endeavor, loved poker, maintaining an almost continuous poker game in his dorm room. Having miraculously evaded the investigative raids of the Coach for three months, Quantrell grew confident that Wobble had relaxed his famous grip and would allow his game room to continue. Right before

Christmas vacation in the late Fifties, Bardwell printed a large sign and mounted it above his door-<u>Quantrell's Casino</u>.

But casinos in a state where gambling is illegal constantly face the danger of raids by law enforcement agents. Gamblers usually know the risks, so Quantrell couldn't have been overly shocked when he returned to his gaming hall after the holidays. Gone was his advertisement. Two, one by four boards had been nailed across his door and a new sign hung in the old one's place - <u>Closed By Order Of Sheriff Wobble Davidson</u>.

DID YOU KNOW?

Four Ole Miss players have won National Back of the Week awards: Paige Cothren, FB against Ark. In 1955; Bobby Franklin, QB against Miss State in 1958; Jake Gibbs, QB against Miss State in 1960; and Archie Manning, QB twice, against Alabama and LSU both in 1969.

I'M PASSING, COACH

In another story, I talked about football players trying to study in Garland Hall. It was difficult to do and many of us used that as an excuse not to do it.

The academic acumen, if it might be so labeled, of the preponderance of football players at Ole Miss in the Nineteen Fifties, was to pass without studying. The perception seemed to exist that anyone could study and pass, and anyone could refuse to study and fail. To refuse to study and yet pass took special talent. Unfortunately, that special talent often included cheating.

Don't ask me how our collective mentality evolved to that position. I don't know. But I do know how it was conveyed to freshmen football players by the varsity. When caught studying, upperclassmen ridiculed us. But that didn't hurt our feelings-we were frantically looking for an excuse not to study anyway.

When we became upperclassmen we taught the new Freshmen Class the principle.

All wasn't lost, though. Those of us who embraced that academic philosophy spent as much time studying as the most intellectual student. We studied constantly about how to pass without studying.

"One night I was actually trying to study," reflected Dewey Patridge. "I had my books all spread out on my desk. I had been at it for awhile when Coach Wobble came into my room."

"Well, what are you doing, Quail?"

Almost embarrassingly, Patridge admitted, "I'm trying to study, Coach."

He said, "I'm proud of you Quail. That's good-you studying. How are you doing in that subject?"

"Coach, I think I'm passing it!"

"Passing!" the Coach exclaimed. "H−l, Quail, you can't pass. You can't even pass what you eat!"

THINKING AHEAD

One difference between football players at Ole Miss in the mid to late Forties from all others was their backgrounds—many of them came back to school from the military, having studied leadership, discipline, authority, and tactics. They had been taught to think under extremely stressful conditions, in some cases actual combat. As a group they may have been more creative than all the rest of us. That certainly appeared to be true with three of them anyway.

In Nineteen Forty-Seven, football players lived in Huddleston Hall, three players to a room, in some cases, quarters probably too close for athletes, even those tempered by the war. Three roommates were Chubby Ellis, Jerry Tiblier, and Bobby Peetes.

One night Bobby, who was a boxer, exclaimed to Chubby, "You want me to show you how I knocked that boy out in the Golden Gloves in Memphis?" Before Chubby could answer, Bobby pounded Jerry, who was facing the mirror, in the back with both fists. Jerry demanded, of course, that he stop, but he wouldn't. Still facing the mirror, the battered one filled a glass with water to splash on Bobby, who upon seeing him do it, quickly grabbed Jerry's clean shirt which was still on a hanger and held it in front of him. Without looking, Tiblier quickly turned and propelled the water into his own shirt.

When Jerry realized he had soaked his own shirt, he filled the container and wet Peetes down again. Bobby reciprocated, and Chubby laughed which brought the ire of both down upon him. A full-fledged three man water fight erupted. When Jerry saturated Chubby's bed, Chubby threw him out of the room in his underwear, locked the door and wouldn't let him back in.

Not to be defeated, Tiblier retrieved a two gallon bucket, filled it with water, went outside and emptied it into the room through the window.

Masculinity demanded retaliation, so Bobby unplugged a lamp, took the electric wire loose, peeled it, attached the naked wire to the doorknob and plugged it back into the wall.

"Jerry's gonna light up like a Christmas tree when he comes back in and grabs that doorknob," Peetes prophesied. But Jerry didn't grab the doorknob. He recruited an old metal, military trunk from the hall closet and threw it against the door. When the metal trunk struck the booby-trap, the dorm electrical system exploded and all the lights went out.

"Bobby and I had dates that night," related Chubby, "but we couldn't get out of the room. Tiblier was still standing there in the dark with a two-gallon bucket of water ready to throw on us, dating clothes and all."

Calling upon all their intellectual resources, they conceived a plan. Chubby and Bobby rolled their dating trousers, underwear, shirts, shoes, and socks up in raincoats, secured them with belts and dropped them to the ground beneath their window.

"Then," Chubby continued, "we both put on Jerry's clothes, disconnected the wire from the wall and doorknob and opened the door." Still standing there was their roomate, wet weapon in hand.

"Please don't wet us!" Peetes quickly begged, "We're dressed for our dates."

With no compassion, even glee, Jerry inundated them and his own clothes with water.

"We stripped Jerry's clothes off right there in the hall, left them with him, and darted out the darkened dorm into the night," Chubby elaborated. "Once outside, we put on our dry clothes and headed for the girls' dorm.

"ALRIGHT! Tell me football players can't think!"

CHAPTER III

BULLY

A letter came from my mother. I was living in Hollywood, playing professional football for the Los Angeles Rams. I think the year was Nineteen Fifty-Eight but I can't be certain about that.

The envelope contained two items. One was the note from mother. The other was an article cut out of a newspaper, probably either the Jackson Clarion Ledger or the Natchez Democrat. I assumed the article was about me. It wasn't, it was about a dog - Bully - Mississippi State's mascot. The clipping announced that Bully had been stolen and Ole Miss students were suspected, probably football players.

"No!", I questioned, with tongue in cheek, "How could anyone possibly think that—-! Not fine, young, wholesome, innocent Ole Miss football players. No one in his right mind could ever come to that dastardly conclusion."

The next article my mother sent me said that Bully had been found in a most unusual place, dressed in a most unusual attire. The Mississippi State people, according to the story, were very upset about Bully's pilgrimage to the Holy Land.

For years, I've tried to get someone to tell me the story.

The Ole Miss people I asked would grin and deny any knowledge of it. They didn't know how he was kidnapped or who did it. I could tell it was a "hush-hush" topic.

The State people I asked would scowl and deny any knowledge about it too. They thought they knew how he was purloined and who did it, but they "couldn't prove it." "But it d--n sure isn't funny," they would declare.

I had just about given up. No one seemed to want to talk about it, so through the years I finally quit asking. I figured I'd go to my grave never knowing what really happened to Bully, sorrow upon sorrow!

I was wrong!

Most of the time I hate being wrong. It seems like I've been wrong most of my life. At least there have always been people around to tell me that—! (I eventually discovered they were right.)

When I was seven years old, I accidentally set the Adams County equipment barn on fire. When lots of people asked me how I did it, I told them that I had struck a match to light a cigarette I had stolen.

"Wrong - wrong - wrong - wrong," they said. "You shouldn't have stolen a cigarette; you shouldn't have smoked a cigarette; you shouldn't have struck a match in the county barn; and you shouldn't have thrown the lighted match onto the greasy floor.

When I was thirteen, I started going steady with a pretty little blond in my class at Crosby Junior High.

"That's wrong," my parents and relatives told me.

I didn't think it was wrong. She was really cute.

I was offered a football scholarship to LSU, when I finished high school at Natchez. One of the assistant coaches came all the way from Baton Rouge to talk to me. "If you come play football for us, we'll give you a lot more than a dinky little 'ol scholarship," he offered.

"What will you give me?"

"Well, I'll tell you but you can't tell anyone else," he beseeched. "That would be wrong for you to tell, and you sure can't tell your Uncle Buster."

I didn't want to do anything wrong so I promised not to tell Uncle Buster.

When I told Uncle Buster, he said I was wrong three times. I was wrong to listen to the offer; and I was wrong to promise I wouldn't tell him; but because I had promised not to, I was wrong to tell.

I got confused on that one.

I came to Ole Miss on a scholarship and fifteen dollars a month laundry money. I thought that was wrong, but I would have been wrong to tell Bus I thought it was wrong. He might have said, "Then you should have gone to LSU." If I had gone to LSU, I would have been wrong, and dead too. Buster would have killed me. So I figured there were things worse than being wrong.

I was wrong every day I practiced football at Ole Miss and every game in which I played. I know I was wrong because all the coaches told me I was--, especially Buster.

I like syllogisms, you know, with a major premise and a minor premise? A fellow can learn a lot by thinking syllogisms, so I applied a syllogism to my situation in football to see if someone else could be wrong other than me.

Lets' see -

> Major Premise= Paige plays football at Ole Miss, first string.
>
> Minor Premise=Paige is wrong, so he's a bad player.
>
> Conclusion= Ole Miss is bad in football.

I didn't bother to offer that touch of learning to my uncle. He would have said I figured it wrong.

After I graduated from Ole Miss I got married. A fellow doesn't even know how to be wrong until he's married.

Then I played professional football. Everytime I missed a block, or a tackle, or a field goal, the coach reminded me I was wrong.

After pro football I entered the grocery business. All the ladies looked at my prices and told me they were wrong.

Finally I sold my supermarkets and went into counseling. My counselees were nice. They didn't tell me I was wrong-they just asked, "Are you certain that's right?"

For five years, Uncle Sam thought I was wrong and said so in letters. "Gather up all your personal and business financial records and report to the Internal Revenue Office," they wrote. We lived in Southaven and Internal Revenue was in Columbus. I had to spend a whole day proving to them I wasn't wrong.

For four years I was nice to the lady at Internal Revenue. I would gather all my financial records and arrange them into neat little categories for her. I would say, "Yes, Ma'am" and "No, Ma'am," with a nice little insecure, frightened smile on my face.

She never found anything wrong but she never looked at me and said it. She just said, "Thank you, Mr. Cothren."

Simple courtesy, I thought, would have required her to say "You did nothing wrong, Mr. Cothren. See you next year," but she never did.

When I got my letter the fifth year, I found a big cardboard box and I dumped all my records into it. I drove to Columbus with locked jaw and clinched teeth. I walked into Ms. Revenue's office; I turned the cardboard box upside down; and I emptied all the papers onto her desk.

She told me, "You're wrong to do that Mr. Cothren."

I walked out of her office and said, "I won't be back."

Most of the time I feel bad when I do something wrong. Dumping those papers on that lady's desk made me feel good! It's probably wrong to feel good about that!

Walking out of her office and saying, "I won't be back," made me feel even better, so I figured, when it comes to the Internal Revenue, it's wrong to do right and it's right to do wrong. I didn't even have to apply a syllogism to discern that truth. I think it was self-evident-some truths are I've been told.

So I was very happy to discover that I would finally learn what had happened to Bully and I can't wait to tell you about it, but I'm not certain about one thing. The person who told me the story is the one who actually stole Bully, who lifted him up out of his dog pen, and introduced him to the glory of Garland Hall.

Would it be wrong to disclose his identity? Maybe so! I think I'll call him "Horse." That's not his real name but it's close and I'm going to write his story exactly as he told it to me.

BROTHERLY LOVE

The entire episode started with Frank Halbert, Hobby Horse, a half-back from Aberdeen. Hobby Horse is a horse of a different color from the one who actually captured Bully, but he was a key figure in the incident.

Frank's older brother Molly played halfback for Mississippi State. Ordinarily I would discount the ability of a boy named Molly, but not in this case. He was a six foot, two hundred pound running back for the Bulldogs. Along with being my personal friend, he was a very tough runner, starting for two years at State. He had one basic problem other than playing for State - Frank.

Blood should be thicker than collegiate commitment, but in the Halbert home, that may not have been true.

Both Frank and Molly were home for the weekend. For some reason, Molly disclosed Bully's hiding place to his brother. Mistake, Mistake, Mistake!

The word had gotten out that Ole Miss was going to steal the mascot.

State people were being very careful not to divulge the location of his kennel, that is everyone except a loving brother. Knowing Molly and Frank as I do, I imagine Frank extracted the information from Molly much as Delilah deceived Samson, "You don't love me if you won't tell me."

For whatever reason, Molly told Frank that Bully was kept in a pen behind a particular fraternity house on the State campus. As soon as Frank arrived back at Ole Miss, he told his teammates.

College football season had ended and both schools were in basketball season. They were scheduled to play each other the following Saturday night in Oxford. Horse and his team, like General Patton laying plans to capture prisoners, began on Monday to formulate a plan to confiscate Bully. By Wednesday night, they had generated what they believed to be a good one.

A short while before midnight two cars left for Starkville. Two hours later they arrived on the Mississippi State campus.

With car lights having been turned off several blocks from their destination, the two vehicles eased to a stop down the street from the fraternity. Horse and three others slipped up the street and around the side of the frat house, being very careful not to make any noise. Peeping around a corner of the house, the invaders spotted the dog pen. In fact they spotted several dog pens. Trying to determine in which pen Bully was housed, the four carefully made their way the remaining few feet to the nearest fence.

"Suddenly all h--l broke loose," Horse shared. "About twenty beagles bounded out of dog houses in the other pens barking like crazy."

"These beagles are Bully's watch dogs," one of the fellows frantically whispered.

"Lights in the fraternity house began to come on," Horse explained. "And not only in that house but in several adjoining houses. People started yelling out the windows. What's going on out there?"

"We'd better get the h--l out of here," one of them groaned.

An instant before they cancelled their mission Bully obligingly trotted out of his house, right to the fence. An estatic Horse quickly reached through the fence and grabbed him. Then he lifted him up on the inside of the pen to one of the raiders who had climbed to the top of the fence and was reaching down on the inside. They had him!

Bully now firmly in their grasp, the detail sprinted toward their singular car, the other one having left when the beagles started barking. A nervous driver had remained in Horse's car with the motor running.

"By the time we reached our car with Bully, Mississippi State students were pouring out of the houses," Horse exclaimed. "Some of them seeing us run toward our car, ran toward theirs.

Finally reaching the vehicle with the dog, they piled in and yelled to the get-away driver, "Get the h—l outa here." Horse and Bully, along with the others jumped into the back seat. In the confusion, the driver did not know they had gotten the mascot. The others assumed he did.

The raiders sped to about a half-mile start on their pursuers.

"They never had a prayer of catching us," declared Horse. "Our driver put the petal to the metal. Probably set a speed record between Starkville and Oxford."

Horse continued, "About ten miles out of Starkville, Bully, in the back seat with me,   f—ted."

"He was probably expressing his displeasure at being captured," I thought out loud.

"I don't know about that," continued Horse. "But it was bad."

"Horse, stop that," the ignorant driver warned. "I'm trying to concentrate on out running these jokers."

"It was the dog," explained Horse.

"Sure it was," responded the driver.

A few minutes later, Bully did it again.

"Stop that, I said!"

"It was the dog," reiterated Horse.

"What do you mean the dog?", looking over his shoulder into the back seat, the driver asked.

"Keep your eyes on the road, Fool," one of the thieves threatened. "You're going to kill us!"

Horse thrust Bully over the top of the front seat to where the driver could see him.

"We got him?"

"We got him! Get this animal to Oxford!"

In record time, they did. About daylight they pulled into the parking lot at Garland Hall.

"What are we gonna' do with him?," one of them asked. "You know they'll be looking for him. Garland will be one of the first places they'll look!"

"I know, I know, but we have to take him in for right now. We'll decide where to keep him later."

I think it's safe to say that in the long history of Rebel versus Bulldog, Bully the State mascot entered the Ole Miss athletic dorm for the very first time.

Courage began to yield to fear in the four marauders, as they hustled their prey into the building.

"We can't keep him here long," one of them surmised.

"You're right about that," another replied. "But we gotta' keep 'im here for awhile."

Later that Morning, with Bully hidden in his room, Horse visited a friend, who worked on the campus, a man who would help them hide the dog, he believed. Horse walked into his shop.

"Got a favor to ask," Horse declared.

"What?" the friend asked.

"Don't you have someone working for you who has dogs?"

"Sure do! Lives just outside of town."

"Reckon he could house one more dog?"

"Probably. Want me to find out?"

"Could you find out this morning?", Horse asked.

"I can find out at noon. Let you know right after lunch."

By noon, every Ole Miss football player knew Bully had come to Oxford. That afternoon Horse and his friends smuggled him out of Garland and into a car. Within a few minutes they arrived at Bully's new, temporary home.

With Bully in his arms, Horse walked to the front door. The black man who lived there came out of his house. He was expecting Horse and they introduced themselves to one another.

"Fine looking dog," the man remarked.

"Thanks! Can you keep him for us a couple of days?", Horse asked.

"Sho' can! Be glad to—!"

"This is a very special dog. He can't be let out of the pen. In fact I'm gonna ask that your children not even play with him. And whatever you do, don't tell anyone he's here. Can you do that for us?"

"Sho'! When you gonna come get him?"

"Saturday morning-that okay?"

"He'll be right here," the man asserted.

"Thanks. See you Saturday morning."

That critical task accomplished, the relieved four headed back to Garland. Chief Tatum met them at the dorm.

Chief Tatum was the head of campus security. A very tall man, and large, he had for years been a special friend of football players. More than once he kept me out of some serious trouble which could have expelled me from school, for which I will always be indebted to him.

While Horse and his crew were securing Bully's living quarters, the Chief had questioned all the football players in the dorm. The four faced the same inquisition. Chief Tatum received the same answer.

"Ya'll know anything about State's Bulldog being stolen?," Chief Tatum asked.

"Chief, we've all heard about it," Horse answered. "Seems like everybody on campus is talking about it."

"Everybody over at Starkville's talking about it too. Everybody in the whole state's talking about it. That's not what I'm asking. What I'm asking is did y'all steal Bully?"

"No, Chief, we didn't," Horse lied. The others shook their heads in agreement.

"Wal', the State folks think y'all did."

"Chief, it's not our fault if they can't keep up with their d−n dog. They think they got any proof Ole Miss football players took him?"

Smiling, Chief Tatum said, "They think y'all did it."

"Wal' Chief, they better have more proof than just thinking," Horse declared.

The two dozen or so Ole Miss football players listening to the dialog chimed in," "Yeah, they'd better have proof, d−n Rednecks ."

"Yeah, they'd better have proof," another echoed.

By Friday morning, not only the State of Mississippi but also the entire Southeastern United States knew about the rustling of Bully. Newspapers and radio spread the news. Bulldog bumper stickers were observed on cars filled with students, cruising around the Ole Miss campus.

The football team wisely maintained a low profile. To a man, all mouths remained shut.

Finally, the day of disclosure came, the day when the truth about Bully's kidnapping would be exposed—the day of the Ole Miss - State basketball game.

It was time to recover Bully. The same contingent who delivered him to his transient home retrieved him and as promised, he was well tended.

Entering Garland, Bully tucked snuggly under his coat, Horse asked a teammate, "You get the water color?"

"Yes, it's mixed up. We're ready to make a Rebel outa' him."

"Good - then let's do it."

They took Bully upstairs to a shower stall. With watercolor, they painted him blue on one side and red on the other.

"D−n stuff wouldn't stick. As fast as we put it on him, he would shake real hard and shake it all off. If we could have held him still until he dried it might'a worked," Horse explained.

But it didn't work. The amateur painters finally gave up on the watercolor. Someone suggested regular house paint, but someone else advised that leaded paint might hurt Bully.

"I don't think paint will hurt him," one athlete said. "As soon as the State folks get him, they'll wash the paint off. Besides, we'll just put it on his hair."

A vote was taken - paint won. A little while later, one of the fellows hustled into the shower with two small cans of paint, one red, one blue.

Bully tried to shake the paint off, he couldn't. But he did get loose. No one wanted to hold him after he had been painted. Shaking, as wet dogs always do, he trotted down the hall, leaving red and blue dog tracks on the tile floor.

"Chief Tatum's coming," shouted a freshman, posted as a guard, "and some fellows are with him."

"Freshman," an upperclassmen excitedly yelled. "Go down-stairs and see which door Chief comes in. Then send a runner up here to tell us!"

Several Freshmen hustled downstairs. In a minute one came bounding back up the stairs.

"He's coming in the far door."

"Good," responded one of the fellows. "Let's get Bully out of Garland through the other door."

Scooping up Bully, paint and all, the upperclassman burst out the door.

"Where are you taking him?," someone asked.

"I have a friend who said he'd hide him in his room if we need him to — !," came the reply.

"He a football player?"

"No!"

About the time Bully and his "handler" left Garland through one door, Chief Tatum, a Deputy Sheriff, and a young man in civilian clothes entered through the other door.

"By the time they got into the dorm," Horse reflected, "most of us had gotten back to our rooms. Everything looked normal."

Things may have looked normal, but Chief still searched every room. Everyone denied knowledge about Bully.

"Turned out that third fellow was the President of the Mississippi State student body." exclaimed Horse. "He'd heard we had Bully in Garland. Turned out he was almost right.

When the three men got to Horse's room, Chief asked, "Horse, word has it that you were in on stealing Bully. You know anything about it?"

"Sure don't, Chief!," Horse lied.

"What are these red and blue dog tracks doing on the hall floor outside your room, then?"

"Those aren't dog tracks, Chief. I know they look like it. One of these smart a-s guys painted 'em on the floor to make it like a dog left 'em-trying to get me in trouble."

"Yeah, sure," the State student body President said. "Some story!"

"Then search the rooms, d--nit. You won't find a dog here."

TO SMUGGLE A DOG

Two guards were posted at all the doors leading into the gymnasium. Every Ole Miss student was being thoroughly inspected.

"What are we gonna' do, Horse?," one of them asked. "We can't bring Bully in through the doors."

"Let's leave him in the room for right now," Horse responded, "and go on in. Maybe we can figure out something."

The gym was packed. Usually the football players sat together at basketball games, unless they had dates. By the time Horse and his friends got inside, the only seats not taken were directly behind the Varsity football coaches. A little reluctantly, they sat down there. Whispering, they discussed possible ways to smuggle Bully into the building. They were having trouble.

Suddenly, one of the Varsity coaches turned around and looked straight at Horse, "Have y'all got that dog?"

"Yes sir," hesitatingly admitted Horse, "but I don't know what good it's gonna do us. We can't get him into the gym."

Reaching into his pocket the coach pulled out a key ring and handed it to Horse. Quietly he said, "This is a key to the door at the end of the gym opening out into the swimming pool area. You can bring him in through that door. You'll have to figure out how to get him over the fence."

The chain link fence was eight feet high. It encircled the swimming pool.

"Quick," Horse whispered to one of the others, "You go get Bully. Don't forget his beanie and flag. Come to the far end of the pool, it ought to be dark down there. I'll throw a volleyball net over to you and you wrap the dog in it and let him down over the fence. Without the dog you can come on back in through the front door and send all the freshmen (football players) down here. We gotta' be ready by half time."

The plan worked perfectly. Bully was in the gym. He and a contingent of freshmen football players waited together in an anteroom on the west end of the gymnasium. They weren't forced to wait long.

The buzzer sounded to end the first half of the basketball game and the players left the floor. Immediately, the door which separated the adjoining room and the gymnasium floor swung open. Through the doors marched thirty Ole Miss freshmen football players. In front of them pranced the proud bulldog - blue on one side and red on the other; an Ole Miss beanie cap bound to his head by a rubber band under his chin; and a Rebel flag taped to his tail. As though he had been training for the event all his life, Bully entered the basketball floor under one goal and trotted straight down the middle of the court to the other one. Behind him marched the Ole Miss freshmen football players.

The Ole Miss Student Body cheered; the State fans jeered and rushed to rescue their well-dressed mascot.

In the immortal words of Sir Winston Churchill, "It was Bully's finest hour."

Sadly the complete story, for truth and honesty's sake, must be told. Because of the lead in the paint, several weeks later Bully died. State people were incensed over his death, understandably. Ole Miss fans maintained however, that Bully may not have expired because of the paint, but from grief.

"He was a Rebel for only a day and then he was taken back to Starkville and forced to be a Bulldog again. Who would want to live after suffering that humiliation?", they asked!

In the meantime, I'm glad I was wrong. I'm at peace now, filled with contentment, knowing the true story of Bully. Never again will I stare at a dark ceiling in the middle of the night pondering, "I wonder what really happened the night Bully was stolen."

Ah, sleep, sweet sleep!

CHAPTER IV

ADJUSTING TO CAMPUS LIFE
INTRODUCTION

Oxford has at this writing been chosen by several publications, Fortune Magazine being the most noteworthy, one of this nation's best retirement cities. That comes as no surprise for many who love Oxford and appreciate all it offers: nice restaurants, nightlife, the quaint Square, cultural opportunities, and a safe environment. But Oxford hasn't always offered such amenities. In fact Oxford offered only one of these cultural advantages before the late Nineteen Sixties, as all older Ole Miss graduates know, a secure environment.

I came to Ole Miss from the rural Homochitto National Forest of Southwest Mississippi, but I arrived via Natchez. In the early Fifties, Natchez was a "rip-roaring" river town with nightlife, live entertainers like Jerry Lee Lewis, nice restaurants and beautiful historic homes. It was a wet town with liquor stores in a dry state, one of them being the Famous Corner on Main Street, across from the Eola Hotel. Someone once said, "Natchez wakes up at mid-night and goes to sleep at eight in the morning." Main Street in Natchez looked a little like Bourbon Street in microcosm, especially on weekends. Natchez-Under-The-Hill offered two "wild" nightclubs, the Pirates Club and the Blue Cat Club. Jerry Lee got his start there.

What a cultural shock for many students who enrolled at Ole Miss in the late Forties, Fifties, and early Sixties, though not so much for me! I knew Oxford because of the truckload of Poole relatives who had preceded me there. I loved the town. It was the home of Ole Miss.

But it was also a little boring, dusty southern village. Kiami's drive-in, two walk-in theatres and a drive-in theatre completed the entertainment possibilities; oh yes, and a skating rink, which didn't help me much. I didn't know how to skate. I grew up in the country on a gravel road. The only things upon which I ever skated were wet corncobs when I ran bare-foot through the barnyard.

Weekends often found a number of students heading out of town, unless the University had booked a band for a dance. With the absence of students, the boredom for the rest of us intensified.

For football players, success in those days bred even more boredom.

We practiced football through Christmas holidays in order to play in the many Bowl games to which we were invited. The football players and the basketball players occupied the campus alone.

Football players back then possessed the capacity to pull pranks anytime, but their abilities, desires, and opportunities expanded during that lonely week between Christmas and New Years. Thank goodness for the tolerance of Campus Security and the sufferance of the citizens of Oxford. Their pity for our plight must have strengthened their patience.

Belatedly, Thank you!

IT'S INCOMING!

Whoever invented torpedoes probably had no idea what they did for the morale of the Ole Miss football players at Christmas time after all the other students departed for home and left us on the campus alone to practice for a Bowl game; not the kind of torpedo one might find on a ship. I'm talking about the kind with which Rebel football players could get into trouble, the type which exploded when thrown against something hard, or when shot against something hard with a slingshot.

Back in the late Fifties few policemen were needed to maintain peace in Oxford. Those few worked out of a small station on the south side of the square near where the restaurant, City Grocery, now offers delicious food. It occupied a very narrow, deep little building with a glass front. Probably, no more than four or five policemen were ever on duty at one time and like the Maytag repairman, they usually faced few if any adversaries - that is until the week between Christmas and New Years when Ole Miss was playing in a Bowl. Business increased considerably then, thanks to a combination of athletic boredom and the invention of torpedoes. Thank God the prevailing attitude of college "pranks" excluded criminal intent. Today football players might discover themselves behind bars.

Every Ole Miss football team during those years included at least one player who could well have been labeled "Minister of Torpedoes." In Nineteen Fifty-Four, that player was Houston Patton, a quarterback from north Alabama. If it could be done with a torpedo, Houston and his army of trained torpedo artillerymen could do it. They could hit a moving car at fifty paces eight out of ten tries.

One night Houston and his draftees positioned themselves on top of several buildings around the Square, and near the two theatres, just a block off the square. They were fully armed with a bag of torpedoes and they were "ready." Houston had given the command to his troops, once their positions had been established, to "fire at will." Some players posted themselves behind the shrubbery surrounding the Courthouse as observers, not so much forward observers, just observers. I was in that group. We wanted to see the show.

"Fire at will," meant to fire at anything on the street that moved and at the police station, even though it didn't move. Admittedly, back in Fifty-Four not much moved around the Square at night but that failed to stop the artillery. For about twenty minutes the noise and the confusion were awesome, the steady explosions of torpedoes filling the air at the rate of about twenty five per minute.

The first detonation hurled the police toward their two cars. The civilian M.P.'s drove several miles around the Square during the battle looking for the invaders, in vain. Both cars took several direct hits. Civilians retreated under the canopies of the various businesses.

The observers observed very little of the spectacle because we were frantically digging foxholes behind the Courthouse shrubbery as the police cars circled the square, a feat made difficult because we dug with our hands.

The raging battle finally ended when Coach Vaught, in his brand new automobile, appeared on the scene, probably at the behest of the police. It wasn't his presence alone which forced the soldiers to withdraw, however. It was the errant torpedo which exploded on the roof of his new car. The dark and dented area remained on it for as long as he owned it, I think.

Normally, artillerymen aren't recognized for their foot speed but Houston's cannoneers, without vehicles, were back at Garland almost by the time the sound of the last exploding projectile cleared the air.

DID YOU KNOW?

Parker Hall led the nation in scoring with 73 points in 1938.

THAT'S NO NOBEL

With little dispute, William Faulkner still reigns as Oxford's most noteworthy and well-known citizen. By various accepted social standards, the Nobel-winning recluse diverged from other people in many ways. Intellectual geniuses always do. Liberal Arts differ from Engineering, and the mind of a writer deviates from the mind of a pragmatist. The greater the mind of the writer, the greater the dissimilarity. Whatever else William Faulkner might have been, everyone now presently recognizes the uniqueness of his mind revealed in the eminence of his work.

I find it very difficult to believe now, that some of us taunted Mr. Faulkner when we encountered him inebriated, staggering slowly either toward the Square or away from it, toward home. If to most people he was "different," to football players in the early Fifties, he was much more than different. He was desparate.

Later in life I realized that minds capable of traversing almost supernaturally deep into any artistic area, care little about the rejection of "normal" people, whatever that means. William Faulkner certainly seemed to remain unconcerned about other's opinions of him until the day he died.

Some people, however, appreciated Mr. Faulkner, even back then. One of them was Ms. Topps, an English professor. She and Mr. Faulkner had become close friends and he agreed to do her a favor. He had promised to evaluate the term papers of some of her freshmen students, Billy Ray Adams being one of them. She sent Billy Ray, another fellow, and two girls with their work to Mr. Faulkner's home.

Standing before the great writer with apprehension, the four students awaited his evaluations. Sternly, he fixed his gaze upon them. Then reaching toward one of the girls, he took her thesis, read about one paragraph and thrust it back to her.

"This isn't worth a s—t," he remarked.

Turning toward the other girl he took her paper, read for a few seconds and handed it back to her.

"You don't have it, Baby."

He then read the other boy's work, or at least a few sentences of it.

"Yours isn't any better than those two."

Then Mr. Faulkner turned toward the future All-American fullback.

"Let me have yours," he gruffly demanded.

"Mr. Faulkner," Billy Ray answered, "If these three wrote papers as bad as you say they are, let me assure you that mine ain't gonna be worth a s—t either, and I'm sorry I wasted your time."

With that, Mr. Faulkner invited them to leave which they were more than anxious to do.

From that moment, Billy Ray accepted the fact that he might not win the Nobel Prize in the field of literature.

DID YOU KNOW?

The Ole Miss football team, first to use air travel for an away game, flew to Philadelphia, Oct 1, 1937, for a game with Temple.

SQUIRREL STEW, ANYONE?

Some yarns concerning athletic life at Ole Miss in the late Forties, Fifties, and early Sixties might best be left untold. The following tale may be one of them. Oh well, what the heck, I've been in trouble before.

Permit me to reestablish the social stage of the era for college students in general, and for Ole Miss football players in particular. When pranks occurred then, seldom was criminal intent considered. Even in the Age of Pranks, one might move outside the wide bounds of acceptance, however. The following episode maneuvers perilously close, so I'll withhold the names of the participants in order to protect the guilty.

Ole Miss football players in the Fifties often found themselves torn emotionally. Almost every year, we were invited to play in a Bowl game, a great honor, especially in those days. There were only four major Bowls; the Sugar, Rose, Orange, and Cotton Bowls. The Gator Bowl was considered to be a minor Bowl, in which "Ole Miss will not participate," so declared our coaching staff in Nineteen Fifty-Three. Things have changed!

Therefore to play in a Bowl game required the coaches and football players to sacrifice Christmas vacation, not a small oblation for young men who had not been home since August. The honor of playing in a Bowl game carried with it the anguish of missing Christmas with our families. Because we played Mississippi State on Saturday after Thanksgiving every year, we had already missed that holiday at home.

To make matters worse, Oxford in those years failed to qualify as the most exciting college town in which one could be educated. Nightlife consisted of a drive-in theatre, two walk-in theatres, a drive-in hamburger stand, skating rink, and a bowling alley and no television. Players who grew up in Memphis, Jackson, the Gulf Coast, and even Natchez experienced cultural shock upon enrolling at Ole Miss, as mentioned in Chapter III. Campus life offered students their most exciting endeavors, if it might be so labeled.

Campus life, however, ceased to exist during Christmas holidays; all the other students had gone home. Life, for the athletes, degenerated into massive boredom. We searched for something to do other than practice football, attend team meetings, eat, and sleep. If any football player possessed an aptitude for trouble it usually emerged during this time.

We shot fireworks. After all it was Christmas and many people in Mississippi celebrate the holidays doing it, so we did it too. We weren't supposed to, at least not on the campus, but we did it anyway. Campus Security, apparently realizing our dilemma, granted great latitude. Unless a Roman Candle or Sky Rocket propelled through a classroom or dormitory window, which sometimes happened, they usually ignored us. Bored football players are capable of conducting some pretty ferocious fireworks wars when unimpeded by the police.

In Nineteen Fifty-Four we were practicing during the holidays to play in the Sugar Bowl. Two of our largest linemen were especially bored. One had come to Ole Miss from a moderately large town, the other one re-enrolled in Ole Miss after spending a couple of years in the army. Both were outdoorsmen, hunters and fishermen.

Whatever else boredom might accomplish, good or bad, it does engender creativity. The two linemen devised a new purpose for firecrackers. They went squirrel hunting with them.

With their .22 rifles hidden in their pant legs, a bag full of firecrackers, and a cigarette lighter, they rambled into the Grove one day, where they flawlessly implemented their plan. After exploding two or three firecrackers, they then shot a squirrel. In that sequence, they "hunted" until they had harvested fifty or so. The blast of the rifle sounded so much like a firecracker that Campus Security evidently made no distinction between the two.

"D—n Grove had too many squirrels anyway," one of them declared to some teammates. "Somebody needed to thin 'em out a little. Might as well a'been us."

The two hunters enlisted the rest of the team to help dress the squirrels and then they talked the cafeteria workers into cooking them, with the coach's permission of course.

One big strapping country boy was overheard saying, as he moved through the serving line, "Oh Boy! I ain't had no squirrel since I been a-playin' football at Ole Miss."

The two shooters may have inadvertently been right. No one seemed to miss the squirrels; at least no one, to my knowledge, was ever arrested for shooting them.

FIRST TIME EVER I SAW HER FACE

Many unusual events occurred while I was at Ole Miss. We won the SEC football championship two years in a row, 1954 and 1955, only the second time that had ever been done by any school. By the last game of my senior year, I held every national field goal record, simply because I was the only field goal kicker. When I kicked six in 1955, only nine were kicked in all of college football, including my six. And of course Eagle Day was our quarterback. Almost everything he did was unusual.

Perhaps, however, the strangest phenomenon occurred when two Miss Americas attended Ole Miss, Mary Ann Mobley and Lynda Lee Mead, at the same time. Both were very beautiful young women, of course, but they were much more than that. They were also "Favorites," with other students, and both were especially close to football players. I went to Natchez High with Lynda Lee and the two were good friends at Ole Miss (I'm bragging now.)

Bull Churchwell recently remarked, "I remember the very first time I saw Mary Ann Mobley. I can even remember what she had on —! She wore an orange skirt and vest, and a green blouse."

"Most people do, Bull," I answered. "Lynda Lee, too." Both of them quickly captured the audience's attention.

"It was about dark," Bull continued. "We had just finished football practice and were walking back to the dorm. It was the first day of school and we saw a crowd of people on and around the tennis court. Someone asked, 'What's goin' on, a fight?'"

"No!," one of the other players answered. "That's the 'Welcome Back, Students' dance."

As they neared the court, the band struck up another song and some of the players, including Bull who was a freshman and Don Williams, an upperclassman, ventured toward the music. Several other freshman players went with them.

"The crowd, which we had seen from a distance," Bull explained, "had encircled two dancers. One of them was Mary Ann. She would dance with one fellow about five seconds and then another one would cut-in! No one boy got to dance with her more than five or six seconds."

Don Williams wanted to dance with Mary Ann and he possessed "something" which would assure it, which none of the other male students had - two big freshmen football players, Bojack Bowman and Bull. Both weighed in at well over two hundred and forty pounds, huge football players in Nineteen Fifty-Seven.

Don pulled the two freshmen over to one side.

"Freshmen," Don threatened, "I'm gonna' dance with Mary Ann. And when I start dancing with her, I don't want to feel one d—n hand tap me on the shoulder. Now come on."

"All three of us went out on the dance floor," Bull explained. "While Don danced with Mary Ann, we followed them around the dance floor. When other fellows came out to cut in, we told them 'Naw, fellow, you don't want to do that. You just go on back over there and wait 'til Don gets through!'"

Don danced with Mary Ann three songs, and then he nodded toward his two guards. They knew what he meant, and backed away from their posts.

"Come on, let's go eat," the upper classman commanded.

"When we walked off the dance floor, Bull glanced back toward Mary Ann. The crowd of males had re-gathered around her.

Every upperclassman football player had a freshman to do his bidding. I never thought about using mine as a guard on the dance floor, but it was a great idea.

DID YOU KNOW?

Ole Miss has supplied 13 NFL first round draft picks.

GET OUTA' THAT HAY

Not every player who signed with Ole Miss found the first year to be a period of ecstasy, especially boys from South Mississippi. In the Fifties, Oxford was a long way from Jackson and points South. Few of us made it home before the Christmas vacation and even then, the coaches kept quite a number of Frosh on campus during the holidays to practice against the varsity, when the Rebels were playing in a Bowl.

I remember envying the players who lived within a weekend driving distance of Oxford — Memphis, Corinth, Tupelo, Grenada. Even if the coaches restricted the freshmen from going home during football season, their parents could visit and bring some food, money, and parental sympathy.

After football season had ended, going home for South Mississippi boys presented several problems, the primary one being the highways. Highway 6 to Batesville and Tupelo, Highway 7 to Grenada, and Highway 51 South were two lanes and bogged down through the middle of every little town. Traveling from Oxford to Natchez took eight hours if I had a ride, much longer if I hitchhiked. Going home presented such a problem many of us found it to be hardly worth the trouble. By the time we got there, we had to turn around and go back.

"Oh, how I wish Ole Miss had been located on the Gulf Coast," we often cried.

In the fall of Nineteen Fifty-Two, four good Ole Miss Freshmen football players from South Mississippi became extremely disenchanted and home sick: Buddy Alliston from Florence, Eagle Day from Columbia, Billy Goat Sullivan from Sullivan's Hollow, and Billy Yelverton from Jackson. Together they examined their options after practice one night.

Eagle said, "I tell you what - let's go play at Mississippi Southern. I know some guys down there and we'll be close to home."

That sounded great to all four of them so that night they packed their clothes, "What few we had back in those days," Buddy admitted.

Early the next morning the four wayfarers slipped out of the dorm undetected by Wobble, no small feat in itself. Nervously they slipped down to Highway 6, thumbs raised. Before long, a sympathetic traveler on his way to Clarksdale gave them a ride to Highway 51 in Batesville.

"We have escaped," they thought. "We're on our way now."

Before long a big hay truck heading South on 51 stopped for them.

"Fellows," the driver said, "I'm taking a load of hay to just south of Grenada. How far y'all going?"

"To Jackson," came back the collective reply.

"You're welcome to ride to Grenada. Get on top of the hay."

In those days Grenada was a considerable distance from Oxford. If Batesville offered a degree of safety from the coaches, then Grenada offered more.

The four ramblers tossed their bags of clothes up on the hay and then one by one they climbed up.

"Hay makes a pretty good bed!", one of them judged.

The four settled down for what they thought would be a peaceful hour and half ride to the sanctuary of Grenada. The truck was slow but the danger of being retrieved had passed!

After about fifteen minutes, all four of them were curled up on the hay, dozing. "This is the way to travel," they surmised - "Cool air, lying down, free gas - only way to travel."

"Suddenly we were aroused from our semi-conscious state by a loud car horn blowing right behind us," Buddy remembered. "We poked our heads up out of the hay - not really believing that we needed to be concerned. We had slipped away undetected. Our getaway had been clean."

Four heads leaning over the back of the hay truck, gazed straight down upon Coach Vaught, who was still bearing down on the car horn, and Coach Kinard.

"Pull that truck over," Vaught, leaning out the window of his station wagon shouted to the driver.

By the time he stopped, both coaches were standing at the rear of the truck, hands on hips, squinting at the four travelers, who wanted, too late, to hide under the hay.

"Boys, empty your butts off that truck with your clothes," Coach Vaught commanded.

"What'll we do?", one of them whispered.

"We'll empty our butts off this truck and take our clothes," Buddy answered.

And they did.

"We climbed in Coach's station wagon with our clothes. Coach Vaught turned the car around and took us back to Oxford. No one said a word about our leaving all the way back, not even the coaches."

"How did they know where to find you," I asked Buddy.

"I have no idea. But they sure found us."

"Did Coach put y'all in the stadium?," meaning to run laps up and down it.

"No" replied Buddy. "Not only did they not punish us, but no one ever mentioned our little AWOL venture again."

That doesn't surprise me. Three of the four deserters eventually became starters at Ole Miss and ended up their football careers in the National Football League. For coaches Vaught and Kinard, and Ole Miss football, that short trip to a point about ten miles south of Batesville proved to be a very productive re-recruitment one.

DID YOU KNOW?

Gene Hickerson, Ole Miss tackle 1953 - 57, won the best blocker in the NFL Award in 1968 for the Cleveland Browns.

LAUREL AND HARDY

Fifteen dollars a month for laundry! That's what every Ole Miss football player received, and was it welcome?! We lived off that fifteen dollars, which in today's economy might equal a hundred. We dated with it. We saw movies with it. We visited the grill with it. And sometimes we bought clothes with it, which surprisingly, we could do in those days. A nice shirt cost five dollars, a pair of trousers seven-fifty.

Eddie Crawford, a lanky halfback from Jackson, Tennessee, and Richard Weiss, a large tackle from Clarksdale were teammates and close friends. After receiving their laundry money one day, they faced a monumental decision - what to do with it. Carefully considering all their options, they decided to go to Harmon's.

Harmon's was a clothing store on the Square. It competed with Carl Coor's out on the campus, and carried a complete line of men's clothing, even hats.

Not many students wore hats in those days, except for the Freshmen men the first semester of school. They wore Ole Miss beanies to cover their bald heads, which had fallen victim to the upperclassmen's scissors. So Eddie and Richard decided they would really attract some attention if they wore hats.

Standing before the extended rack of men's hats, two great minds working together, they made their joint decision.

"We'll take these two," they said to the clerk, after each found his respective size.

"These are really nice," encouraged the salesman. "Ya'll will look sharp in them."

The hats were typical "Joe College style," flat and narrow brim. The athletes admired themselves in the mirror.

"They really do look good on us, don't they?," Eddie hopefully asked Richard.

"Sure do," Richard responded.

The fastidious dressers walked back to the campus, completely aware of admiring glances from passing cars. Not only did the hats look nice but they knew they looked nice in the hats. Made them look intelligent too, they thought.

New clothes in those days demanded a visit to the Grill. If students weren't in class, they could probably be found at the Grill. The two made their entrance.

"Wow," one girl exclaimed. "Those are really nice hats!"

"Where did you get them?" a male student asked.

"Makes you two meatheads look pretty smart," a teammate remarked. "Think I'll get one of those. How much you pay for 'em?"

Their confidence soared.

After all the accolades subsided in the Grill, Richard turned toward Eddie. "Come go with me to the coaches' office. I gotta' pick up something."

Just before the two well-dressed college students turned off the sidewalk into the coach's office, Wobble walked out of it, briskly. Meeting the two, his expression never changing, his eyes fixed upon their heads, he muttered, "Laurel and Hardy," and kept walking right on by them.

Laurel and Hardy stopped dead in their tracks as Wobble passed. They watched as he continued to walk away, waiting for him to turn or smile or say something else, anything. He never looked back.

Their confidence now shattered, the two football players hastened to Garland Hall where they "dis-robed" their heads and hid their hats.

They never wore them again.

DID YOU KNOW?

Junie Hovious led the nation in punt returns, a 15.1 yard average in 1940.

THE PILOT

As I mentioned in another story, some tales are probably better left unstated, forgotten: the following is one of them, but it's so funny, it cries to be told. I hope no one gets into trouble. For what it's worth, the main character, a very good friend and teammate of mine and a great football player, is deceased. I hope the Statute of Limitations has expired for the rest of us.

In the beginning of this book, I evaluated the college culture of the Nineteen Fifties by declaring a lack of criminal intent. College pranks were first considered innocent until proven guilty. Such is the following story.

Armed Forces Day at Ole Miss in the Fifties was held in the Spring. All the branches of service displayed their hardware on the campus in an attempt to lure graduating R.O.T.C. seniors into their division. The artillery exhibited 105 Howitzers and 155 Howitzers, for example. They would be postured around the campus for students to examine. Armor displayed its tanks. Several could be seen scattered around the grassy area between the Library and the hospital, the building which now houses R.O.T.C. The Air Force, unable to land its fixed wing aircraft on the campus, of course, never the less displayed its helicopters. They usually occupied the area adjacent to Garland Dorm, immediately in front of the hospital.

By Friday night prior to Armed Forces Day, all the military hardware was in place - howitzers, tanks, a helicopter, machine guns, mortars, etc.

On Friday night before the day of military display, the main character and a couple of his teammates visited Marks, Mississippi. Holly Springs and Marks afforded the two nearest watering holes, Holly Springs offering the Haba Grill and Marks, a small beer joint on Highway 6 east of town.

The athletes choose Marks. Haba Grill would be too crowded on Friday nights, they reasoned. Fewer Ole Miss students would frequent the Delta town. Besides Marks was farther from Oxford. They were less likely to be caught by the coaches.

"We had a great time at the beer joint," one of the fellows told me. "We probably drank eight or ten beers apiece. There were several nice looking girls to talk to and we didn't get caught."

They each bought a couple of more beers for the road, and headed back to Oxford. About forty-five minutes later, they arrived at Garland, parked the car and walked around the building toward the front door. There, some thirty yards away sat the helicopter.

The three of them walked over to the machine. After looking it over completely, two of the fellows walked on into Garland, but the main character lingered. Several minutes passed.

Suddenly, the late night quiescent air around Garland erupted under the thrust of a mighty engine.

Sprinting back outside, the two friends gasped at what they saw. The helicopter hovered about ten feet off the ground.

"That thing was revved up, and blue flames were exploding from the exhausts," one of the friends exclaimed.

"Man, that would be the very thing to go frog gigging in!" the other one loudly surmised.

Garland Dorm emptied, as the football players quickly established their observation positions around the airborne aircraft.

"Who's flying that thing?," a player yelled, trying to be heard above the roar of the powerful motor.

"I don't know," someone screamed.

"I do!" one of the beer drinkers confessed. "It's_____(he revealed the pilot's name.)

"I didn't know he could fly a helicopter," another person shouted.

"He can't," came an informed reply.

"He can now."

"I wonder if he knows how to land it?"

"We're about to find out," someone answered. The machine tilted toward the ground and crashed.

The pilot's teammates dashed to the wrecked vehicle and pulled their friend out.

"We'd better get him away from here and hide him," someone warned.

With flashing red and blue lights rapidly approaching, the football players quickly retreated back into Garland. Within minutes, military personnel, including M.P.'s surrounded the wounded bird.

The next day FBI investigators were called into the mystery. They questioned many of the athletes, none of whom knew anything.

"No Sir, we sure don't know who did it," one of them lied. "But he musta' been some kinda' fast. By the time we got out of the dorm, he had run plum' off!"

One of the pilot's friends who was there, remarked, "You know, if he had altered the pitch of those propeller blades just a little, he would have been the first person to go into orbit."

The mystery of the Ghost Pilot remains to this day.

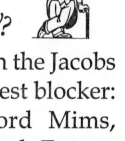

DID YOU KNOW?

Four Ole Miss players have won the Jacobs Blocking Trophy as the SEC's best blocker: Buddy Bowen, 1947; Crawford Mims, 1953; Paige Cothren, 1955; and Everett Lindsay in 1992.

WHAT PRICE A STATE BEANIE?

For a freshman football player at Ole Miss in the Vaught years, one of the most exciting events was going home for the first time. About mid-season, Wobble sometimes released the Freshman team for the rare visit. Players looked forward, not only to seeing Mom and Dad, but also to visiting with old friends, rehearsing all the exciting and humorous events connected with being an Ole Miss freshman football player.

By the time Billy Ray Adams had played football for Wobble a couple of months, he had already learned to fear him, to respect him, to avoid him whenever possible, and to obey him.

On a Wednesday, Wobble told Billy Ray and his teammates they could go home on Friday afternoon after class. Practice would be cancelled. Speaking very somberly to them the freshman coach said,

"Now let me tell you something. This will be your firstvisit home. I want you to go home and have a good time and be back when you're supposed to be, by bed check Sunday night. Stay out of trouble and listen to me, now, listen. Don't bring your a-ses back up here without a Mississippi State Beanie."

"Well," Billy Ray remembered, "that wasn't gonna be hard for me to do in Columbus." (Billy Ray grew up in Columbus, Mississippi only twenty miles from the State campus at Starkville.)

Lee High of Columbus was playing football at home that Friday night. Billy Ray and one of his high school classmates, a student at Mississippi State, went to the game. Lee High's stadium was built into the side of a hill and fans entered it from the top. Walking down through the student section, Billy Ray spotted dozens of State freshmen wearing their beanies. About ten of them sat on one row. All were tall, so they looked like State's freshmen basketball team to Billy Ray.

"D—n," Billy Ray thought, "Look at the beanies. This is going to be easy pickin's."

As they walked down the stadium, Billy Ray suddenly reached down and yanked a beanie off one of the basketball player's heads.

"What are you doing?" his friend excitedly asked, as the victim jerked his head toward the pair and started to stand. Billy Ray explained Wobble's command.

"H—l, I might as well get me one!" his State friend replied.

He then jerked a beanie off another freshman's head.

The two thieves quickly walked to where their Lee High friends were awaiting the kickoff and sat down.

In disbelief, the two beguiled State freshmen fixed their gazes upon Billy Ray and Miller, his friend. Then all the State students, including the two who had their hats stolen, started organizing.

"We could tell they were preparing to come get their beanies," Billy Ray recalled, "and the friendly group into which we had retreated weren't going to rescue us."

Billy Ray quickly turned and handed the two beanies to a Lee High girl sitting directly behind him.

"Keep these for me," Billy Ray implored.

Finally the State entourage stood in front of Billy Ray and Miller. An upper classman was their spokesman.

"I represent Mississippi State," he threatened, "and I want the beanies."

"Do I look like I have any beanies?" Billy Ray arrogantly replied.

"We know you got the beanies."

"Well, I don't have your beanies!" Billy Ray countered.

"Well, you son-of-a-b—-h!"

"Pop, he hit me on the jaw," Billy Ray declared, "and a full scale fight erupted."

A cop finally disrupted the fight. When he heard the story, he said, "Billy Ray, we're going to have to take you down to the station."

"I knew the cop," Billy Ray exclaimed. "His son was a Lee High school mate of mine."

"Oh man," Billy Ray begged, "do you have to?"

"Well, I tell you what, walk on up to the top of the stadium and wait for us there."

The policeman then handcuffed the Bulldog "spokesman," brought him to where Adams was waiting and drove both of them to the police station.

"Chief Vickery was a long time friend," Billy Ray explained, "a three-hundred pound man."

"Now boys," the chief said to the two brawlers, "what y'all need to do is shake hands, be friends, and I'll let y'all go."

That sounded reasonable to Billy Ray, but two policemen who were standing out of the chief's sight looked at Billy Ray, shook their heads vigorously back and forth, and silently said, "No, no, don't do it."

"I ain't shakin' his hand!" Billy Ray asserted, not understanding why the two had warned him not to do it.

"What'd you say boy?", the chief asked. "I'll keep your a-s here all weekend!"

"Well, I ain't shakin' his hand."

"Get out'a here then!", the chief commanded, with a smile.

"Miller had gotten the beanies from the girl. Before I left to go back to Oxford on Sunday, he gave me his. I had two beanies to take back to school. I was anxious to plop them down in front of Wobble."

Billy Ray reported to his coach with the two beanies. "This is really gonna be good," the fullback thought.

"You dumb a-s, what did you do?" Wobble demanded, staring at the Maroon hats.

"Well Coach, you told me not to come back without a Mississippi State beanie so I brought you two."

"My God," Wobble exclaimed, "I was just kidding. Any dumb fool would have known that!"

I MIGHT HAVE PASSED THE PLATE

Rex Reed Boggan was a huge Ole Miss football player in the Nineteen Fifties, six four, two hundred sixty pounds. Will T. Black was a small one, even for those pre-monster days, five feet eight inches tall, one hundred and sixty-five pounds. While their physical similarities were few, they shared at least one mutual interest. Each believed a fellow ought to shoot a few fireworks during Christmas and for both, the most desirable of all fireworks, which best to them represented the Spirit of Christmas was the Roman Candle. The ball of "light" exiting the cardboard tube would best illustrate the "Light of the World" exiting Heaven and coming into this world. And of course, such a beautiful expression of the true meaning of Christmas cried out to be seen.

To Mutt and Jeff the most obvious platform from which to preach the Christmas Story seemed to be the Oxford Square. Assuming their altars on the west side of the Courthouse they preached the message, one Roman Candle after another.

Somehow, the Police failed to correlate that which the two football players were desperately attempting to illustrate and the safety of the buildings around the Square. The two tried to explain to them that most of the fireballs had found their way skyward and had dissipated before falling back to the earth. The police reminded them that they, the police, had observed several fireballs bouncing on the street under and around moving cars and toward several retail stores.

Rex Reed responded by telling the officers that he wasn't aware of any stray messages emanating from either of the evangelists, as he continued to fire his candle over the gendarmes' heads. Will T., the smaller of the two stopped firing.

The police announced that the two of them would have to be taken to the Police Station.

Rex Reed, all two hundred and sixty pounds of muscle, explained to the police that he really didn't want to go, as he lit another Roman Candle.

A bystander related, "Rex Reed was still firing his Roman Candle as poor little Will T. was carted off to the Police Station. Oxford's two policemen, both of whom were Will T.'s size, wisely placed discretion before valor. Or it might have been that a larger preacher should better convey the Christmas message.

I CLEANED IT YESTERDAY, SIR

By the time Dewey Patridge enrolled at Ole Miss, the Second World War had been over almost ten years and no other war loomed anywhere in sight. But football players always looked for easy courses to take, and R.O.T.C. provided the athletes with one. We could take it for four semesters or if we wanted to graduate with a commission in the reserves, for all four years, eight semesters.

The course itself consisted of two hours of classwork each week and a two hour drill, held from 1:00-3:00 P.M. each Thursday. Every Cadet in the Army R.O.T.C. was issued a cal.30 M-1 rifle, which had to be cleaned weekly.

Football players hated drill and most of us disliked having to clean our rifles. We hated drill because we didn't like being ordered around by one hundred and twenty-pound intellectual fraternity boys. Besides, we got all the physical exercise we needed at football practice.

We disdained cleaning the rifles because it was a "waste of time." After all, they had not been fired and probably wouldn't be. We reasoned they weren't dirty. We griped about having to do it, incessantly.

One day Cadet Bull Churchwell, a big tackle from Lucedale told his cadet friend Dewey, "Quail, you don't have to clean that rifle."

"Bull, I can't stand any more demerits."

"I'll show you how to do it," Bull retorted. "You know those Frat Cats-they're gonna always clean their rifles. Go on down to the supply room (where the rifles were kept), sit around and chew the fat with them, and watch 'em."

"Yeah, but what good's that gonna do me?"

"Let me finish. Watch 'em. When one of them comes in, cleans his rifle and leaves, take his rifle up front and let the Sgt. Inspect it."

"That's not a bad idea, Bull. That's pretty good."

Several months after Dewey embarked upon his new weapon-cleaning program, Army R.O.T.C. had a surprise Federal Inspection.

"My d—n rifle hadn't been cleaned in four or five months," Dewey admitted. "Since the beginning of the first semester, that thing hadn't been touched."

The inspecting Colonel worked his way down the line of men until finally he stood in front of Cadet Patridge. Dewey thrust his rifle out,— the

Colonel, with white gloves, took it.

"My rifle was sticking out, now Paige," Dewey told me. "It was, shall we say - different."

The Colonel, with great stupefaction asked, "Son, when was the last time you cleaned this rifle?"

"Yesterday, Sir!"

The Colonel "threw" the rifle back at Patridge and shouted, "Yesterday? Six months ago yesterday, maybe. That's two hundred demerits."

"I marched off the demerits every day for two weeks, cursing Bull every step," Dewey complained.

"I was just trying to help the boy," Bull declared.

DID YOU KNOW?

Paige Cothren led the Nation two straight years in field goals, kicking six both years, 1955 and 1956.

THE DUCK HUNT

If you get to the final chapter in this book, The Pooles, you will read there that the majority of Pooles were, in their youth, hunters and fishermen. Ray was an exception and I have to admit that I was a lot like him. To both of us, a pretty girl in town held more appeal than a squirrel slithering up a tree or a perch flopping at the end of a fishing line. Later in life, however, both of us have drifted back toward our roots. I learned to enjoy hunting quail, due primarily to the exercise. Sometimes we walked fifteen miles a day, which allowed me to practice gluttony at the supper table.

Late one afternoon in January, Nineteen Fifty-Six, Jimmy McDowell, then sports Editor of the State Times newspaper in Jackson, Mississippi, and I were sitting in my dorm room talking. Ole Miss had just defeated TCU in the Cotton Bowl and we were exulting over our great victory, the Rebel's first major Bowl win. Suddenly, my Uncle Ray Poole walked into the room.

"Ya'll," he exclaimed, "I have never seen anything like I saw today. I was riding around out near Abbeville and I saw a lake that was covered with ducks."

"Where was it?", I asked.

"You turn left at Abbeville and it's just a couple of miles down the gravel road."

Then turning toward Jimmy, Ray asked, "You want to go out there early in the morning with me Jimmy? We can kill a tub full of ducks in no time."

"Ray, I've never been duck hunting in my life," the redhead confessed. "I don't care a thing about it."

"You want to go, Paige?", Ray pleaded.

"Sure! Is anyone else going?"

"Everybody but Bruiser is out of town. He has never been duck hunting either but I'll ask him." (Bruiser Kinard was offensive line coach)

"What time you want me to be ready?" I asked.

"Wal', we can't shoot ducks before daylight and daylight comes around six-thirty. I'll pick you up at six. I'll honk."

The sound of his car horn two stories beneath my window sent me scrambling down the stairs with my shotgun. The air was frigid as I turned the corner of Garland Hall; Ray and Bruiser were waiting in the car.

"Had anything to eat?," Bruiser asked me.

"No sir."

"Here's a piece of cake," he said, thrusting it behind his head to me in the back seat.

"Here's coffee," Ray suggested.

The cake was great and the coffee both warm and satisfying. I had just finished both when Ray brought the car to a halt at the side of the dark gravel road just ten miles or so from Oxford.

"The lake is just a hundred yards down the hill to the left there," Ray explained. "I can't understand why more people don't know about it. You'll see in a minute -ducks will blacken the sky."

"I couldn't find you any waders, Paige," Ray commented. "But you can stand on the levee. You'll kill as many as we do."

In the dark, we climbed over a fence separating the woods from the road, Ray and Bruiser carefully avoiding the barbs which would rip holes in their rubber pants. We creeped through the deep underbrush being careful to make no more noise than necessary. Ray, walking in front of Bruiser and me, suddenly stopped. So did we.

"Listen to that," Ray excitedly petitioned.

From fifty yards away the quacks of a million ducks, it seemed, reverberated up the hill.

"Let's be quiet from here on," our leader cautioned. "We'll get in position before daylight."

Slowly we crept toward the sound until it was almost deafening and we stood on the water's edge. In the dark Ray pointed to the right and I saw the levee about thirty yards away.

"Get out on the levee, Paige," Ray whispered, "Bruiser and I are gonna wade out into the lake."

As I turned to ease toward my position Ray put one foot into the water. We all jumped at the sound-"crack."

"D—n water has a thin layer of ice on it," one of them mused. "It's gonna be hard to be quiet!"

"We've got to get out in the pond, though, We'll be as quiet as possible."

I could hear them slowly and carefully wade out into the water as I slipped quietly toward the levee. By the time I got to the middle of the dam, the noise of breaking ice had stopped. Apparently it had not disturbed the ducks, or if they were frightened, they were afraid to fly at night. None rose up from its roost. I wondered if they were frozen onto the ice, admitting to myself an ignorance of duck hunting. I had only killed one duck in my entire life.

Sitting down in the middle of the levee, I waited for daylight. The ducks were still emitting their vociferous music, suggesting an attempt at harmony. I secretly hoped they were singing a funeral dirge. Out of sheer boredom I glanced around, and spotted light shining from a house at the far end of the levee, estimating it was three hundred yards away, toward the south. I'll betcha the sun will come up right over there, I thought, right over Ray and Bruiser's heads. Later when it did, I was proud of my homing instincts. The R.O.T.C. had taught me well.

The raven sky stretched above my head like a celestial blanket held in front of an immense light with millions of tiny holes punched in its vast surface. I had occupied my solitary seat on the levee for about ten minutes, perusing the heavens, listening to the incessant sonance of the ducks, wondering how they would free themselves from the ice, when the first dim light of the dawn oozed into the eastern horizon.

Suddenly the mystic quiet was shattered by an explosion, a gun blast, no more than a hundred yards away-followed by a loud "crack".

"That must have been the duck hitting the ice," I thought.

Finally I was able to see my surroundings. The lake stretched all the way to the light, but seemed to be shallow most of the way, for buck bushes, which could only survive in shallow water, grew every ten feet or so, stopping perhaps a hundred yards short of the house. Their branches, like magnolia trees, grew in every direction, impeding my view of my co-hunters, but not of the ducks-they were everywhere, as numerous as Ray had declared and their pre-dawn cries had indicated. The first shot had awakened them and the light encouraged them to evacuate-in waves they flew, thousands upon thousands. As soon as one wave left, another wave more numerous than the last would appear, diving in to feed among the buck bushes.

For ten or fifteen minutes at least, the sound of a firing shotgun and the subsequent crash of a trophy through the ice never abated, sounding more like war than war.

I did not see the man until he was upon me, twenty yards or so down the levee in the direction of the house. He had no gun and the slight smile on his face indicated friendliness. I was proud of my several slain fowl which had fallen on the levee-most of them had not and the other two hunters would have to retrieve those for me.

The stranger spoke first.

"Good morning. There certainly are lots of ducks out here, aren't there?"

"There sure are," I responded, "I've never seen anything like it."

"Having much luck?", he asked.

"I think so. I can't see my partners but I imagine they have knocked down a good many. I've been hearing dead ducks hit the ice."

"I live in that house at the end of the levee," he informed me, "and I've been listening to the shooting. Sounds like a war down here."

"We've heated our gun barrels some," I calmly agreed.

"You do know you're on a Federal Game Reserve, don't you?"

"Sir!?!"

"You're on a Federal Game Reserve. It's illegal to hunt here. I'm the Federal Game Warden."

"No, Sir. We didn't know that!"

"Call your friends and tell them to gather up their ducks and come on out," he commanded.

"Yes, sir."

"Ray, Ray," I cried at the top of my voice, hoping to verbally penetrate a crack in the barrage-they were still 'hunting'. I finally pierced through the thunder. The guns silenced.

"Ray, there's a man out here on the levee who says we're on a Federal Game Reserve and he's a Federal Game Warden. He says to gather up your ducks and come out."

"What?", he asked.

I repeated my message, with some tones of urgency. I wanted mature companionship desperately.

"Okay", he replied.

We could hear them whispering but we couldn't tell what they were saying. I knew what was going through their minds.

Finally, we heard the hunters coming toward us, their every step announced by the breaking ice. A few minutes later they stepped upon the levee, each with a shotgun in one hand and three ducks in the other. Both men looked intently at their adversary, who stared fervently back at them.

"Is that all the ducks you've killed? This has sounded like a war down here," the federal agent asked, unbelieving.

"None of us have ever duck hunted before," Ray explained. "We couldn't hit 'em!"

"You certainly couldn't," he agreed. "One duck for every twenty shots! Anyway you're hunting on a Federal Game Reserve. Here's a summons. The J.P. is in Abbeville. You'll need to see him today. I'll call and tell him you're coming."

"We may have another duck or two out there officer. I hate to leave them. Could we circle back and see if we can find any more?"

"You've paid for them," the agent barked. "It's okay with me."

The place looked different in daylight. The trail to the car was clear. I started back.

"Wait," Ray beseeched. "Let the game warden get home and we'll get those ducks."

Twenty minutes later, the three of us arrived back at the car, each carrying at least fifteen ducks. We dumped them into the trunk and pulled off our hunting gear, Ray turned his auto toward Abbeville.

"I've got a plan," Bruiser announced, as we approached the Justice of the Peace's small shotgun house. "Let me do the talking."

We knocked on the Judge's door.

"Come on in," came the reply, "I ben' spectin' yew."

The Justice was lying on his couch in his tiny living room and made no effort to rise when we entered. He had not shaved in several days and a wad of chewing tobacco pushed the whiskers on his right cheek out even farther. He wore overalls and a gallon syrup can, his spittoon, sat on the floor near his head, half-filled with dark liquid.

Whut 'ken I do fer yew boys?", he asked.

"Well Judge," Bruiser answered, "I think you already know why we're here. But before we talk about that, I'd like to talk to you about something else."

"Go 'head."

Then with all the eloquence our offensive line coach could muster, and it was considerable, Bruiser explained that he and Ray were football coaches at Ole Miss; that I was a player and poor; how none of us realized we were hunting on a Federal Game Reserve; that we had not killed many ducks; we were very sorry; and that if he could see his way to forget the whole thing, we would make it worthwhile. Lowering his voice a little, Bruiser glanced around the room. "We'll see that you get four free football tickets for every home game next fall!"

The Judge remained stoic on his couch for a full twenty seconds. Then he narrowed his eyes, raised up onto one elbow and centered his spittoon with a half-cup of tobacco juice.

"I ain't never 'ben t' one 'o them 'aire futball games - I wouldn't walk cross a'ter road, rat 'ter t' see one free. 'Yew owe me sum money."

We paid him. I can't remember how much but we settled up, got in Ray's car and headed back to Oxford, an exciting hunting trip spoiled and our attempt to evade prosecution failed. No one said a word for five minutes, until Bruiser broke the silence.

"How in h—l do you reckon a fellow could live all his life just eight miles from Hemingway Stadium and never see a game?"

"I don't know," Ray answered, "but I wasn't any more impressed with him than he was with us."

A minute later Bruiser responded.

"Well, that was d—n little."

CHAPTER V

THE EAGLE

INTRODUCTION

I was a freshman at Ole Miss the first time I saw Herman Sidney (Eagle) Day up close. I had heard of him all through his high school years. Along with about twenty other first year football players, I was herded into his room at Garland Hall, knowing not why. I quickly found out. It was our second day on the campus.

"Freshmen," the Sophomore began, "I know you know who I am. I'm Eagle Day. You probably came to Ole Miss just so you could tell your children and grandchildren some day that you played football with Eagle Day."

Then he laughed with the weird sounding, rhymthic chortle which I would hear so often the next three years - "Unh-ah,unh-ah,unh-ah," —-his voice rising on the "Unh" and dropping a few octaves on the "ah."

"I'm from Columbia," Eagle continued. "There are four highways going into Columbia, and if you ever go through there, you'll know that's where I'm from because on all four roads you'll see a big billboard which says 'Columbia, Mississippi - Home of Hugh White and Eagle Day - Unh-ah, unh-ah, unh-ah." (Hugh White was Governor of Mississippi at the time.)

"Freshmen, when you go back home this summer and decide to write me a letter to impress all your high school buddies, just address it, Eagle Day, Mississippi. I'll get it, unh-ah, unh-ah, unh-ah."

"I'm sure you already know this, but I played all three sports at Columbia. I was all they had! 'Course that was enough!"

Then Eagle followed the declaration with his customary giggle.

"In the fourth quarter of our high school football games, my 'lil 'ol team would be so tired! I'd call time out and gather 'em around me. 'Boys', I'd say, 'I know you're tired and those big 'ol players across the line from you have beaten you up pretty bad. 'Course on account of me we're thirty points ahead so don't even try to block them any more - - I'll run over them,' Unh-ah, unh-ah, unh-ah."

Eagle was on a roll. Freshmen lived under the authority of upperclassmen. We were a captured audience and had never heard his verbal auto-biography. I was fascinated and the other freshmen, if not fascinated, were certainly bewildered. None of us had ever heard anything like this before.

"The basketball game would be about over and we'd be ahead by twenty or thirty points. I'd collect my weary little boys over to one side of the court. 'Fellows, it's late in the game and you're exhausted. If you have the ball in your hand and don't know what to do with it, just pass it to me. I'll shoot! 'Unh-ah, unh-ah, unh-ah.'"

Becoming as acquainted with Eagle in the following three years as anyone could, I believe he would have shot it, too - - in a heartbeat.

When Eagle finished his soliloquy, he sent us out and brought anoth-er group in - -, until all the freshmen had heard.

From that first day, like Jonathan loved David in the Old Testament, my heart was knit to Eagle. I enjoyed his company, and being the country boy I was, I enjoyed his self-glorifying stories. I thought they were funny then - and I still do.

He Was Different

Eagle was different. I had never known, nor would I ever come to know an athlete like him. He boasted of his past and future accomplishments and made me laugh. His bragging was so apparent, it became transparent. I thought I could see all the way through it to a veritable heart.

Eagle would never have admitted it, but I believe he wanted people to know he really wasn't arrogant - - self-confident perhaps, but not arrogant. To have conceded that though, would have dismantled the mystique, some-thing he wasn't willing to do. He elevated the level of his self-promotion so high, people would be forced to see it was done in a "spirit of jocosity," I believe he thought.

I believe it, but I certainly can't prove it. I would need his verifica-tion to prove it, but preserving the mystique prohibits him from providing that.

Many of my friends however, would disagree with my analysis of Eagle.

I had never heard a football player self-extol at all. I had certainly never heard one do it like Eagle. In one fell swoop, my ears traveled from a void on the subject to the maximum. I listened to Eagle's bragging with wonder, amazement, and a touch of envy.

Many times, I had wanted to vaunt myself and my athletic accomplishments. In high school, I even wanted to flaunt my grades. (That desire quickly mutated at Ole Miss.) I lacked the courage. If the deeds of my body had fallen short of the words of my mouth, as they most assuredly would, the ensuing censure by my teammates would have been too shameful to bear. So I suppressed my yearning to self-extol.

Eagle didn't!

Because vaunting oneself takes intestinal fortitude and extreme self-confidence, coupled with a total disregard for other's opinions, I respected Eagle. I may not have been in the majority, but I had to respect him. He was our quarterback and he called my plays.

If I had boasted, I would most certainly have embarrassed myself. I would also have embarrassed my Uncle Bus. I learned early in my football career at Ole Miss not to disconcert Uncle Bus. To have done that would have produced far more than embarrassment for me. Besides I wasn't that much of a gambler. The odds, when considering the consequences, were just too great.

Eagle never seemed to worry about falling short of his words. When he failed, he simply reverted to his unusual cachinnation and ignored his teammates' derision.

The Ole Miss quarterback had indeed been a great high school athlete. He played all three sports, as I mentioned, and made All-State in all three. He received high school All-American acknowledgements in football and baseball, both of which he played at Ole Miss. He came to the University as a highly recruited football player. He would not disappoint Ole Miss fans.

Not every teammate was as impressed with Eagle as was I. Not every coach was either. Coach John Vaught was one of them.

Whether it was Eagle's extreme self-confidence or his tendency to believe he knew as much about football as the coaches, I don't know. But Coach Vaught had, by Nineteen Fifty-Five, lost most of his faith in Eagle. It may have been because of Eagle's song and dance.

Eagle sang two songs about himself- - one he wrote and one he borrowed from a popular movie. The one he wrote became his "workout"song. He developed a prance to accompany the words and he performed it at some point in almost every practice.

"Ra Ra Ra Boom De Aye.

My Name is Eagle Day.

I love to run and play,

Come every Saturday!

On the words 'boom' in the first line; 'Eagle' in the second line; 'run' in the third line; and the syllable 'Sat' in the fourth line, he would alternatingly kick one leg and then the other up into the air, as though he were punting a football. At the conclusion of the four-line song, he would stop, slightly bend both knees, thrust both arms straight out to his side, and bow. The process would be duplicated several times before a coach finally funneled him into the practice session.

Many of the football players cringed, shook their heads, and turned the other way. The coaches tried to ignore his little song and dance until it was time to begin practice. A few players, I was one of them, thought it was hilarious.

Looking at Coach Vaught, Eagle sometimes threatened, "I'm going to run out on the field Saturday, doing it!", meaning before a game.

"If you run out on the field doing that, I'm going to run you off the field permanently," Coach Vaught countered.

Sometimes Eagle would strut into the crowded Student Union, which we called the Grill, singing his workout song. Usually though, he reserved his other song for the Grill.

Oh yes, they call me Mister Touchdown.

Oh yes, they call me Mister T.

I can run, and kick, and throw

Give me that football

And look at me go!

Most of the regular students seemed to enjoy the song. They held football players in pretty high esteem back then, anyway. Whether or not they liked it was totally inconsequential to Eagle though. He would have performed even if they had insisted that he not—!

I thought that song was funny, too.

The Season

By the fall of Nineteen Fifty-Five, as I wrote earlier, Coach Vaught had lost most of his confidence in the senior quarterback. On Monday, September 12, he was demoted to the second team and replaced by a very promising Junior from Drew, John Wallace Blalack. We were beginning the final week of preparation for our first game against Georgia in Atlanta, Saturday, September 17.

Eagle must have been dejected and perhaps even angered by the rejection but he never displayed it. His demeanor remained the same and his song and dance continued. Dangling at the end of a long, unclimbable emotional rope, his confidence never seemed to waver.

Wednesday, September 14, three days before the opening game, Blalack was injured in practice. The prognosis was bad - he wouldn't be able to play Saturday. Coach Vaught was forced to reinstate Eagle into the starting line up. An undaunted Eagle ran out onto the practice field in a red jersey, the color of the starting eleven-"Ra Ra Ra Boom De Aye—."

I marveled at his tenacity. My surprise existed, not so much at the ease with which he transferred back onto the starting team, but that he revealed absolutely no ill will at having been demoted in the first place — an unflappable male Molly Brown.

Eagle was set to lead Ole Miss to a great season.

We beat Georgia 26 to 13. Eagle passed for more than 250 yards; he rushed for about 100 yards; and he punted for more than a 40-yard average. Three of his punts sailed out of bounds inside the Bulldog's ten-yard line. He even played good defense that night.

Herman Sidney Day was now permanently engrafted back onto the starting football team at Ole Miss.

We ended the Nineteen Fifty-Five season with a 9 -1 record, our only loss being to Kentucky, 21 to 14 in a controversial game. We scored two other touchdowns which the officials called back. They would not identify the offenders against whom they "threw the flag." Coach Vaught threatened, to no avail, to contest the game.

After we beat Mississippi State 26 - 0 in our final game of the regular season, we were crowned Southeastern Conference Champions and invited to play the Southwest Conference Champions, TCU, in the Nineteen Fifty-Six Cotton Bowl. We had won the SEC Championship two years in a row, only the second time that had ever been done.

Eagle performed brilliantly that year. Among many other honors, he was chosen first team All-SEC and first team All-South. He earned and deserved the respect of all our coaches and every player - and he received it.

The Cotton Bowl

I really thought he would do it! I believed Eagle would run out onto the Cotton Bowl field singing "Ra Ra Ra Boom De Aye." It was his last game for the Rebels; his last opportunity to display his theatrical talents, which were extremely suspect; his final occasion to frustrate his coach; and his concluding chance to exhibit his self-confidence, as he called it, before his home state fans, many of whom had come to the game, others who were watching on television.

"Why didn't you do it, Eagle?", I asked him after our warm-up.

"Come on man, it's time to get serious," Eagle retorted. "We have a game to play, a really big game."

"That was true three months ago too, Eagle."

It must have taken every fiber of his being to resist the temptation.

TCU's best football player was Jim Swink, a consensus All-American. He had rushed for more than fourteen hundred yards in a ten game season, mostly against eight man fronts, and had scored twenty-four touchdowns. He ran on his heels, the first running back I had ever seen do that. It gave him tremendous balance and enabled him to turn ninety degrees without slowing down. He led the nation in kick-off and punt return yardage, and ran six back for touchdowns; an extremely dangerous runner in an open field.

After the game a friend asked, "Paige, what was tackling Swink like?"

"Like tackling a small rope dangling from a limber tree limb."

The sky was blue, the air was crisp, and Cotton Bowl Stadium packed as we ran out onto the field to start the game. Eagle looked serious.

Ole Miss had played in only two major bowl games before Nineteen Fifty-Five and had lost them both. With only four minutes to go in the game, it looked like we were going to make it three.

Swink had scored twice, once on a thirty-four yard run from scrimmage. TCU was leading us 13 to 7. We had the ball on TCU's forty-two yard line, but it was fourth down with four yards to go for a first down. Less than four minutes were left in the game and we had no time outs. Ole Miss was in trouble.

The one immutable rule for Ole Miss quarterbacks was obedience. Rejecting Coach Vaught's will always resulted in swift and severe retribution. I had never seen an exception, but I was about to - - -!

Sometimes because of the rule of "limited substitution," Coach Vaught had trouble making his will known to the quarterback. Coaching from the sidelines was illegal and if caught, resulted in a fifteen-yard penalty. But the decision of whether or not to punt was so important Coach Vaught had devised a subtle system of conveying his desire to the signal caller. He would stand at the intersection of the fifty-yard line and the sideline, so he could be easily located by the quarterback; turn his back to the field; and flex his right leg as though it was cramping. That meant, "punt." The absence of that little exercise told the team, "go for it."

Eagle cautiously, so as not to be detected by an official, glanced over toward Coach Vaught. He was flexing his right leg.

Our quarterback turned back toward his team. Speaking in the third person as he often did, he exclaimed, "Coach Vaught said 'punt.' 'Ol Eagle ain't too smart but 'ol Eagle knows this isn't any time to punt. Sprint out left."

Everyone in the huddle experienced the same shock. Our eyes widened and we gasped.

One of the Ole Miss linemen frantically cautioned, "Eagle, you can't do that. Coach Vaught said 'punt.'"

"Sprint out left," Eagle forcefully repeated. "On two."

Then the quarterback looked directly at me.

"Paige, I'm probably gonna' hit you."

Seldom does one person gain such a clear, deep, yet unintentional picture of another man's soul. When Eagle confessed, "'Ol Eagle ain't too smart," he was telling the eleven players on the field and all who would ever hear the story, 'for four years you thought I was arrogant. I was just playing a game. I was having fun.' It was as if he was saying, 'Before I walk off this field, I want you to know the truth.'

When he defied Coach Vaught's clear command to punt, he exhibited true self-confidence and courage.

In the calling of that play, we see his humility; in his act we glimpse his confidence.

"Break," Eagle barked out, meaning to break the huddle.

The play, "sprint out left," sent three pass receivers on 'out' pass patterns, to the left side of the field. The left end ran a 25 yard out; the left halfback a 15 yard out, and the fullback slipped into the left flat, 5 yards deep. After taking the ball from center, Eagle would sprint to his left. If a receiver became open, he of course would throw the ball to him. But if the end and left halfback were both covered, then Eagle directed his attention to the defensive cornerback on that side of the field. If the cornerback covered the fullback, Eagle would run the ball. If the cornerback came up to contain the quarterback, Eagle would pass the ball to me, the fullback.

TCU's cornerback left me and came up to tackle Eagle. I was open.

Eagle on the run to his left fired the pass right into my stomach. Eleven yards later, we had a first down on TCU's 31 yard line. Ole Miss fans went wild.

The next play, Eagle called "Sprint out right." "It worked to the left, let's see if it's open to the right."

It wasn't. The right end, the right halfback and I were covered. But Eagle wasn't. He tucked the ball under his arm and scrambled to TCU's 5 yard line. Billy Lott, a sophomore halfback scored around our right end the next play. I kicked the extra point and in the immortal words of Walter Stewart, "Ole Miss by D—n."

Ole Miss had won its first major bowl game -Hotty Toddy!! Ra Ra Ra Boom De Aye!

Two people earned a ride off the field on the backs of the players that day, Coach Vaught and Eagle Day. Eagle won "Outstanding Back" and Buddy Alliston, our left guard, received the "Outstanding Lineman" award.

From that day, our quarterback would no longer be known as the Arrogant One. He would forever live in Ole Miss football history as "The Mississippi Gambler."

The players' respect and appreciation for Eagle had grown immensely during the football season, not only for his athletic ability and his self-confidence, both of which were so visible, but for his toughness. More than once, I saw him reach up to his bloody face, grasp his broken nose with both hands and pull it off his cheekbone to where it felt straight to him. For further fine-tuning, he would look at me through watery eyes and ask, "Does it look straight, Paige?," never entertaining even the thought of leaving the field.

"Just a touch to the left, Eagle."

He Did It To Me

In the three years I played football with Eagle, I grew, ah,er,frustrated with him only once.

We were playing Houston in Jackson. Eagle was the quarterback and I was the fullback. Eagle called a play in the huddle. When we got to the line of scrimmage, he saw that Houston's defensive alignment, probably expecting a roll out, had left a huge gap right up the middle.

Eagle changed the play at the line of scrimmage.

"Red, forty eight trap."

Red was our live change color that night. Forty-eight trap was my play right up the middle. Buddy Alliston pulled and trapped the defensive left tackle. I gained 15 yards.

We huddled and Eagle called another play. When we settled at the line to run it, that same gap reappeared.

"Red, forty eight trap," Eagle yelled.

I groaned out loud!

A split second before Gene Dubuisson snapped the ball, I heard Eagle laugh with that now familiar giggle.

By the time I got to the line with the ball, Houston had sent eleven men to that spot. I was creamed.

"Eagle, thanks a lot, d—n it," I screamed, as I squirmed out from under a thousand pounds of defensive flesh. "When you audible with the word 'trap' and then we trap, that tells them our live color and the play! They knew what we were going to run!"

"Just wanted to see how tough you are!"

"I don't believe that. Stupidity caught up with you again!"

"Unh-ah, unh-ah, unh-ah!"

We Lost Touch

In Nineteen Fifty-Six; Fifty-Seven; and Fifty-Eight, Eagle played for

Winnipeg in the tough Canadian League, where he made All-Canadian. I played with the L.A.Rams in Fifty-Seven and Fifty-Eight. Eagle and I had tried to stay in touch with one another, but in the summer of Fifty-Nine we lost contact. I had no idea where he was - or the team for whom he was playing, although I assumed he still played for Winnipeg, until one Sunday morning. I was lying in my bunk at the Rams Training Camp in Redlands, California, seventy-five miles east of Los Angeles. I opened the L.A.Times to the sports section. The sports headline jumped off the page at me.

"Eagle Day Says He's Best"

Unknown to me, Eagle had signed with the Washington Redskins, who already had two fine quarterbacks, Ralph Gugglielmo and Eddie LeBaron. In an interview with the three quarterbacks, Eagle had declared to a L.A.Times sports reporter that although the other two men were good quarterbacks, never the less, he was much better. The reporter wrote a major story about it.

The Redskins were training at Occidental College in Pasadena.

After Sunday lunch, I drove the two hours to Pasadena. Stopping at the entrance to the college, I asked and received directions to the Redskins dormitory. A young lady sat at the information desk in the lobby.

"Can you direct me to Eagle Day's room?"

Looking down at a list of names, she answered, "Certainly! He's in room (she gave me the room number) straight down the hall to the left."

When I neared Eagle's room I could hear his voice. Stopping at the partially open door, I peeped into the room. Eagle sat near the window, ten or twelve other players sat and stood around the room.

"Rookies," the immutable quarterback cajoled, "I know you know who I am — —."

I pushed the door open and stepped inside the room. Eagle turned toward me. His eyes widened-his jaw dropped. For a moment -just for a fleeting moment I thought I saw a touch of humble uncertainty in his face. It quickly passed as that familiar sound filled the air.

"Unh-ah, unh-ah, unh-ah"

Eagle and I have remained close friends throughout the years. Seeing each other again, after a brief separation, he never fails to announce to everyone around, "Here's the fullback who kept those defensive ends off me."

And I never fail to reply, "And here's the quarterback who gave Ole Miss its first major bowl victory."

Sometime way back there before our brains aged, we must have made a silent commitment to one another not to let anyone forget —- or did we?

It's been so long, I can't remember.

CHAPTER VI

NOT ANOTHER PRACTICE!?

One thought and one thought only dominated every Ole Miss football player's mind while he was standing in the class registration lines in the late Forties, Fifties, and early Sixties-get morning classes. Getting football-friendly professors was important too, but not critical. Morning classes were!

Morning classes allowed us to take a nap before our ominous 3:00 P.M. death trek down to the killing field, ah, the practice field. Back in those years, a football player's perfect schedule, if playing football allowed perfection into a schedule, included fifteen hours of the easiest subjects taught by profs who liked football, followed by lunch, followed by a nap from 1:00 to 2:15.

Football practice in high school was fun, for the most part. Young bodies were very resilient, egos were growing, and cheerleaders were often present. High school coaches had not, from professional necessity developed the killer instinct. Back then high school sports were just that, and winning though important wasn't everything. I'm not certain about the Nineteen Nineties!

Football practice in the pros was fun, for the most part. It wasn't the greatest fun I've ever had and it wasn't as much fun as high school football practice, but it was easier than college. We attended no classes and the players' ages were close to the ages of the coaches. Pro football clearly differed from the college sport too in that it was a job, a profession. Getting paid helped.

Injured pro football players received special attention from the coaches. When I played, each professional team could carry only thirty-five players with no taxi squad, nor reserves. The coaches wanted their players healed by Sunday so they could play, so they would win, so the coaches could work for another year. Practice might be forfeited for healing purposes.

College football practice was a practice horse of a different hue. Back in the afore-mentioned years, Ole Miss and other colleges could sign as many players to scholarships as each school wanted. The NCAA had not yet seized authority and power from schools by which it limited athletic scholarships.

Ole Miss signed ninety-two freshmen in Nineteen Fifty-Three, my freshman year. Wobble inherited a dormitory full of headaches and Ole Miss sported a practice field full of football players. So what if a few couldn't handle the "torture" and left the team! Many more good players remained.

And practice was torture, or close to it!

In an interview by Sport Magazine in Nineteen Fifty-Six, Buster Poole stated calmly, almost apologetically, that playing football at Ole Miss was "probably the hardest work that Paige will ever do."

Forty-two years later, I'll make it official. He was right. Further, nothing else I've done was hard enough to come in second.

I own a large thick book entitled The Synonym Finder, one thousand three hundred eighty-eight pages of words, all the words in the English language and all their synonyms. Adequate words to accurately describe football practice at Ole Miss in the Nineteen Fifties cannot be found, even in that book.

At 2:15 P.M. each practice day, the agony began. That's when the alarm clock shattered my afternoon nap if my class schedule allowed one; that's when the nausea feeling awakened in the pit of my stomach, and I swung my reluctant legs off the bed onto the floor; that's when I pushed myself out of my room and joined my disinclined teammates for the long somber migration to the football field. If a football player ever indicated a proclivity toward sullenness, it usually surfaced between Garland Dorm and the practice field. We were all certain that "today" would be the day of our demise, our departure from the earth. Somewhere along the excursion every player would either imagine or verbalize (or both) the words "I'm not gonna' make it today!" Part of that statement may have gushed from wishful thinking. "If the heat doesn't get me, the hitting probably will, and if the hitting doesn't get me, Uncle Bus will," I imagined.

Water and tape were taboo on the Ole Miss practice field in the Fifties. Water would "soften the muscles" and indicated an affinity for indulgence. Nothing could destroy a football player's character faster than an indulgent nature. Voluntary liquid deprivation tempered the mettle of the athlete in those days. In extreme thirst, the barometer by which the authenticity of the steel of nerve might be measured was the rejection of water. And so we got no water in practice, regardless of the temperature or the length of the workout.

Oh how we prayed for rain! Oh the beauty of storm clouds and lightening! And when our prayers were answered, I loved being tackled. I learned how to fall face down in a water puddle, and how to time my run so that the tackler and I arrived at the mudhole at the same moment.

If the lack of water afforded a measuring device by which the intestinal fortitude of a football player might be measured, the rejection of tape gauged his pain tolerance and his self-worth, or so our coaches seemed to believe.

Personally I loved tape just like I loved water. I would have been happy to have authenticated my manhood some other way but I never got a vote.

As a matter of fact, football practice at Ole Miss depicted a pure totalitarian form of athletic government. As mentioned in both the prologue and introduction, our coaches owned absolute control of our lives. And while we may have resented it internally, though I don't remember doing so, the coaches certainly never knew it!

The severity of practices and our apprehension of them; the coaches total control; and our fear of them all combined to create situations which were funny at the time and which have become much more humorous with the passing years.

WALK CAREFULLY AROUND THE DEAD

At some point on the first day of fall football practice, whether in the meeting room or on the football field, Wobble Davidson, the freshman football, coach always gathered the freshmen around him for their verbal introduction to the mentality of Ole Miss athletics. Such was the case following the first day of practice in Nineteen Fifty.

The long, hot second practice of the day had just ended-the twenty 50 yards sprints had been run, the ten 2 minute grass drills had finally ceased in the 100 degree heat. The late afternoon sun glanced off the white stadium wall, a barrier which deflected the fickle south wind around the practice field, a wind which held little healing for thermal bodies anyway.

Most of the athletes stood in various painful contortions, pine trees in the midst of a storm, bent over in various angles. Their sweaty stomachs and chests heaved almost in unison, as though at the command of a drill sergeant - in, - out -in, out! Salty liquid fell like a rushing mountain stream from the faces, running down their arms, dripping from the fingers, sloshing in their football shoes, then called cleats. A few had fallen to one knee, some past there to their backs, their glazed eyes staring endlessly past the small floating clouds into space.

Into the midst of all of that, stepped Wobble, moving around the bodies, until he stood in the middle of them. The figures grew even more silent.

"Front and center, men," the Coach yelled recalling his old military days.

The exhausted warriors began to stir, some ever so slowly.

"On the double, move it. On one knee."

Oblivious of the Coach's intent, the freshmen glanced nervously at one another, most of them strangers, having only met the day before.

"Freshmen," Wobble began.

At his voice, all of the young men looked fervently into the Coach's face, hoping for good news, for comforting words, for compassionate words.

"If you'll keep your mouths shut," he continued, "trust no living soul, and WALK CAREFULLY AROUND THE DEAD, you might make it here."

If concern had preoccupied the minds of the young athletes before that statement, it suddenly erupted into a massive over-flow after it.

"Is he serious?," someone whispered. Everyone, not really expecting an answer, hoped a player who perhaps knew he was only joking would say so. Anxious eyes searched other faces.

"Lord I hope not!," ventured an optimistic but guarded response.

"I guess we'll soon find out," someone else mused.

Ninety sets of worried ears found listening to the rest of Wobble's directive to be difficult until he got to the part about the Co-eds, for whom the coach devised another name.

"Now, men," he continued, "don't get involved with any one of those cute little split - t—ls you're gonna see running around the campus. Girls are just like street cars, another one will be along in a little while."

To some degree, fear produced by Wobble's first statement yielded to the levity of the second one. In both declarations, the beginning football players glimpsed the character of the man who would predominantly influence their lives for the next four years.

They could not then have known it.

DID YOU KNOW?

Barney Poole made All-American at three different colleges: North Carolina 1943; Army 1944 & 1946; and Ole Miss 1947 & 1948.

THE TIGER

I hated Thursday practices during the football season. I was the only one who hated Thursday practices more than Monday, Tuesday, and Wednesday practices. Thursday practices were supposed to be a semi-light workout, and they were - - for everyone except me. Thursdays we worked on punt protection. I played fullback.

Of all the possible mistakes which could be made in a football game, Coach Vaught most loathed having a punt blocked. To say that getting a punt blocked was his pet peeve was putting it more than mildly. He would not endure it, and the culprit who caused it was in trouble. A blocked punt was anathema to Johnny Vaught.

I was promoted from second team to first team early in my sophomore year in part because the first string fullback caused a punt to be blocked in a game. Trying to decide which of the two defensive ends he should block, he kept retreating until he retreated into our own punter. The punted ball ricocheted off his rear-end backward over our punter's head.

In punt protection, the fullback and the punter were the only two men who lined up more than two yards off the line of scrimmage, the punter about twelve yards deep, the fullback about five. The fullback's blocking responsibility was the defensive left end, on the fullback's right. Every block on punt protection was important but the fullback's block on the end was critical. Every other defensive player was impeded on the line of scrimmage. Not the defensive left end. No one touched him on the line. He belonged to the fullback, and by the time he got to the stationary blocker he was going full speed. He seemed to afford the defensive team the most likely chance of blocking the punt, and of course Coach Vaught knew that.

The biggest, meanest, fastest, hardest end on our team was Tiger Adams. His body fat was zero, if that's possible. About twenty pounds heavier than me, he was muscle and bone and he wasn't named Tiger for nothing. He pounced - - especially on punt-protecting fullbacks like me. He ran bent over and after five yards he was going full speed. I had to wait on him to get to me.

Tiger loved Thursdays. We practiced punt protection for one hour. I hated Thursdays. I had to block Tiger, or try to. No beauty on the Ole Miss campus could make my heart race like blocking Tiger Adams on Thursday afternoons. No football game could get me as excited or as worried.

"Run over him, Tiger," the defensive coach yelled. "Don't let him block you!"

"You'd better block him," Bruiser yelled.

The defensive coach was my Uncle Buster Poole. Buster was the grandfather whom I never knew, my teacher, my coach, my advisor, my counselor and on Thursdays my enemy.

I wanted to write my mother, his sister, or maybe Mama Poole and say, "Do you know that on Thursdays your son tries to have me killed." I would have, too, but I didn't want Buster to tell the rest of the team that I told Mama on him. Besides, Mama might approve.

So, for four years, every Thursday I faced Tiger.

"Block him, Paige," Coach Vaught would yell. "You'd better not let him run over you!"

How more miserable can life get? I faced an end who wanted to flatten me like a pancake; an Uncle who concurred; and a head coach who demanded that I prevent it. I never could understand how a defensive coach and a head coach on the same team could oppose one another so viciously, with me the target for both.

My head still rings. And when I suffer a really scary nightmare, Tiger Adams always seems to be in it.

"GOL-LEE, STONE"

Jerry Stone, about whom I have already written, started for Ole Miss as a center in Nineteen Fifty-Six. We were freshmen together and finished together. Jerry came to Ole Miss from Summit, Mississippi, via McComb just as I came from Crosby via Natchez. We collided with each other in all three sports when Crosby played Summit and then our senior years, when Natchez played McComb. Jerry was a vicious competitor and he had a mean elbow back in the days when football players could legitimately throw an elbow. More than one opposing player felt the pain of it, yours truly included, as I wrote earlier.

I think I know when Jerry covenanted with himself to crush my head with his elbow. We were seniors in high school and he played right end for McComb. I played middle linebacker on defense for Natchez.

Three times in our game with McComb, Jerry jumped high to catch short passes in my area. Three times I caught him in the air, slammed my right shoulder into his belly and drove him into the ground. The last time he looked up at me with fire in his eyes and said, "I'm gonna get your a - s, Cothren."

He finally did. I told you about it in Chapter 1.

I think Jerry's dad taught him how to throw his elbow. His dad, Hook Stone, coached the Southwest Junior College football team. Surely when Jerry was a little boy Hook said, "Now son, here's how you throw a football; and here's how you catch a football; and here's how you kick a football; and son, here's the most important thing. Here's how you throw an elbow."

He listened!

When we were freshmen, one of the many fullbacks who came to Ole Miss that year was Billy Bails, from Osyka, Mississippi. Billy was without question one of the toughest runners I have ever seen. He stood six feet, two inches tall and weighed two hundred and ten pounds; a big back in Nineteen Fifty-Three. He had very little neck, very little chest, and very little stomach. It seemed to me that his crotch lay no more than twelve inches below his chin. He sported the biggest and longest legs I have ever seen on a six foot, two inch body. And when he ran the football, he pumped his powerful legs up past his two ears. Everyone hated tackling him.

Billy was a country boy. Many of us were in those days, but Bails perhaps more so. He talked with a slow country drawl, and thank goodness, he never seemed to lose his temper. A mad Billy Bails would have killed tacklers, not just run over them.

Buddy Harbin, a freshman with Stone and me tells the story. He insists that it's his favorite Jerry Stone tale.

"We were practicing one day in Vaught Valley when Jerry, who was playing defense at linebacker, yelled at me, 'Watch this, Roomie.'"(Note: Vaught Valley was the lower practice field.)

Jerry was speaking to Buddy. As you probably surmised, the two roomed together.

"Billy Bails ran the ball off tackle and Jerry popped him under the chin with the meanest elbow I ever saw. Blood flew everywhere and Billy's chin needed a dozen stitches to close it. When Billy got his eyes uncrossed, he looked up from the ground at Jerry and said in his slow South Mississippi drawl, "Gol-lee, Stone, I'm on yo side!"

When I faced Billy Bails, I wanted to attack with an elbow, too. I sure' didn't want to put my body in front of him.

DID YOU KNOW?

The first college football game ever played in Jackson pitted the Ole Miss Rebels against Alabama, Oct.27, 1894. The score: Rebels 6 - Alabama 0.

ALL I CAN SPARE

Wobble represented the personification of patience when coaching a football player who really wanted to play, who would hustle and play with a little pain. He had very little patience though with a boy who would toil just enough to keep his scholarship but not enough to improve his abilities. The coach's lack of sufferance with a loafer sometimes journeyed down less than a diplomatic path.

Such was an end from the Delta who came to Ole Miss in the late Fifties. He was blessed with great talent but he was lazy. For that reason he was given a partial scholarship which he had to earn. He was on the bubble, so to speak. Everyone agreed, however, that he possessed the physical ability to be a great end at Ole Miss.

One day in a scrimmage, the end was hit pretty hard and continued to lie on the ground after the play had ended. The other players had moved back away from the fallen comrade, secretly grateful that his failure to arise from the ground granted a temporary respite. All eyes were fixed on the stricken one, as helmets were removed and players sank to one knee, an endeavor allowed when practice slowed.

Wobble, knowing the end wasn't hurt, bounded over to the wounded warrior, looked down at him, and said, "I wish you would get your lazy a -s off the ground and do something — hit somebody, do something!"

The lethargic athlete pushed himself off the ground until, with moans and groans, he stood erect before the disapproving coach. His hands on his hips, his displeasure with Wobble evident, the chided end, in his deep Delta accent, retorted, "Coach, I'm giving you all I can spare," creating a two-syllable word out of "spare."

Before the sound of the word "spare" fully cleared his mouth, the athlete was an ex-athlete and on his way to the dressing room, a victim of Wobble's impatience with indolence.

TAPE? YOU NEED NO TAPE!

Back in the Fifties and early Sixties, Ole Miss football players were expected to play hurt—that's play WHEN they were hurt, not play LIKE they were hurt—and not by the players but by the coaches. The second from the last thing I wanted to do was play football when I was hurt. The last thing I ever wanted to do was not play after the coaches told me to —-! The coaches scared me worse than being hurt.

The rule of limited substitution had been imposed upon college football. Simply stated, limited substitution meant that a player who started the quarter could leave the game and return only one time. If he left a second time in the same quarter, he couldn't return to the game that quarter. Likewise when a player, who had not started the quarter came into the game, and then left, he could not return to the field that quarter. Therefore, a player, especially a starter, had better be genuinely hurt if he took himself out of the game. Remember, in those days, every player played both offense and defense.

Does all this sound complicated to you? Pity the poor officials faced with the task of keeping up with it. They did more writing than officiating.

Because of limited substitution, coaching responsibility included teaching players to "play through" pain. I never was really fond of doing that, "playing through" pain. The phrase stressed the notion that the player controlled the pain. When I hurt, I always felt like the pain was controlling me.

Anyway, we had to play even though we were hurt unless the injury included structural damage. A broken arm or a broken leg usually excused a player from practice and maybe even from a game. Just about anything less than a broken bone, however, might not be reason enough to leave the field.

One day in a full contact scrimmage, my little finger on my right hand slipped under the opposing ball carrier's thigh pad and folded back almost to my wrist where it stayed. The pain propelled me out from under the pile of sweaty players yelling, "Doc, Doc."

Doc Knight, I knew, could with great compassion recognize my problem and resolve it. And being unceremoniously void of all pride, yelling at the top of my voice, I anxiously looked for him. Before Doc got to me, however, my Uncle Buster Poole did.

He waved Doc back to the sideline, much to my silent chagrin. Then with his left hand he grabbed my right wrist and with his right hand, he grabbed my displaced finger. At that moment, I was uncertain whether he intended to restore it to its rightful place or just break it off. Moments later, though it seemed longer, Bus snapped my finger back into place.

The pain was awesome.

"Will you let Doc tape my finger?", I pleaded, glancing expectantly toward Doc Knight.

"Tape? Tape?, You don't need any tape."

Waving Doc and his tape away, Buster repeated, "Look Paige, it's back in place. You don't need any tape."

I thought I needed tape. I wanted tape. But I didn't get any tape, not that day.

I got some tape the following day though. I got it in the training room before I ran out onto the practice field. I got lots of tape. My right hand was barely visible underneath it.

I tried to hide my taped hand from Bus but that was hard to do. He finally spotted the large clump of white at the end of my right arm. Walking over to me he asked, "Think you have enough tape on that hand, Paige?"

"Yes, Sir!"

I think he was teasing.

YES, YES!! THE PLAYERS CRIED

When Ole Miss journeyed to Jackson in Nineteen Fifty-Six to play Tulane, we had won fourteen straight football games, including a 14 to 13 win over TCU in the Cotton Bowl following the Nineteen Fifty-Five season. The Tulane game was played in the midst of two storms, one from the heavens and one from the Green Wave, who won the game 10 to 3. The next week we traveled to Little Rock and were shut out by Arkansas 14 to 0. Ole Miss had lost two games in a row, an aberration for a proud school.

The Ole Miss fans were distressed; the student body was exasperated; the coaches were ferocious; and the players were emotionally distraught in small part because of the losses but primarily because the coaches were ferocious. Ferocious coaches conduct long hard practices and long hard practices depress football players. Depressed football players are notoriously unsuccessful. But Ole Miss had Doc Knight, trainer.

Doc Knight always attacked declining emotional states of Ole Miss football players. After a loss, he encouraged. After a coach's censure, he consoled. When we "screwed up," he exhorted. When hurt, he doctored us. And when we were "down" emotionally, as I mentioned, he sought to inspire us. And boy, after two losses, we were "down", so down as someone said, we could have "slid under a snake's belly!"

Sometimes Doc Knight's methods of inspiration though, moved toward the unorthodox, at least in light of the Nineteen Fifties concept of unorthodox, and certainly in regard to the coaches' view of it.

Doc assembled a loud speaker system in our dressing room. (I still wonder how he did it over the weekend) Upon entering the dressing room Monday afternoon for the first practice following our loss to Arkansas, we were greeted by loud band music - "Dixie," the Ole Miss Fight Song, "Forward Rebels," and several other inspirational musical arrangements. We assumed the coaches directed Doc to install the esprit-de-corps builder until Wobble entered the building.

If Wobble abhorred anything more than cigarettes and loafing, it had to have been artificial emotional stimuli, a dislike possessed by the other coaches but mastered by the freshman coach. To him, Doc's creation epitomized artificial emotional stimuli.

The players were packed into the noisy den of our dressing room, in different stages of undress and dress when Wobble, entering the room, encountered the orchestral score reverberating off the ceiling. He stopped as though he had collided with an invisible wall. Within a second only the sound of music could be heard as fifty silent heads turned toward the coach in apprehensive anticipation. To all who heard his retort, it will live, if not in infamy, certainly in posterity.

"The next d - n thing Doc's gonna try to PIPE in here is WOMEN." (Not exactly the word Wobble used.)

"Yes! Yes!," chorused a room full of hopeful voices.

So far as I know, much to our chagrin, Doc never even tried to implement Wobble's notion. We may never know whether it was because of the music or the exciting idea, but the inspired Rebels won the next few games.

DID YOU KNOW?

Only one family has placed 14 or more of its members into college football as players: the Pooles of Ole Miss.

SEMIHOLE TRIBE?

Football practice seldom lulled at Ole Miss under Coach Vaught and his staff. I remember few "timeouts" and no water breaks. The NCAA had not yet imposed its rules upon colleges and universities limiting the length and number of practices. Had they done so, the schools would probably have ignored them and continued to practice as long as they desired. We practiced from 3 P.M. until dark every day, except the days before games, when we only worked one and one-half hours.

Actually, I wanted shorter practices. In fact, in retrospect, I think all the players would have voted for shorter practices. Had we been given the decision, I imagine our practices would have been so short, they would have ceased to exist altogether.

One day in Nineteen Fifty-Eight, practice lulled for a few minutes. Dewey Patridge and the other players fell to one knee.

I never could understand why the coaches let players fall to only one knee. Why not to two knees? If falling to one knee was okay, then falling to two knees would be even better. They let us alternate knees. We could rest on one for a while and then upon the other one, but not both of them at the same time.

Someday I'm going to try to work up the courage to ask Coach Vaught about that.

Anyway Dewey was resting on one knee talking to Coach Hovious. Wobble was standing nearby.

"Indian," Coach Hovious asked Dewey, "how much Indian blood you got in you?"

"I don't know Coach, I got a good bit in me."

"Which tribe you from?"

Wobble who had been listening to the conversation suddenly retorted, "He's from the Semihole Tribe."

Hovious looked at Wobble, "What the h —l is that?"

"He's a half-a - s Indian."

THE ROOTER

In the early Nineteen Fifties, freshmen football players gave little if any consideration to disobeying Wobble either in the dormitory or on the football field. In the same way, the six-gun equalized the Old West, bringing every man, regardless of his size, to a common plateau; a small thin man might be left standing over a large muscular dying one, a smoking pistol in his hand, so every young man who played freshman football under Wobble was brought to a common denominator, - - fear of the Coach. Regardless of our high school athletic reputations, regardless of our sizes, regardless of our families financial conditions, regardless of our family relationships with other Ole Miss coaches, regardless of our intellectual abilities, all us evolved, sooner or later, to the place of Wobble-fear.

Fear of a coach forces a football player to obey. The obedience may be contaminated with selfishness, self-preservation, or even a desire to please the object of the fear. The fear may be punctuated with a desire to be a star, a Saturday afternoon hero. But its presence, whatever the cause, forces a young man to expend great energy giving his best.

Fear mixed with humor however, causes the one who possesses it to respect the object of the fear. Respect technically differs from fear. One may fear without respecting but he cannot respect without fearing.

Wobble manifested the ability to make young men fear him but when he effectuated punishment with humor, it produced respect. By the way, the "innocent" bystanders found the applied discipline funnier than those disciplined, of course, but they usually laughed with reservation, knowing their time was coming.

Horace Williams, a lineman at Ole Miss in the early Fifties found a companionship of fear with all the other freshmen at Ole Miss. While his fear of the coach, as evidenced by his obedience, might seem a little extreme, few of the other players doubted they would have done the same thing had they received the same command.

Horace was a small lineman, even for the early Fifties. He was being handled-beaten by the big tackle across the line one day in a scrimmage. So Horace did what all smaller linemen do against larger adversaries - he submarined. To submarine means to get lower than your opponent in order to protect your area of responsibility. But the lower Horace got, the lower his blocker got, until finally Horace was diving into the ground on every play-with Wobble yelling.

"Williams, quit sticking your head into the ground."

Finally the coach stopped the scrimmage. Turning to Horace he said, "Williams you like sticking your head into the ground so much, I'm going to let you do it the rest of the day!"

Wobble then made Horace move over to the edge of the field, put his head on the ground with his hands behind his back, on his feet, not his knees as one might think.

"Now charge," Wobble commanded.

Without hesitation and without questioning his coach Horace started pushing himself around the practice field, his helmeted head on the turf, his hands behind his back, his rear-end up in the air, and his feet pumping against the ground.

Laughing, teammate Charlie Duck remembered, "What I couldn't get over is that Horace never looked up. His forehead was on the ground, which meant his eyes had to be closed and he never looked up. I think I would have looked up to see where I was going."

The fact is, he never looked up the rest of the day. Horace kept rooting and the team kept practicing, forgetting about him, until he rooted close by.

Toward the end of practice someone asked, "Where's Horace?"

His trail, clearly visible, was never the less hard to follow because he criss-crossed so many times.

"There he is, in the hedge," finally one of the searchers called out.

The chain link fences around the huge practice field at Ole Miss were designed to keep unwanted visitors out. The hedges which had been planted just inside the fences kept opposing spies from watching practice.

Sometime in Horace's journey, he had pushed himself through the hedge and into the fence. That's where the student managers found him, unconscious.

"Blood must have gone to his head," someone surmised.

When extricated from his leafy tomb, Horace quickly recovered.

Some forty-six years later, while gathering information for this book, Charlie Duck, one of Horace's best friends, was telling me the story at an annual gathering of M-Club Alumni in Memphis. Wobble walked up. I asked, "Coach do you remember when you made Horace Williams - - -?"

He interrupted me before I could finish.

"- - put his head on the ground, and his hands behind his back and charge?", he asked.

"Yes, you remember it then?"

"D - - nest sight I've ever seen. I couldn't make him keep his head off the ground so I figured he liked it." "Only thing," the Coach continued, "he pushed up piles of dirt everywhere. We had to re-groom the whole practice field."

DID YOU KNOW?

Paige Cothren led the NFL in field goals and field goal percentage for the L.A. Rams in 1958.

WHAT KIND OF DEFENSE?

Although I can't prove this, never the less I believe it may be true! Wobble occupied the coaching position of "Terminator," among multitudinous other duties. Oh, he wasn't a terminator in the normal sense of the word. He killed no one. He terminated Ole Miss football players' complacency, our lack of effort, our imperturbable attitudes. And, failing to dislodge those undesirable characteristics from us, then he might have been influential in disengaging us from the team. His way of disclosing our failures with short, pithy statements often penetrated to the very core of the problem.

One year in the Mid-Fifties, the Rebs had lost two football games in a row. That year, we had very little depth and four of the starters had suffered catastrophic injuries, three of them being season ending - -! Morale was low after the sixth game, and it seemed as though the team had just about decided to "hang it up."

Because of a lack of depth and experience, Coach Vaught had, at the beginning of the season, announced a reward system for superior effort. The recompense consisted of shirts - - from The Carl Coors Shop in the Student Union Building. A key block, for example, resulting in a score, procured one shirt. A saving tackle to prevent a score received two, etc.

The potential of receiving beautiful new shirts had helped but had not quelled the Rebels slide into an emotional abyss.

On the first Monday after the second loss, Wobble arrived at the field house before the other coaches. As each player arrived to dress for practice, he directed him to sit in the dressing room bleachers used for team meetings. One by one we sat down quietly until everyone had arrived.

"You Prima Donnas," Wobble started, "you think you have it made here. You don't!"

Then position by position, he began to reprimand us.

"You ends, - - when a ball is thrown toward you, you aren't going for it. You'll just let the d - - n thing fall to the ground - - and you tackles and guards, you're just sitting there. You couldn't knock a whore off a P - - s pot. You centers are just as bad. And you backs, - - you're supposed to run the football not walk the football, and when you aren't running the football, you're supposed to block. Have any of you thought about blocking someone? It would be nice. Then when you get on defense you just sit on your b—ts. No wonder you've lost two games in a row. Get off your a -ses and hit somebody. You know the school pays a lot of money for your shoulder pads - - I don't know why! Seems like you've made up your minds not to use them...etc. etc. etc."

The chiding lasted for twelve hours, it seemed, but actually about ten minutes. Then Wobble stopped talking and looked at us. A minute or two passed, no one said a word, until he looked at each of us directly in the eye. Then he spoke - - softly.

"You know what you people have?"

He hesitated, giving the question time to sink in .

"A shirt offense and a s - - t defense.

With that, he turned and walked out of the room.

I'm not certain how long we sat there before anyone said anything or moved. We wanted to laugh but were afraid, not knowing if we were sup- posed to —! I imagine everyone else was thinking the same thing I was, " We'd better figure out some way to win. We don't want to be known as a shirt offense and a s - - t defense."

NOT WHILE YOU'RE RUNNING

Three "Mama's" played football at Ole Miss during the Vaught years. One was Mama Hitt, who played in the late Forties. One was Mama Hurst, who played in the Mid-Fifties and one was Mama Shute who played in the late Fifties.

I'm not certain why Hitt was nicknamed Mama but Hurst and Shute were so named in part because they were large and built in such a way that their protruding stomachs made them look pregnant.

I played with Mama Hurst. He was a fullback. Pregnant or not, "she" could and would run over you. Though she may have been blessed with some mothering instincts, they certainly stopped at the point of impact with tacklers.

Mama Shute was a large lineman, a highly sought-after high school player, but he had a weight problem. Every fall he reported to football practice substantially massive.

Shute's second year Ole Miss Red-shirted him. He had reported in about twenty-five pounds too heavy.

"Wobble, the Red-shirt coach, was determined to get the weight off him," one of Shute's teammates declared. "He was running him to death."

In sprints, Wobble ran behind Mama shouting, "Run Mama! Pick it up! Get in shape, Mama. Run!"

One hot afternoon session in two a day practices, Wobble was pushing Mama to "Run, Mama, run!"

"Mama got to moaning and groaning real loud," his teammate explained, "while he was running, with Wobble right behind him."

"I can't go, I can't go!," Mama cried out to his coach, slowing down and bending over in obvious pain.

"What the h - -l's wrong with you?", the Coach asked.

"I got to go the bathroom!"

"What you got to do?", Wobble asked.

"I don't know!"

"You don't know?" the Coach exclaimed. "Well you got to do one or the other."

"I got to s - - t!" the tired lineman exclaimed, probably hoping that particular urge indicated more urgency than the other.

"Get your a - s to running," the Coach commanded. "I've never seen anyone do that while they were running."

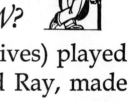

DID YOU KNOW?

Five Ole Miss Pooles (or relatives) played in the NFL. Two, Buster and Ray, made All-Pro three years each.

ARROWHEAD

Wobble was a prolific nickname originator. He must have spent hours devising the appellations. When I suggested that it must have taken him a long while to conceive them, a teammate forcefully declared, "H - - l no! That was just the way his mind worked."

The teammate was probably right. Wobble owned an extensive vocabulary, and he possessed enough interest in each player to perceive the person's unusual characteristics, the ability to exaggerate it, and then the wisdom to name it.

In the fall of Nineteen Fifty-Six, Dewey Patridge, a halfback from Philadelphia, Mississippi, was a freshman. Like all freshmen of that era, he remembers vividly the first time his freshman team went "down the hill" to scrimmage the varsity. Two fears existed for every freshman their first year at Ole Miss: going down the hill, and getting caught breaking a rule by Wobble.

Going down the hill meant descending the bank between the freshman area, immediately behind the stadium, and to the lower field where the varsity practiced.

"Wobble really hadn't noticed me," Dewey explained. "I was running third string on the freshman team. We went down the hill the first time and you, Paige, Jerry Baker and Big Mama Hurst kept hurting our defensive halfbacks. Finally Wobble had to put me in."

"Who is that d - - n Indian-looking boy," he asked.

"Dewey Patridge, from Philadelphia, Coach, and he does have some Indian blood in him," a manager answered.

From that day, Indian became one of Wobble's names for Dewey.

A while later "Indian" developed a cyst behind his left ear.

"I finally talked Doc Knight into letting me to go to the doctor to have it cut out," Dewey explained. "It was deep and it was sore."

That afternoon Dewey reported for practice, his head almost completely bandaged. "I looked like a war veteran from 1812," Dewey admitted. "I had bandages from my neck to the top of my head."

"What the' h - - l's wrong with you, Indian?" Wobble asked.

"Coach, I had something cut out of my head."

"Probably one of those d - - n arrowheads you got down on the reservation!!"

From that day Dewey was identified by three nicknames, "Quail," "Indian," and then by "Arrowhead."

"When they took that arrow out of his head wasn't anything left," Wobble surmised.

DID YOU KNOW?

Jimmy Patton, Ole Miss halfback 1952 - 56 both played and coached for the N.Y. Giants at the same time. He made All-Pro five straight years, 1958-62.

WITH HIS LEG, COACH?

One of the two greatest fullbacks ever to wear the Red and Blue was Charlie Flowers. No, the other one wasn't me, as badly as I hate to admit that, it was John "Kayo" Dottley. Both of them are justifiably members of the National Collegiate Football Hall of Fame.

Charlie came to Ole Miss as an unlikely candidate for consensus All-American. By his own admission, his two legs were only two blood vessels down to his feet. Great fullbacks are supposed to have big legs. Mine weren't, so I did calf-muscle exercises every night before I went to bed, trying in vain to enlarge them. By the time Charlie got to Oxford, he had already given up on making his bigger.

With legs so small, I never could figure why it hurt so much to hit him. Neither could many others.

Probably in part because he had small legs, Charlie hated the fifty-yard sprints the coaches made us run at the end of each practice. We started running the sprints immediately after we thought we were going to die from the practice itself.

Charlie and his teammates had run about half of the prescribed number of sprints when Charlie "knew" he was dying. The temperature had burned into the mid-Nineties, the humidity languished at about 90%, and Charlie had ten more fifty-yard sprints to run. He was bent over at his waist, his hands resting on his knees sweat spilling affluently from his body. Splattered against a bloody wall, Charlie thought he was "done for —."

"What the h - - l's wrong with you, Flowers?," caustically yelled Wobble.

"I'm not gonna make it Coach!"

"Not going to make it, H - - l," Wobble retorted. "I saw a soldier get his leg shot off in the South Pacific, pick it up and use it for a crutch to walk half a mile. What do you mean you're not going to make it?"

"Once for all and forever, amen, I knew I would get no compassion from Wobble," Charlie muttered.

He finished his sprints.

RUNNING ON AN ACRE OF WHAT?

In the early Nineteen Fifties Ole Miss signed a halfback from one of the larger high schools in the State. He was a very handsome, very muscular, very fast, and very talented young man. He had blond-white hair which he kept neatly greased and shaped into ducktails, the style of his day. He was smart and so fast that he ran both the one hundred yard dash and the two-twenty for Doc Knight's track team. (Doc was the track coach in those days.) But he had one glaring weakness - he didn't like to hit or to be hit. On offense his problem was less apparent. Halfbacks were to run to daylight and he did that — in a hurry. But football players in those days played both ways, offense and defense. On defense, a player had to tackle the opposing ball carrier, which required sticking your head and shoulder into him. My friend did that poorly, thereby continually procuring the coaches condemnation. But even when running the ball, he tended to decelerate in order to reduce the force of impact when about to be tackled a maneuver which the coaches labeled "Tip-toeing," or worse.

Wobble bristled over a football player who shied away from contact. He often bridled that player with a nickname which depicted the fallacy, so he christened my friend "Milk Toast," the color of his hair supporting the epithet.

One day in a scrimmage, Milk Toast, running the ball, broke through a huge hole in the line. When the two defensive halfbacks came up to make the tackle, he throttled down.

Wobble, standing about ten yards behind the geared down athlete yelled, "Milk Toast, you look like you're running on an acre of boobs". (Wobble used another word).

The picture painted in our minds of a football player wearing cleats running on a field of women's breasts must be an original. What a portrait to hang over the fireplace!

At any rate an entire coaching staff and football team found itself bent over in laughter. I wonder if the image is as humorous to you ladies!

WE WERE EXPENDABLE

Things started changing in the late Nineteen Sixties. Football players began to determine "if" and "how badly" they were hurt. In the Seventies and Eighties, they began to be listened to in regard to whether or not they were hurt too badly to play. Now, in the late Nineties it seems, especially to old timers like me, that the players have become the sole determinant of whether or not they should be practicing and/or playing.

In the late Forties, Fifties, and early Sixties the coaches, with some humble and guarded advice from Doc Knight and rare counsel from a doctor, made the decisions. I don't ever remember being asked how badly an injury hurt. When Coach Vaught asked, "Can you go, son, can you go," the decision had already been made. He expected you to go. The question had little to do with gathering information - - it had everything to do with commitment, the coach's commitment. He had already committed the player to play.

Players, therefore, in those years knew they were expendable so we were reluctant to admit we were hurt. Coaches essentially ignored the player's injuries until the injury itself demanded notice. Ole Miss coaches had played with that mentality, so they coached with it. That acumen prevailed as the "norm," which meant that any variance from the norm must of course be abnormal. To refrain from acting and being "tough" was an unacceptable deviation from the norm. The tougher the practices, the more indomitable the players became.

According to the normal disposition of mind, therefore, for the era, the coaches owed the players the task of making them more invincible. To "Be" invincible, one must "Think" invincible, and "Act" invincible. Hard practices and accepting the notion that injuries, even serious ones, ought to be viewed casually was part of the hardening process. Pain was incidental and the memory of it would later become humorous, "so ignore it," we were silently told.

We did and it has! When we older ex-players get together and remember, we laugh at the coaches' responses and reactions to our injuries.

For you to view the following seven short stories as humorous therefore, you must first understand that we, the former players do. Then try to comprehend the casual mode of regarding injuries in those days. Hopefully the tales will contain some amusement for you.

Oh well, maybe not!

A Terrible Way to Get "Pinned"

In Nineteen Fifty Six, Milk Toast pushed up out of a scrimmage pile groaning and holding his left hand over his upper right shoulder. His right arm was dangling.

Wobble had named my friend Milk Toast in part because he often thought he was hurt worse than he was —, or believed he was really hurt when he wasn't hurt at all. Today some might say he had a low tolerance for pain, not a desirable attribute for an Ole Miss football player in the Fifties.

Anyway, Wobble grasped Milk Toast's right hand with both of his hands and shook his right arm vigorously.

"You're alright, Milk Toast," the coach assured him. "Get back in there."

Milk Toast continued to scrimmage - - until a red spot appeared on his white jersey, near his right shoulder. Doc Knight lifted his shirt and motioned for Wobble to look.

The halfback had broken his collarbone and one end of it, as he continued to scrimmage, had finally worked its way though the skin.

"Well h - - l, Milk Toast," the coach exhorted. "You should have told me you were hurt."

The injured halfback underwent an operation to have the broken collarbone pinned back together. Two months later he was operated on again to have the pin removed.

The preceding story might sound cruel now, when reflected against the mirror of modern opinion of football injuries. But that friend, who remained one until he passed away, and I laughed about it many times.

Run it out, Paige

My friend and I also laughed about my foot many times. I admit however, that I thought his collarbone break was funnier than my foot wound.

In the early part of the Nineteen Fifty-Four season, I developed a severe pain in my right foot, at least it was severe to me. Running backs need their feet. They use their feet on every play. I assumed, therefore, that since my feet were so important, I needed to determine the source of the pain. I wanted to see a doctor.

"Run it out, Paige," my Uncle Buster Poole responded. "Keep it loosened; run it out."

I ran every day. I practiced and played the rest of the season. I ran, and ran, and ran.

I wanted to ask Uncle Bus what that meant - - to run it out but I was afraid he might think I wasn't running enough and make me run some more. I think he meant that if I ran enough the pain would go away.

After the season ended, it finally went away.

Four years later I was playing for the L.A. Rams. The arch of my right foot started hurting. I went to the doctor, who x-rayed it.

Holding the x-ray up to the light, the doctor turned to me and asked, "When did you break this bone in your foot?"

I had forgotten! But then I remembered. I told the doctor the story. He grimaced.

"I'm surprised it showed up on the x-ray," I said to him. "I thought I had run it out."

Tough as a Rock

In Nineteen Fifty-Four, a large handsome boy from the Mississippi Delta played tackle at Ole Miss. Actually, he didn't play in games much. He wasn't there that long. Wobble nicknamed him Rock because he looked like a big Rock Hudson.

Like Milk Toast, Rock, a very nice young man, seemed to have a low tolerance for pain. For that reason, the coaches perhaps believed that he needed "toughing up" a little.

One day in practice, Rock was hit very hard from the side by another huge lineman, All-American Rex Reed Boggan. Rock struggled to get up.

"Get off the ground," Uncle Bus yelled.

"Coach, I hurt my leg," Rock countered.

"You're not hurt, Rock," Bus answered. "get up, get in the huddle."

Rock finally struggled to his feet and returned to the defensive huddle.

He scrimmaged the rest of the day. Then, with the rest of us he suffered through grass drills, those dastardly exercises of falling onto the ground and rising again to the chant of Coach Bruiser Kinard yelling, "front - up - back - up - front - back - up." Finally he "ran" wind sprints with the rest of us if his running could be labeled that —! Tiptoeing on his painful leg, he finished far last on each sprint.

You're running like a rock," the coaches yelled.

Rock got no faster.

Finally practice ended. Rock limped into the dressing room, showered, dressed and left. That night he moved out of the athletic dorm.

A few days later I saw him on the campus. He was still limping.

"Hi Rock," I greeted. "How you doin'?"

He pulled up his pants leg and pointed to the cast.

"I broke the thing."

Turned out he had broken the small bone in his leg.

When told about Rock's injury, one of the coaches declared, "I don't know why Rock quit. He still had one good leg!"

Practice Takes Precedence

Operating under the aforementioned attitude, practice at Ole Miss took precedence over everything short of death. Occasionally it even threatened to exceed that - -, although our coaching staff would certainly deny it, and properly so!

To be honest, I never doubted that practice would continue if I broke my neck on the practice field. And few days passed without the thought coursing though my mind that "today might be the day that I have a heat stroke, or heart attack, or get my neck broken." Periodically, in the toughest practices, I think I even welcomed it, if only subconsciously.

Billy Oswalt played for Ole Miss in the late Fifties. One day in an extremely tough practice, Billy received a terrific blow to his head rendering him unconscious. He swallowed his tongue.

Billy Ray Adams tells the story.

"Oswalt was lying on the field dying, I guess. He was gagging, couldn't breathe. His jaws were locked. Doc Knight couldn't get his mouth open to pull his tongue out of his throat so he ran over to his medical bag on the sidelines and back, having retrieved a small medical instrument with which he could pry open Billy's jaws."

"Thank goodness, Doc brought the instrument on the field. Billy looked like he was dying to us. It took Doc a while tò get his jaws open and get his tongue out."

Wobble disdainfully looked down upon the operation. Finally he said, "Doc, looks like he's gonna make it. Could you move him off the d - - n field so we can get back to practice?"

Doc obeyed. He moved Oswalt over to the sideline and Billy started awakening. He made it.

"Thing about it is," one of his teammates remarked years later, "Wobble's request seemed perfectly reasonable to us then."

Oh my, how times do change!

We'll Play on Top of Him

Along about that same time, Freddy Roberts, a fullback, took a hard lick in the face during a scrimmage.

A teammate remembers, "He was laid out on the field, blood flooding from his nose. Doc was feverishly working on him, trying to stem the red tide."

"Doc," Wobble proclaimed, "If you don't get him off the field, we're going to play on top of him!"

With the help of a manager, Freddy was pulled to the sideline by his arms.

Cold as a Cucumber

All of which reminded Doug Elmore of the plight of Gibbs Goodwin.

"One day Gibbs got knocked cold as a cucumber in a freshman scrimmage, lying face down. I thought he was dead and no one was paying any attention to him. He wasn't moving a muscle, just lying there. I said, 'He's dead'!"

Wobble said, "S—t, lets move up ten yards and get out of the way," which they did.

Finally Doc came out on the field and rolled Gibbs over.

"Blood was spurting from his nose," Doug continued, "H - - l, I thought he was dead. I couldn't even call the next play."

Is He Dead?

Although Gibb's plight did not occur everyday, neither was it isolated. Forty years ago football pads and helmets were much inferior to those worn by players today. Face masks delayed their entrance into the game until Nineteen Fifty-Five and then they consisted of one small, non-protective, round plastic bar. Few players came through Ole Miss, or any other college for that matter, who avoided being knocked unconscious at one time or another.

Bo Ball certainly didn't escape!

Bo was red-shirted his sophomore year, and the red-shirt team, which ran the opposing teams offenses and defenses, was scrimmaging the varsity.

"Bo was knocked cold as a wedge," one of his teammates remembered. "He was just lying there on the ground, face down."

Wobble, who coached the red-shirt team as well as the freshman yelled, "Get up, Bo."

Bo didn't move.

"Wobble walked over to where the fallen warrior lay and looked down at him for a second or two. Then he stuck his foot right under Bo's side and flipped him over," the teammate continued. "While he was flipping him, Wobble said, 'Let's see if he's dead'!"

Bo flopped onto his back. Blood was running from his nose and out of the corner of his mouth.

"Yeah, I believe he IS dead," Wobble asserted. "Let's move on up the field a little way."

Bo wasn't dead, but neither was he conscious; nor did his condition halt practice.

Both Gibbs and Bo recovered. They had to - - Wobble demanded it!

THAT'S NO BLOOD!!

Like schools and athletic programs everywhere, Ole Miss has signed its share of tough guys, football players who could fight. During my years at Ole Miss, we had Billy Yelverton, a six feet four inch, 220-pound tackle who ran a ten flat hundred. Billy loved to fight. While at Ole Miss he won the Mid-South Golden Gloves Heavyweight Championship held in Memphis. I saw him whip a sailor from the Naval Air Base in Millington, Tennessee, out at Sardis Lake one day until the fellow's face disappeared under a mask of swollen, bloody tissue. Billy knocked all of his front teeth out. Blood from his face, nose, and mouth washed bits of tooth enamel all the way down the front of his body.

During Reed Davis' playing career at Ole Miss, the tough guy, according to him, was Tommy Lucas. Nicknamed ToJo for obvious reasons, he was mean.

"He was tough," explained Reed. "When you lined up in front of him, you knew what was coming at you - - shoulder pads, elbows, and fists."

One day in a scrimmage, Tommy had been working on Reed for a quite a while.

"After about thirty minutes of it," remembered Reed, "he had me punchy. He had hit me with elbows and fists so much that I quite playing football and just started ducking."

It paid off.

"I saw the knuckles coming straight at my face and I ducked. Freddie Roberts happened to stop right behind me. Tommy's fist caught him flush in the face and he crumpled on the ground like a sack of potatoes."

Freddie was lying on his face, out cold, a pool of blood beginning to spread out around his helmeted, comatose head. The players gathered around him but no coach noticed.

"Freddie hadn't moved a muscle for ten or twelve seconds," Reed continued, "and the pool of blood around his head was expanding rapidly. I decided I needed to do something."

Reed hollered at Wobble who was coaching a small group over near the sideline.

"Coach, you'd better come see about Freddie. He's really bleeding!"

Wobble casually glanced over toward Reed's fallen comrade and strolled over to where he was lying. He looked down at him for a moment, slid his right foot under Freddie's chest, flipped him over, and after a quick observation, offered his medical summation.

"H - -l that's no blood! My hemorrhoids bleed more than that every morning."

Vintage Wobble!

NUBBIN
A SPECIAL MAN

This work was never intended to be a treatise on social change nor a critique of the doctrine of social and political correctness. But to tell an extremely humorous story about a very special person, the concepts must be discussed.

Truth is static, of course. But truth must always be understood against the background of cultural mores and standards at the time of the truth. A diamond's beauty cannot be fully appreciated until it is placed upon a black velvet cloth. The teachings of the apostle Paul, woman's greatest single liberator, cannot be understood nor esteemed if evaluated by female rights of today. But when measured by woman's rights of his day, his inspired thoughts were revolutionary (I Corinthians 7:4b.)

So it is with this story about one of the most beloved people ever associated with the University of Mississippi, one of the hardest working, and one of the most intelligent, Billy (Nub) Sanders. Nub, or Nubbin as many of us lovingly and respectfully called him was, during the aforementioned years, Ole Miss' Equipment Manager. He was stricken with cerebral palsy which changed his physical appearance and rendered his speech almost unintelligible, until his hearers trained their ears. That didn't take long for freshmen football players after learning that Nubbin ran the equipment room with an uncompromising iron fist. When Nubbin addressed the players in that stern, serious tone which he had fully mastered, we soon learned we had better know what he was saying. He tolerated no foolishness from any of us, not even the biggest and meanest.

I faced a dilemma in penning this story. I could remain socially correct and not write it at all; or I could be true to my own person, ignore social correctness and tell the story. I could not do both. I think Nubbin would agree with my decision.

I'm too old to change. I refuse to adhere to the overly sensitive concepts of being socially and politically correct. No one has ever been socially correct with me. Let's see, in my life time, I have been called, to my face and behind my back: "Jug-Butt," (I can't imagine why, I've backed up to many mirrors and I've seen no jugs); "Red-neck" (No, No, - I went to Ole Miss); "Stupid" (I have my Master's Degree, took four years of Greek and taught it, college level); "Rural" (I didn't even like the Grand Ole Opry when we used out door toilets); "Black Sheep S.O.B of my family (That one might have been true); "Meat-head" (I played football at Ole Miss in the Fifties, what can I say?); "Super-stud" (Heh,Heh, I really don't know now, I mean - - -); "Fanatic" (The word fan derives from it); "Religious Fanatic" (I am a fan of what the Lord did for us); "Sinner" (Yup!); "Weird" (I liked Sophomore Lit, — I'm sorry!); and "Party Animal" (Dad-gummit, I thought I was invisible); just to list a few.

And all those descriptive cognomina were conferred upon me by people who loved me. I might have listed epithets bestowed upon me by enemies, but I couldn't write the nasty things in this book and an entire paragraph of first and last letters with dots in between would have been very boring.

I don't ever remember getting my "feelings" hurt at being called all those names because I had been taught as a child not to wear my feelings on my sleeves, not to be hyper-sensitive, and not to be obsessed by other's opinions and descriptions of me. Thank goodness! That instruction came in handy my freshman year in Oxford. But then again I might have allowed my feelings to be hurt if I had known, as modern America knows, I could have gotten something out of it.

Anyway, I'm old fashioned. I believe truth ought to pre-empt feelings. If I'm born with big floppy ears, I shouldn't rise up in righteous indignation when my friends call me "Ears," or "Floppy." Denying they are big and floppy doesn't eliminate them nor change them - - it only moves me into dishonesty and publishes my shame and embarrassment about them, revealing an image problem in me.

The old adage, popular when I was in grammar school, might well serve us today. Concerning the scourge of head-lice, our teachers would say, "Now children, it's not wrong to HAVE lice, it's just wrong to KEEP them." I was in high school before I finally figured that out. The teachers were exhorting us to change the bad things within our power to change and accept the rest, with no self-degradation, I might add.

Nubbin had cerebral palsy, not his fault. The paralysis is characterized by involuntary motions, difficulty in control of the voluntary muscles, as well as slurred speech. In Nub's case, he walked on the tips of his toes. He never denied having the handicap, nor did he ever seem wounded by the telling of his stories, and he certainly had no image problem.

So much for my sermon. I hope the story about Nub doesn't offend you. If what I've said so far does bother you, you will be irritated at the account and you might do well by not reading it. My motives are pure in writing it. Nubbin and I were very, very close during my playing days at Ole Miss and pretty close afterwards. I can assure you, I respect no man nor the memory of any man more. (Nubbin passed on in the Mid-Nineteen Nineties. The Ole Miss family grieved.) I want him to be remembered, not only in the hearts and minds of those who played at Ole Miss, as he most assuredly will, but on the printed page as well. He overcame his disability. Only the great do that! If you have a problem with the story, please assign it to me, not to Ole Miss.

Sometimes It's Tough To Order

Playing football games in Memphis in the Fifties meant traveling to the city in two large buses, playing the game, eating the post-game meal at the Peabody Hotel, and then motoring back to Oxford. Sometimes, the coaches would remain in Memphis and eat together in various restaurants.

One night after a game, the coaches and Nub went to Jim's Steak House. The waitress, before taking their dinner orders, asked if they wanted anything from the bar. One by one the coaches ordered drinks until finally it was Nub's turn. Looking up into her eyes he enthusiastically decreed, "I'd tade' ah Schitz," (I'll take a Schlitz,) unable to sound the "l" in Schlitz.

The waitress stiffened, leaned back, slanted her eyes and barked, "What did you say?"

"I'd tade' ah Schitz."

I can't understand you!

"D - -n it, deve' me ah Budwiser!"

A Genius

I guess it's because I had so much trouble with Math that I admired Nub's mathematical mind. Our dressing room contained more than one hundred lockers, all secured by a combination lock, each requiring the memorization of three numbers. It took me a week to trust my memory enough to throw my piece of paper away. Nubbin knew the combination of all the locks. I stand amazed. It would take me the rest of my life to do that, and I still wouldn't throw the paper away.

That's why playing cards and dominos were so difficult for me. I could parse a verb or diagram a sentence, but numbers were anathema.

Not so for Nubbin. He was recognized as the team's best "Hearts" player. No one could beat him including the coaches and Doc Knight. He and Doc would engage in ferocious Hearts battles, but the Equipment Manager almost always won. He could remember every card that hit the table.

As adept at numbers as he was, he was just as energetic about retrieving stolen, ah, that is to say, borrowed property.

Football players are notorious about - ah - borrowing athletic socks, shorts, jocks, t-shirts, jerseys, and even footballs from the Athletic Department. A week into fall practice most players' rooms were, in my years, crammed with UMAA memorabilia. Once a month, Nub, who had a master key, would, while we were on the field practicing, search our rooms and reclaim the items. He never mentioned our thefts and we never mentioned his emancipation of the goods, but we knew he had gotten them.

The next day the "borrowing" would continue. A month later another raid would occur.

Billy (Nub) Sanders is a name which will never disappear from the mental and emotional pages of those who knew him well. The courage which he exhibited in his life may never be bettered, even by those who attack one another on the Ole Miss practice field and in Vaught-Hemingway Stadium. All our lives have been uncommonly garnished by knowing him.

May the Lord rest his precious soul.

CHAPTER VII

RAY, BUSTER, AND WOBBLE MADE ME DO IT!

By the time I reached my early thirties, I found my self fully invested with good, old fashioned self-confidence, a kind which thought it could do anything —- especially anything physical. After all, I had survived my Uncle Ray while growing up. I endured Wobble my freshman year at Ole Miss, and withstood three years under my Uncle Buster on the varsity. Then I weathered playing in the National Football League for Sid Gilman, the coach of the Los Angeles Rams, considered by many of his players to be as tough or tougher than any coach in the history of the league.

By the time I was thirty, I lived in a large, lovely home; owned three supermarkets; was Chairman of the Board of a local newspaper; married to a lovely wife; and the father of two beautiful children. My self-confidence had magnified into pride.

From years of counseling, I recognize two kinds of pride, the good kind and the bad kind.

Our Creator had the good kind, of course. He created the world, stepped back, looked at it and said, "It is good," indicating an inner satisfaction at doing something really well.

The bad kind contains arrogance. It believes it can do anything, whether or not it has ever been done before. Generally speaking, that kind of pride is unteachable.

That was me, unteachable (notice I used past tense) and that characteristic nudged me into some trouble.

I'll explain! But first, please let me clarify why I decided to include this story in a book on Ole Miss athletic humor. It's simple. Had I not been born into the Poole family and played football at Ole Miss, it wouldn't have happened. The seeds planted in me long ago and the genes which carried them to fruition produced in me the perfect soil in which to nourish pride.

The Phone Call

I got the call from Larry in December, a few years after I had retired from pro football. I don't remember the year.

Larry Morris was an All-American linebacker at Georgia Tech in the early Fifties. He was drafted by the Rams and we became very close friends, living in the same apartment complex with our wives and traveling to football practices together each day. After several years with Los Angeles, the Rams traded him to the Chicago Bears, who then released him to Atlanta in an expansion draft.

Larry telephoned me from Atlanta. He and his wife Kay had become avid snow skiers and wanted my wife and me, along with some of their friends from Atlanta, to go on a skiing trip to North Carolina.

I had never been on snow skis, but I had always wanted to learn, and I figured this might be a great opportunity. Skiing shouldn't be very hard for me, after all, I was a pretty good athlete at Ole Miss and with the Rams. In fact, I could probably start watching it on television and essentially master the sport before we got to Atlanta.

At first I wondered why the skiers on television seemed to lean forward, but then I figured that out. Skiing down a mountain produced a strong wind against the bodies. Leaning forward equalized that force.

Then I noticed how they flexed their knees. I reasoned they did that in order to absorb the shock of skiing over bumps, which I later learned are called moguls.

By the time we packed to go to Atlanta, I pretty well knew how to ski.

We rode with Larry and Kay in a ten vehicle convoy to Maggie Valley, North Carolina. The temperature wallowed in the mid-twenties.

No Snow

We had one serious and immediate problem. There was no snow.

Now, I come from the country and I had never skied, and I knew very little about the sport, but I knew in order to ski, you had to have snow.

"Not to worry," Larry promised, "there would be snow in the morning."

I looked at Larry askance. "How in the world do you know that Larry? There isn't a cloud in the sky!"

Larry explained. I thought he was pulling my leg until Kay validated his explanation.

"They are going to make the snow."

"Come on, Larry!" I doubted, "How can they make snow?"

The temperature would be in the mid-teens that night. The resort workers would mix certain chemicals with water and with several large machine-gun looking instruments attached to rubber hoses carrying the chemicals and water, spray the mixture into the frigid air. It would fall back to the slope as snow.

"Wow," in ignorance I remarked. "A technological marvel."

Much to my delight, early the next morning, the slope was covered with snow.

Larry gathered the group together for an early breakfast. That slope was the only one in the state with snowmaking equipment. It would be very crowded.

"Think you'll have much trouble learning to ski?", Larry asked.

His question irritated me. Had he forgotten my athletic ability?

"I don't think so Larry, I've been watching a good bit of it on television. Think I've pretty well got it down."

"I don't think you will either," agreed Larry. "I've always admired your coordination."

On the slope, Larry gathered all of us around him.

"I've made arrangements for those of you who have never skied to get lessons."

Motioning toward a young man who was standing nearby, Larry introduced him to us.

The instructor stood about 5 feet, 6 inches and weighed about 125 pounds. He wore black, shiny, very tight ski pants which revealed more than they should have.

"All off't you who have not skied before, come 'mit me," he commanded in a thick foreign accent.

Ten or twelve new skiers started out toward the kiddy slope with the teacher. I stood my ground.

"Aren't you gonna take a lesson?", Larry asked.

"Please take a lesson," my wife implored.

If they thought I had regressed so much athletically that a small, sissy looking foreigner was going to teach me, they were crazy.

"I don't need a lesson. I'll teach myself."

Then turning toward Larry, I suggested, "Larry, just show me what to do. I catch on quickly."

Leaning over toward me so the others couldn't hear, Larry whispered, "Paige, you don't really need a lesson. You're a natural athlete. I'll show you what to do."

I agreed with him.

"He's going to break his neck," I heard someone remark from the group of students now making their way toward the kiddy slope.

The Slope

The slope was only about four hundred yards long and relatively wide. The first hundred yards were pretty gentle, then it rose up sharply to a flat area on top which was accessed by a rope-pull traveling up the right side of the slope.

Larry helped me put on my boots and skies; handed me my two poles and, showing me how to push myself along, helped me slide over to the rope lift.

"Paige, stand with the rope touching your right leg like this. Make sure your skies are parallel and pointing up the slope. Put your hand through the leather loops of your ski poles. Then, with both hands gradually tighten your grip on the rope - don't grab it suddenly, it will jerk you down."

Larry and I let the rope pull us up to where the slope angled sharply upward.

"Turn loose here," he barked over his shoulder.

Together, we skied back down the hundred yards to where the snow ended, to the line of skiers which was rapidly forming to catch the lift.

It was as natural as breathing. Of course, the slope was gentle where I skied but I could tell I was created for the sport. Having learned how to catch the lift, I skied down the gentle incline four or five times. Larry had skied down from the top several times.

The line of skiers waiting to catch the lift stretched all the way across the slope, three or four people deep. It took fifteen minutes to move from the back of the line to the rope. The slope was crowded.

I was about half way up the line when I felt an arm slip around my shoulder. Turning my head, I looked directly into Larry's eyes.

"I have never seen anything like it."

I knew what he was talking about —. He had been watching me ski.

He repeated, "I have never seen anything like it."

"What's that Larry?," trying to conceal my pleasure.

"You!"

"Me?," I asked acting completely surprised.

"You!" he echoed. "Paige, I've been skiing for five years and I have never seen anyone catch on as quickly as you."

"Oh, come on, Larry," I replied, secretly agreeing with him.

"No, it's true, Paige. You haven't fallen a single time have you?"

"Well, no," I answered shuffling my skis, trying to appear humble.

"Paige, you're already skiing as well as I am, which is really discouraging to me. It's taken me five years to learn to ski as well as you, your first time."

"Well, I did put a lot of thought into it before I came over here," I confidently laughed.

"You're ready for the top," my friend asserted.

For a few minutes I hesitated. Larry was looking at me as we neared the rope, waiting for a response, an answer. I carefully considered my reply, not wanting to openly flaunt my massive amount of self-confidence, but I knew I was ready for the top.

"I don't know, Larry."

"You're ready," he repeated. "You're wasting your time down here on the beginner part of the slope. Besides, it takes too long to catch the lift to go up only a hundred yards.

"I don't know."

"Come on," he insisted. "We'll go up together."

From the top of the slope, I got my first view down. Our small cabins, in which we were all staying at the base of the slope, looked much smaller. The skiers, stretching out across the snow lining up to catch the lift, looked like a multi-colored worm.

The confident smile quickly abandoned my face, my miniscule common sense challenging my corpulent pride.

"I don't know about this, Larry," I blurted out, finally facing the truth.

It was too late! Larry saw me weakening. He intensified his argument.

"Now wait a minute, Paige, listen to me - just listen to me! The reason it looks a lot steeper from up here, is that from this spot, you can see the entire gist of the slope at once."

I had no idea what he was talking about, but I figured it made sense to him. Not wanting to admit ignorance, and with a non-analytical brain void of all mathematical erudition, I agreed with Larry.

"That makes sense. Here I go."

And I went —fast, with skis parallel. I don't know how fast a five-foot, ten inch, 210 pound man can go down a mountain on a pair of skis, but whatever it is, that's how fast I went- I think it would be about the same speed as falling out of an airplane without a parachute.

Two miracles occurred on the trip down, one I can explain, one I can't.

I didn't fall. I don't know how I kept from it, but leaning into the wind, with knees bent like I'd seen on television, I made it all the way to the bottom.

I didn't hit anyone. I can explain that, I think. The news about the run away skier seemed to precede me. The other skiers separated, leaving me a clear trail to the bottom. People up the slope yelled and people farther down got out of the way.

"Snowplow!", about half the way down the slope a man yelled as I went by.

"Snowplow! Did he say snowplow? Where?"

I knew he was kidding. I had seen snowplows in Philadelphia when I played with the Eagles. There was no snowplow out there - kind of like yelling "bicycle" to an infielder catching a pop fly.

The line of waiting skiers at the lift kept getting closer and closer. People everywhere were yelling, "Snowplow."

I began to wonder if that word might have a different meaning. I didn't have much time to think about it.

About seventy-five yards from the line of skiers stretched all the way across the snow, I decided it was time to slow down.

I wanted to slow down - I tried to slow down - but I didn't slow down. In fact, my speed didn't change. I started getting worried.

All eyes were riveted on me.

"How DO I stop?" I wondered. The awful truth shattered my complacency, not to mention my self-confidence. I didn't KNOW how to stop.

"I can't stop!," out of desperation I yelled to the line of skiers, which by now was almost upon me.

I hollered too late. Nothing else was left to do but hit the "dirt." On my back, skis and ski poles in the air, I granulated the line of skiers. Some were lying on the snow, some off the snow on the muddy ground. Skis, poles, legs and arms of about ten people were intertwined. I lay on the bottom of the pile. Trickles of blood eased out of some of the victims, moans exuded from all of us. I was struggling to get up and help others up, my mother having taught me well. She said, "If you ever knock down a lady, apologize and help her up."

I had ladies down every where, and men too.

Suddenly, I felt a tremendous tug on both my arms. I looked up through the bodies into the face of the little Austrian ski instructor, who had grabbed the bottom end of my ski poles. He was furious.

"You kan't haff these enny mor' - you kil' someone vid' theem", he screamed as he yanked my poles from my hands. Apparently I had crashed into the skiers with my arms over my face and the sharp ends of the poles pointing at the sufferers.

No more than thirty seconds after the little Austrian relieved me of my ski poles, we heard a loud, frantic "Ho, Ho, Ho!"

I turned my head just in time to see a large Atlanta Falcon rookie football player from our group slam into the line of skiers, about ten yards to my left. The Austrian ski instructor bounded over strewn bodies to where the big football player lay, ripped his ski poles off his hands, bent over, looked down into his face, and fervently declared, "Ho, Ho, Ho, iss verdy insufficient!"

Unbeknown to me, Larry had convinced his teammate to go to the top a few minutes before he talked me into it. But the big rookie balked. Thinking they were skiing down together, Larry started down the slope, looked back, saw his friend had remained at the top, came straight to me and took me up. After he launched me, he turned to his catatonic companion and said, "Look there - Paige is ten years older than you and already retired and he's going down. You're young and in great shape. You're afraid?"

Larry shamed him into following me.

I was still trying to help my victims get up and get their skis back on when I heard it: deep laughter, so deep that the person laughing was gasping for breath. It was coming from about halfway up the slope. I searched a moment before I spotted him. He was lying on his back, slowly sliding down the mountain, his mirth preceding him. It was Larry.

Then I understood. From the first phone call inviting me to come, he had set me up, and not only me, but several others.

It's reasonable to assume, isn't it, that all my athletic accomplishments ought to qualify me to ski without taking lessons? After all, I survived Ray, Wobble, and Buster. That ought to count for something.

CHAPTER VIII

GAME-DAY AT OLE MISS

At this writing, I am 62 years old. Maybe it was my age, or maybe it was the era in which I played football at Ole Miss; maybe my love for the Rebels caused it; perhaps my fear of the coaches; but game day at Ole Miss is still unlike any other day of my life. Back then, the organized player walk through the Grove was still in the future, thus unavailable to season our emotions.

We walked from Garland Dorm to the field house and stadium but we avoided the Grove. The Grove consisted of parties, food, drink, laughter, and enthusiastic conversation about everything, not just the football game. By canonical decree, football players on game day must brandish a game face. Walking through the Grove might alter it.

I was never really certain what my game face was supposed to look like. I thought about standing in front of the little mirror fastened above my lavatory and experimenting with different facial expressions, but I was afraid my roommate would catch me, or worse, Wobble. I studied all the other players. Maybe I could get an understanding of what a game-face was supposed to look like from them, but they seemed to be searching my face for it. After all I was Buster Poole's nephew. That should have given me some idea, but it didn't.

Finally from trial and error, from looking at older players, and from coach's veiled comments, I decided that game faces ought to appear more serious than other faces on other days. From that, I reasoned that I manifested a pretty good game-face. I was certainly serious about getting hit, except my eyes seemed to glaze over when I thought about it. Someone told me fear caused that. I knew I had some fear on game day but I never knew whether it came from the prospect of getting hit or from the fear of Buster if I didn't hit the fellow on the other team hard enough. I knew I had some fear though because on game-day girls looked no better than boys to me. On the way to the football field one Saturday morning, I met an Ole Miss Beauty on the sidewalk. I called her "Sir." Fear had the same effect on me as the five-hundred dollar vaccination I took years later in preparation for prostate surgery. The shot was supposed to eliminate certain desires. It did! I called an attractive blond "Sir" the day after that shot, too.

At any rate, walking through the Grove unsupervised might destroy our game faces. That's why we avoided it.

Game days also made me sweat, even before warm-ups. I think standing in front of a firing squad does the same thing to you. Playing in college football games made me hot. Thinking about playing in college football games also made me hot. I guess it was nervousness.

Nervousness in some people causes them to laugh - at everything. Those players had it tougher than I did. They had to preserve their game-faces while they were nervously laughing. I just sweat. Maintaining a game face while sweating was easier!

Some of my teammates would arrive at the field house three hours before the game started, slip into their pad-less uniforms, find a place to lie down, and go to sleep. I always admired that, probably because I couldn't do it. I couldn't sleep much the night before the game either. I couldn't even sleep the night after the game. Starting at the end of practice on Friday my eyes started widening. Then on Saturday morning, they glazed over. They stayed wide until the enemy left town. The first time I got hit the glaze left my eyes and I always got hit on the kickoff, especially if Ole Miss kicked to start the game.

I kicked off for Ole Miss and I kicked off a lot because Coach Vaught loved to kick off. Sometimes I think he would have kicked off after the other team had scored if the referee had let him.

We also kicked off a lot because we scored a lot!

Opposing teams like to hit kick-off kickers. They can't hit punters; they can't hit extra point kickers; they can't hit field goal kickers. But they can sure hit kick-off kickers.

I always knew who was supposed to hit me after I kicked off. It was the man who lined up right in front of me fifteen yards away. While I was placing the ball on the tee, he would be staring at me. I knew what he was thinking, - "Kill, Kill, Kill." While I was running toward the football he would be running toward me.

Sometimes I would try to stare him down, but I was never very good at staring at someone who was staring at me. I always envied boxers who could stare right into each other's eyes from a few inches away just before the bout begins. When I tried staring at the fellow who wanted to kill me, I started smiling real big. That wasn't good. My smile usually intensified his scowl which made me self-conscious and caused me to lose some concentration. That made me kick badly.

Besides, when I smiled, I lost my game-face.

HOW ARE THE FANS TAKING IT, COACH?

Not every funny story that involved Wobble, evolved from Wobble. Such was the story of freshman Jake, an Ole Miss defensive back.

The Ole Miss freshman team, coached by, of course, Wobble, traveled to Baton Rouge in the early Sixties to play the LSU Frosh. The tiger's offense revolved around a big fast running back. Toward the end of the game the big LSU back broke loose and churned toward the Ole Miss goal line. Only Jake stood between him and an LSU touchdown. The two collided on the five yard line. The tiger back blasted over Jake into the end zone, leaving him prostrate upon the ground. He moved "nary a muscle," and appeared to be hurt very badly. The players thought he was dead.

In those days, coaches seldom ventured onto a football field to check on a hurt player. If anyone went, it was usually the trainer. But Jake seemed to be hurt very badly. He appeared comatose, so the trainer and Wobble hurried out onto the field to the fallen warrior. Leaning down over him, the coach, attempting to force the sound of his voice into what appeared to be a lifeless brain, yelled, "Jake—Jake, are you alright? Can you hear me, Jake?"

Opening one eye, and looking up at Wobble, the corpse responded, "I'm alright, Coach, but how are my fans taking it?"

Needless to say, Jake's career suddenly ended at Ole Miss. I wonder if Wobble ever visited a hurt player on the field again.

BUSTER, BARNEY AND A MOUTH FULL OF TEETH

James E. (Buster) Poole was one of the greatest ends ever to wear the Red and Blue of Ole Miss, and without a doubt one of the greatest ever to play for money. He was a New York Giant from Nineteen Thirty-Seven until Nineteen Forty-Two. After serving in the Navy during the war years, he ended his career with the Giants in Nineteen Forty-Six. The following year new Ole Miss head coach John Vaught hired him as his first assistant coach.

Buster blazed the trail for the rest of the Poole family (there were fourteen of us) to come to Ole Miss. It wasn't easy for him. Growing up on a farm in the middle of the Homochitto National Forest in Southwest Mississippi, his rural high school offered only three grades. To graduate from high school, he would be forced to leave home, which he did. The football coach at Natchez High School and a few interested Natchez businessmen recruited him. Natchez was fifty difficult, graveled miles from Homochitto. The coach found him a plush home, a room in D'Evereux, a large antebellum home in Natchez. After living a couple of weeks in total luxury, Buster went home. When the Natchez coach went to the Poole farm to retrieve him, the big country boy explained why he left.

"It was too rich for my blood Coach. Besides, I can't live next door to such a pretty girl." The owner of D'Evereux's beautiful daughter apparently presented too much of a temptation to the big, innocent farm boy.

When the coach promised to find him another room, Buster reluctantly went back to Natchez with him. His next home was the county jail, where he lived in his own private cell. Everything was fine at the jail until a year's end audit revealed an inflated food bill. Scratch one county jail resident.

After being thrown out of the Adams County jail, the coach housed Bus in a large attic over a hardware store on Main Street, where he lived alone the rest of the school year. He graduated from Natchez High School with honors. In describing his attic residence, Bus said, "I had a bed, a small table, a light bulb hanging from the ceiling, and two meals a day. I thought I had life made."

As a result of Buster's athletic exploits at Natchez, Tad Smith, Ole Miss's Athletic Director made a summer trip to Mama Poole's home and recruited Buster back to Oxford. Thus began the Poole odyssey at Ole Miss, where as I mentioned, fourteen young men from the Poole family played football. Poole Drive on the campus honors the family.

Barney, Buster's younger brother, played eight years of college football. He played at Ole Miss in Nineteen Forty-One and Nineteen Forty-Two. When World War II erupted, he transferred to the University of North Carolina, which had been converted into a Marine pre-flight school. Playing with the Tarheels was considered military football and didn't debit Barney's college eligibility. After one year at North Carolina, Barney transferred to West Point where he played in Nineteen Forty-Four, Forty-Five, and Forty-Six. Since playing at North Carolina and West Point was considered military and not collegiate football, Barney still had two years of college eligibility left. Buster wanted Barney to play those two years at Ole Miss.

To do that however, Barney had to flunk out of West Point, which he didn't want to do, though NOT because he didn't want to return to Ole Miss. He was a good student. He just simply didn't want to fail a course. If he elected not to flunk, he would have graduated and spent the ensuing five years on active duty. Buster and his other younger brother Ray had both served in the South Pacific and he, Buster, argued, "Since the war is over, Barney, it would be foolish for you to waste five years in the army. You'll be too old to play pro ball by the time you get out."

Finally Barney relented to the wishes of his older brother, who would now become his coach at Ole Miss.

Buster became as tough a coach as he had been a player, and he had been a zealous player, regarded as one of the most aggressive ends ever to play pro ball. Sammy Baugh, the perennial All-Pro Quarterback for the Washington Redskins has been credited with saying, "When we play the New York Giants and Buster Poole, I have two thoughts in my mind. Throw the ball quickly and run like h—l." In those days quarterbacks could be legally roughed, as long as they were standing.

By the time Barney labored through eight years of college football, he had made first team All-American four years and second team All-American one year. That's still a national record and not likely to be broken. For all of that, Barney is a member of the National College Football Hall of Fame.

Brother Buster, however, was less impressed with Barney and the rest of the Poole family as the fans and the press. He demanded a maximum athletic effort from us and he showed us no favor. He expected us to be as tough as was he when he played.

In Nineteen Forty-Eight, Barney's last year, Ole Miss played Tulane in New Orleans. In the midst of the game from his left end position, Barney caught a short pass over the middle and was tackled from behind. As he was falling, the opposite side linebacker placed an elbow across Barney's mouth, which of course was unprotected by a "yet-to-be-invented" face mask. Barney lost eight teeth, four knocked completely out and four broken off even with the gums. The blow rendered Barney semi-conscious and true to his tested character, he struggled to get onto his feet.

Buster, watching his younger brother squirming on the ground, yelled from the Ole Miss sideline, "Barney get up - - doesn't look good wallowing around on the field. Get up!"

Barney couldn't get up, at least not quickly. Finally with the aid of the Tulane trainer, he stumbled off the field on the Tulane side of the stadium. Slowly he made his way around the end of the field alternatingly falling to one knee, then the other, struggling to his feet, and staggering a few more yards until he faced his brother at the Ole Miss bench. Blood and bits of enamel ran down his chin and soaked his jersey fading his number 89 under a mushy crust of red. Then Barney opened his mouth and revealed the ghastly vacuum where once eight teeth had lodged.

Buster recoiled momentarily and softened slightly, as evidenced by his reflection.

"Well, Barney, it does look kinda' bad but then you don't need teeth to play football."

After the smelling salts had revived him, Barney played the rest of the game.

Years later when I had two teeth broken off against Kentucky, I opted to stay in the game. I knew Bus would demand to know why I had come off the field and I also knew why he would send me right back on - - - a football player doesn't need teeth to play football!

I TRIED TO COACH

Ole Miss was playing Kentucky. It was Nineteen Fifty-Eight and Ole Miss had a great guard playing for them, Richard (Possum) Price. Possum had been at Ole Miss long enough to develop both fear and respect for the coaching staff, especially Wobble Davidson and Head Coach, Johnny Vaught. Like the rest of us, he learned early the expediency of obedience.

"To obey is better than sacrifice," the Bible teaches but Richard had learned, at Ole Miss, obedience might include sacrifice.

Early in the Kentucky game, Possum squirmed out from under a pile of players with a terrible pain in his foot. Certain it was broken, yet with great reservation, he hobbled toward the Ole Miss bench. Coach Vaught met him about ten yards out on the field.

"Get your a-s back in there, Price," Coach barked.

Without hesitation, Possum turned around and hobbled back onto the field. He played the rest of the game.

By the following Monday, Possum's foot had officially been diagnosed as broken. He was leaning on his crutch at Monday's practice when Coach Vaught walked over to him.

"When did you break your foot, Possum?"

"I think it was in the second quarter, Coach."

"Why in h−1 didn't you come out of the game?," Coach asked.

"I tried to Coach, but you sent me back in−!"

"What the h−1?", Coach Vaught surmised. "You still had one good leg. Besides you probably played better on one than anyone else I could have sent in there on two!"

GET ALL OF IT!

Mentioned in another story, Ole Miss, in Nineteen Fifty-Six, had won fourteen straight games when we traveled by train to play Tulane in Jackson. Ole Miss was expected to win by three or four touchdowns, but everything was against us that night including ourselves and the heavens. At almost the precise moment my toe struck the football to initiate the game, the sky opened and one of the hardest rains I have ever seen fell, and fell, and then fell some more. If the Lord hadn't promised not to do it again, we would have searched for an ark.

The rain fell not only upon the players, but also upon a field pulverized by an afternoon game between Mississippi State and Auburn, melting the loose turf into six inches of mud.

Tulane was no more cooperative than the weather and the mud. The only thing on the field which could float was the Tulane quarterback, Phil (Fig) Newton and he pontooned about forty yards in the fourth quarter to put the Greenies ahead, 10 to 3.

Everyone was frustrated, especially my uncle Buster Poole. Buster was probably the most, ah, ah, competitive, that's it, competitive coach I've ever known. And he wore a small green hat on game days, whether for luck or not I do not know. His competitive nature and tendency toward frustration generated within him the proclivity to kick and stomp his hat.

Someone once decreed to count the times he stomped his hat in one season, but the pollster lost count in the sixth game, stating that the number, even by that time had reached well into double figures.

Buster could kick a chair farther than anyone I have ever seen, too. He coached the defense so when the offense took the field, he usually sat in a metal folding chair. Once, in Hemingway Stadium, about thirty thousand fans saw him kick his chair fifteen yards onto the playing field. From that one act of antagonism emanated a year of reprimand by the Southeastern Conference, which commanded him to sit in the chair during play for the remainder of the season. A violation of that mandate would have resulted in a ban from the sidelines. Miracle of all miracles, he made it.

Those of us who played at Ole Miss under Uncle Bus, knew we had not erred when he said nothing. When we blundered, we knew it. Correction came powerfully and swiftly. The absence of chastisement, not his compliments, meant he was pleased. In four years of playing defense under him, he never paid me a verbal compliment for any act on the football field, but I knew when he was pleased by his silence.

I knew Buster perhaps better than other players. I should have. He was my Uncle and we grew up in the same house, he a few years before me, of course. But we all wanted to please him and we kidded each other about desiring his approval.

"Did Coach Buster brag on you today?", one player would ask another, jokingly.

"No! Maybe tomorrow!"

Against that background, we played Tulane. Even after Fig Newton floated Tulane into the lead, we still had a chance to win the game. Tulane was punting on fourth down from around their own forty yard line.

Buddy Harbin, our starting left end remembers, "I was just as frustrated as everyone else. We should have been winning big - - we were behind. Everything seemed to go against us. I looked over at our bench and Coach Buster had thrown his hat down and stomped it in the mud again, and was yelling, 'Get that ball, get that ball,' meaning block the punt."

Buddy thought, "Alright Coach Bus, I'm going after that ball! I'm gonna' to get it one way or another - - I'm going after that sucker."

At the snap of the ball, Buddy tore into the Tulane backfield untouched on the line of scrimmage. But when a left defensive end finds himself untouched on the line of scrimmage, he knows the fullback, positioned seven yards in front of the punter will probably block him."

"To block a punt," Buddy recalls, "when the fullback was blocking on me, I had to get up high in the air. That rendered me vulnerable to the block of the fullback. All he had to do was hit me about the knees and that would flip me."

(Buddy remembers well. As a blocking fullback, I loved for defensive ends to jump. Usually their feet went straight up and they landed on top of their heads.)

"And when I flip, I know I'm going to hit the ground and hit it hard," Buddy continued. "But jumping gives me a chance to block the punt."

Buddy could still hear Bus yelling, "Get that ball, get that ball," when he left the ground.

"I don't know whether the punter jostled the ball or what happened but I got a hand on it. I got that ball."

Buddy flipped, and he crashed into the muddy ground. Mud covered his head, coated his face, and caked his eyes. Lying on the ground, he was aware however, that he had not fully blocked the punt. Rather than careening back over the punter's head toward our goal-line, the ball had in fact, deflected off Buddy's hand high into the air and fell eight yards downfield, where we recovered it. Because of Buddy's effort, the football had traveled only eight yards.

"I did it - - I did it," Harbin was telling himself as he pushed his dazed and muddy body off the ground. He was trying to dig the mud from his eyes when his substitute, Billy Pruett ran onto the field.

"Buddy, Buddy," Pruett yelled. Coach Poole wants to talk to you."

"He's got to be pleased with that," Harbin thought, as he jogged toward the Ole Miss bench. "I'll get that compliment now. He's gonna finally brag on me!"

Buster met Buddy a few yards out on the field. Grabbing Harbin by the jersey and looking straight into his muddy eyes, Bus yelled, - - "Harbin if you're gonna block the d - -n ball GET ALL OF IT!"

Oh well, so much for commendations! Knowing Uncle Bus as I do, however, I believe Buddy received a semi-compliment. Bus did acknowledge the fact that Buddy had gotten PART OF IT!

LET'S MAKE A DEAL

Louie Brown is a distant cousin and one of my very best friends. We played all three sports together at Natchez High School. He was six feet, two inches tall, one hundred ninety pounds, all muscle, and he played end on the football team. He could run like a deer and catch a football with either hand. He was a grade behind me, so I was a freshman at Ole Miss when the football signing date rolled around Louie's senior year. I went to see him. I wanted him to come to Ole Miss and so did the Ole Miss coaches especially Buster, also a relative.

"Louie," I begged, "sign with us man. I'm selfish, I want you at Ole Miss. We'll have a great time."

"Ole Miss is a country club, Paige. I can't go there!"

I grew up in the country but Louie grew up deeper in the woods than I did.

"Ole Miss isn't a country club, Louie," I retorted. "There isn't but one golf course in Oxford and it's a nine-holer on the campus; doesn't even have a club house! Besides you like to play golf — what's the problem with that?"

"You know what I mean," Louie argued.

"No, I don't."

"Only rich kids go to Ole Miss.", he retorted.

"Rich kids? Am I rich? How can you say that Louie?"

"I got two pair o'blue jeans and four t-shirts," he emphatically declared. "I can't go to Ole Miss with two pair o'blue jeans and four t-shirts."

"Louie," I argued futilely. "You're lying like a dog. I've double dated with you - you forgot about that. I've seen you in dress pants and sports shirts. Besides I went to Ole Miss with only two pairs of blue jeans and one pair of dress pants. The dress pants were Ray's (speaking of my Uncle Ray Poole) hand me downs. Mother shortened the legs, 'course the crotch hung down to my knees. I wasn't all THAT dressed up when I went to Ole Miss."

"Naw", he countered, "I'm goin' to State. I fit in better at State."

"You're gonna be sorry you did that, Louie," I warned.

I really wanted Louie to come to Ole Miss, my best friend, but as bad as losing him to State was, telling Buster was worse.

By the date of the Ole Miss game Louie's sophomore year, he was the Bulldog's starting left end. From my fullback position, he was one of my primary targets. The entire Ole Miss roll-out offensive system depended upon the fullback knocking the end down so our quarterback could get outside. Once outside, he either passed or ran depending upon the actions of the corner back.

The first time we had the ball, Eagle Day our quarterback, who knew how close Louie and I were, looked me squarely in the eye as if to say, "Paige I'm not really sure I can trust you to block him, but we might as well find out early."

"Roll out right!"

I really didn't want to hit Louie but I sure didn't want to face Buster if I didn't.

"Well, Louie, dad-gummit," I thought. "I told you not to go to State."

I was going full speed when I threw that 'ol side body block into Louie. I could tell he didn't believe I'd hit him that hard. He jerked his cleats out of the ground just about the time my body slammed into his knees. His feet flew over his head and his entire lanky body crumpled on top of me.

"D—n, Paige, why'd you do that?"

"Two reasons," I grunted. "I told you not to go to State and I'm afraid of Buster."

We started untangling from each other.

"We gotta work out somethin'," Louie proposed. "It's gonna be a long day."

"What 'cha got in mind, Louie?"

"I'll let you block me one time," he offered, "and then you miss me one time. One and one - that's fair!"

"No way, Louie. I'm so much better than you, I can block you every time if I want to," I bluffed.

By then each of us had extricated himself from the ground and one another, and were walking back to our respective huddles.

"Tell you what I'll do, Louie. I'll go two for one. I'll block you twice and I'll miss you once! That's the best I can do."

"Deal," Louie quickly agreed.

I was surprised he didn't stick out his hand to shake on it. Buster would have seen that for sure.

Oh, for the good 'ol days of college football!

By the way, we beat State twenty-six to nothing, won the SEC, and accepted a Cotton Bowl invitation that day.

We might have beaten 'em even worse if I had offered three to one.

DID YOU KNOW?

The 1910 Ole Miss football team blanked seven of its eight foes in posting a 7-1 record. Vandy won 9-2. Point totals for the year were 144 - 9.

A TEAR-AWAY JERSEY

I have absolutely no idea who did it, but in Nineteen Fifty-Four, someone somewhere invented tear-away football jerseys. They were the rage of college football that year, the new product which would allow running backs to run for much more yardage as they ripped themselves right out of the large, meaty hands of hostile linemen. So the old jerseys were moth-balled, the red ones, the blue ones, the white ones, with their beautiful traditional numbers and three stripes around each sleeve. With much fanfare on the part of the media and our coaches, we assumed our tear-aways, items which would revolutionize college football and make thousand yard rushes of our running backs.

One of our best running backs was Allan (Red) Muirhead from Canton. Along with Lea Pasley, he returned kickoffs and punts, as freshmen, in Nineteen Fifty-Two. They led the nation in punt returns that year.

Red, while he was one of the Rebel's best running backs was certainly not one of the best at abiding by training rules. He loved to party and he had devised and mastered an evacuation plan from Garland Dorm after bed check, which he occasionally implemented even nights before ball games. When explaining his rationale for so doing he once told us, "Man we don't play until one-thirty. I can come in before daylight and still get six hours sleep, and that's all I need!"

All the other players knew about Red's theory and lifestyle, but the "honor among thieves" code prevailed among college football players, so of course no one betrayed him.

Ole Miss was playing North Texas State on Saturday in Oxford; they were not a perennial national powerhouse. The players knew that the second and third teams would probably play most of the game. Red figured he would play very little, being a starter, so on Friday night, he partied. But that Friday night he partied too much.

"I kinda had to pour him into the bed when he came in", his room-mate declared to us that morning.

It was hot that day, in the low nineties, and very humid. The thin, perforated tear-always made the heat a little more bearable—for most of us — not for Red. Nothing could make the heat more bearable for him. He was "sick."

In the early stage of the game, Houston Patton, Ole Miss' quarterback called Red's play, a sweep around left end. Muirhead, the right halfback took the ball and set-sail. He turned the corner okay, but about ten yards down field, his sickness surfaced and he slowed down, which allowed a small North Texas State defensive back to catch him. The defensive back grabbed a handful of tear-away jersey and hurled the afflicted runner to the ground.

On Sunday afternoons, following Saturday games, the football team and coaches assembled for three infernal hours of authoritative evaluation, condemnation, and correction. Coach Buster Poole operated the film projector, probably because he was the more serious coach, and his was the task of identifying error, which he did flawlessly. His eyes were keen, his tongue sharp, and his comments caustic.

Red's "fall from grace" appeared more vivid on the screen than it had on the field. Buster ran the play, and then he ran the film backward. He ran it again and he backed it up again at least ten times. Apprehension increased in the players, Red slouched lower in his chair.

The inevitable utterance finally came!

"D — n a running back who can't tear away from a tear-away jersey."

The laughter which erupted included almost everyone in the room. Neither Red nor Bus thought it was funny.

WHUT DEFENSE YA'LL IN?

Sometimes football players, when placed under a little pressure find themselves in a situation where they need help, no matter from whence it comes.

When Billy Brewer, the former Ole Miss Head Coach was a junior at Ole Miss, he found himself in just such a predicament. Ole Miss was playing Tulane in New Orleans.

"Billy had been playing a good bit on defense," one of his teammates explained, "but we were beating Tulane real good—had 'em by thirty-five or forty points in the last quarter. Coach Vaught decided he'd give 'ol Billy a little experience at quarterback."

Before receiving a snap from center, the quarterback, of course, called out the signals at the line of scrimmage and the ball would be snapped on a pre-arranged count. The entire quarterback cadence consisted of a series of numbers and one color followed by the actual snap count. The first series of numbers denoted the defensive alignment; a "color" either "live" or "dead" followed that; the third part of the cadence announced the play to be run; then the actual snap number was called. For example; the quarterback, before placing his hands under the center would yell:

"*Sixty-two*" - that meant the defense had employed a six man line with two linebackers. If the defense lined up in a five man front with three linebackers, the quarterback would shout "fifty-three."

"*Red*" - A color was employed in order to audibalize or change a play at the line of scrimmage. If Red was the "live" color then the next series of numbers would indicate the new play to be run. If however, "Blue" was the live color and the quarterback yelled "Red," the next series had no importance; they too would be "dead."

"*Thirty-Five Slant*" - This series of numbers indicated an actual play to be run IF the live color had been declared but to be ignored if the dead color had—! In the event a dead color was announced, the original play which had been called in the huddle would be run.

"*Hut one-Hut two*",etc. - The actual snap count which had been designated in the huddle, indicating when the center would snap the football to the quarterback.

The critical part of the information was the first part. The quarterback must identify for his teammates, none of whom could see all the opposing players, the defensive alignment before the play could be run.

When Billy got to the line of scrimmage for his first play, however, he couldn't determine the defense. But that little inconvenience failed to hinder Ole Miss' future Head Coach for long.

"Hey, Podner," Brewer called out to one of the opposing linebackers, "what defense y'all in?"

"Six-two," came back the obliging reply.

"Thanks! - Sixty-Two - Red - Thirty-Five Slant - hut one - hut two—!," barked the Ole Miss quarterback, his dilemma quickly and unusually resolved.

DID YOU KNOW?

Ole Miss has had 36 first team All-Americans; 90 first-team all SEC; and more than 150 pro-football players.

GET UP, BARNEY

Before my uncle Buster Poole, for years the defensive line coach at Ole Miss, passed away we became very close again. I moved to Oxford and Buster, his once great, strong body now riddled with cancer, would hobble with his walking cane into my office and ease himself into a chair. I always tried to lure him into reminiscing about growing up in Homochitto or athletics, primarily football. Invariably when Ray or Barney's athletic prowess was mentioned, Buster would develop a slight smile on his face and declare, "Wa'l, ah, ah, both those boys were great football players but I believe I was just a little bit better."

I never saw my elder uncle play so I can't say if he was better. I only got to see Ray play one game in Nineteen Forty-Six. But I saw Barney play four games in Forty-Seven and Forty-Eight. By Forty-Seven, he had already played six years of college ball; two at Ole Miss, one at North Carolina, and three at West Point. I believe he was one of the best all around ends ever to play the game. Others agree because he was elected to the National College Football Hall of Fame.

On a cool, crisp November afternoon in Nineteen Forty-Seven, Ole Miss played Chattanooga in Oxford. By halftime the Rebels were leading the Moccasins by more than thirty points. Coach Vaught told the starters to undress at the half. They would not play the last two quarters.

"We played State the following week. Coach Vaught wanted to make certain all of our starters were healthy plus he wanted to give the second and third team fellows a chance to play," Barney explained.

Just before the teams left the dressing room for the second half, however, word came down from the pressbox that Charlie Conerly had just broken almost all of the collegiate passing records and that Barney was in striking distance of breaking the record for the most passes caught in one year.

"You both will play the second half," Vaught informed the two, wanting Barney to break the record.

With just a couple of minutes left in the game, Barney had caught eight more passes which infuriated the Chattanooga coaches and players. To them it appeared that Ole Miss was trying to run up the score, a no-no in those days.

"About the last play of the game," Barney remembered, "I caught a short pass near the Ole Miss bench, and the provoked defensive halfback on that side, at the end of a fifteen yard sprint to tackle me, slammed his helmet into my rib-cage. All the oxygen left Hemingway Stadium."

Barney was lying out of bounds in front of the Ole Miss bench and at the feet of his elder brother, gasping for breath. The game had ended, people were leaving the stadium, and Barney couldn't get up, less than a perfect setting for Buster to exhibit brotherly love.

"Get up, Barney," Buster exhorted, looking down into his brother's face with some displeasure.

Barney couldn't breathe, much less get up.

"I could hear him tell me to get up but I couldn't get my breath - - I couldn't get up."

Again, with a little more indignation, Buster repeated his command, "Get up, Barney."

But Barney couldn't get up, he tried again but he couldn't move.

Finally with full exasperation, the elder brother "nudged" Barney in the side with his foot (Nudge is Barney's word. I would have used a stronger one.), and shouted emphatically - - "Barney, get up! It doesn't look good - - and besides, MAMA IS IN THE STANDS."

THAT ISN'T A RIB PAD

On September 17, 1955, Ole Miss played Georgia in Atlanta. We played the night game of a double-header. Georgia Tech had played Miami that afternoon. Ole Miss' offensive success, that year and other years, depended upon the quarterback roll-out play. The quarterback who was Eagle Day in Nineteen Fifty-Five, would receive the ball from center, reverse out, (if roll-out right had been called, he would come out from under center as though he were going left but immediately turn and sprint to our right,) and try to get outside the defensive end, whose responsibility usually included "containing." For the play to succeed, the fullback had to block the end in, a formidable task due to the angle of attack.

Roy Wilkins, later to become my teammate with the L.A. Rams, played left end for Georgia. Roy was a big rugged end who knew how to handle blocking fullbacks. In the middle of the second quarter he pumped his right knee into my left side right in the middle of my cross-body block, a block which is now illegal. I felt like I had been shot in the left side with buck shot. The air left my lungs, and the pain was vicious. I staggered toward the Ole Miss bench. As I neared the Rebel sideline I became vividly aware that every eye was fixed on me. I knew what the coaches were thinking.

"He had better be hurt!"

I knew what the other players were thinking because they knew what the coaches were thinking.

"He had better be hurt."

I was encouraged to see Jerry Baker, the other fullback, running by me onto the field. I knew I had succeeded in missing one play, at least.

My eyes were still on the ground as I passed the coaches. Eye contact might encourage their comments or questions. I just wanted to get to the bench where I knew Doc Knight would be waiting. Sweat rolled down my face as I plopped down. Doc Knight pulled up my jersey. Then he summoned Doctor Varner. That told me I was officially hurt. "At least now, I have evaded the wrath of the coaches," I thought.

Like most players, I had rather be legitimately hurt physically than to suffer the ire of the coaches. Besides, in one platoon football, a restful visit to the bench was always welcome even if the temporary sojourn involved a little physical pain.

"Ah, yes," Doctor Varner exclaimed. "You have a couple of floating ribs."

A "floating" rib has been torn loose from the sternum. I was the proud owner of two of them. Doc Varner stuck his forefinger in between the ribs, separated them, and moved them back into place.

"How long will it be before he can go back in, Doc?", I heard a coach ask.

"Not long," came the medical reply.

Doc Varner placed a piece of hard rubber over the point of separation and Doc Knight bound tape around my upper body to hold it in place.

"How does that feel?," one of them asked.

"Not very good. I can't breathe."

"I can't loosen it!"

"Can you re-tape it?," I countered, biding for more time.

"Get back in there, Cothren," I heard Coach Vaught yell.

Baker didn't look nearly as good running off the field as he had jogging onto it a few plays earlier.

The pain was excruciating and I could barely breathe, but I played the rest of the game, continuing to launch my floating ribs into opposing knees with considerable anticipation.

Oh, how I dreaded practice the following Monday! "Surely, surely my floating ribs would exempt me from practice," I hoped.

I reported to the Coach whom I thought might afford me the greatest possibility of compassion, the brother of my mother, Uncle Bus. I was wrong!

"Uncle Bus," I pleaded, "if I could just wear rib pads, I might be able to practice. I know I could block the ends next Saturday."

"Boy, you're gonna practice this week and block the ends next Saturday, too. Besides, football players at Ole Miss don't wear brassieres.

"Fellows," Bus then proceeded to yell to the dressing room full of players. "We have an Ole Miss football player who wants to wear a brassiere. Have you ever heard of anything like that? An Ole Miss football player who wants to wear a brassiere!!"

I stood there amongst my peers, my teammates, my compatriots, most of whom were now folded over with laughter, a slight forced grin on my face. Before Bus dropped the subject, he almost had me believing I really did want to wear a brassiere.

"I'd wear one of the d—n things if it would get me out of practice," I murmured loud enough to be heard by my teammates but not so loud as to be heard by Buster.

I failed to get my rib pads but I succeeded in having to cross-body block with floating ribs in every practice and every game the rest of the season.

Amazingly, I was awarded the Jacob's Blocking Trophy as the best blocker in the SEC that year.

"Oh, if they only knew—!"

DID YOU KNOW?

Bobby Wilson led the nation with 10 pass interceptions in 1947.

TURN 'EM AROUND BOYS

Ole Miss coaches, from Nineteen Forty-Seven to Mid-Sixties may have been solicitous about some team anxieties, but one "feeling" with which they were notoriously unconcerned was players' emotional sensitivities. Football players who got their feelings hurt easily lasted a very short time in Oxford, if in fact, they even survived recruiting. A player unable to take a good "tail-chewing" lived a miserable life at Ole Miss because sooner or later, probably sooner, he was going to find himself on the receiving end of one. Our coaches were just as apt to do it in a game before thousands of people as they were in practice.

None of the coaches culled anyone. The fact that Billy Kinard was the brother of Coach Bruiser Kinard in no way eliminated him from the possibility. I think the fact that I was Buster Poole's nephew increased the possibility of my receiving one. All my other relatives who played under Uncle Bus, would, I believe, enthusiastically agree.

Our first football game in Nineteen Fifty-Five was against Georgia in Atlanta, September 17. It was unusually hot, in the ninety degree range and humid. In those days, football practice could begin no earlier than September 1st, so we practiced only fourteen days before the game. Reluctantly, I'm certain, the coaches excused practice on Sunday, although we did spend most of Sunday afternoon in meetings and watching film. None of us was in the best of shape due to the few days of practice.

After the Nineteen Fifty-Two season, the NCAA voted to return one-platoon football to the college gridiron, which occurred in time for the Nineteen Fifty-Three season. That meant college football players must play both offense and defense, as well as special teams- limited substitution, it was called. A player who started the quarter could come out of the game that quarter and re-enter it only one time. If he came off the field the second time he could not play again until the next quarter. A player who did not start the quarter could only go into and out of the game one time. Once he came off the field, he could not re-enter the game during that quarter. How football officials kept up with that melange caused all of us to wonder.

Buddy Alliston and Charles Duck were Ole Miss' two excellent guards in Nineteen Fifty-Five, but the Rebels had little depth in that position. The second team guards had accrued minimum playing experience the year before.

By the middle of the fourth quarter that hot night in Atlanta, Buddy had played the entire game and Charles all but two minutes.

Georgia called time out. The welcomed rest gave the two weary linemen time to talk. One of them whispered to the other one, "What do you think Coach would do if I took myself out of the game?"

"I don't know! You gonna try it?"

"Thinkin' about it. What if we both went off at the same time? Reckon that'd work?"

"I'm tired enough to try it," the other one replied.

Each lifted himself off one knee and both jogged toward the Ole Miss bench. Before they got to the sideline, Coach Vaught walking briskly out on the field, met them.

"Where the h—l do you think you're going?" the Coach demanded.

"Coach, we're tired. We thought maybe the other guards could rest us a while," Buddy nervously answered, hoping that collective bargaining might influence the Coach.

"Get your butts back on that field."

With that command the two disappointed guards made a silent U-turn back onto the field. They played the rest of the game.

So much for collective bargaining on the Ole Miss football team.

WHAT HAPPENED!?! WHAT HAPPENED?!?

Ole Miss enjoyed a great football season in Nineteen Fifty-Four. We lost one game 6 - 0 to Arkansas in Little Rock. Buddy Benson, an Arkansas halfback threw a wounded duck desperation pass to Preston Carpenter in the final few minutes of the game for the win. Ole Miss gained more than four hundred yards that day to only about one hundred for Arkansas, most of theirs on that pass play. But we still won the SEC Championship and were invited to play Navy in the Sugar Bowl.

The game was televised for the first time and Ole Miss would play on television for the first time. The day was less than glorious for the Rebels inspite of the tube or perhaps because of it. I'm not certain that we country boys knew how to be televised.

Our misfortune started on the very first play, the kick-off. We won the toss and elected to kick with the wind. I was the Ole Miss kicker. When I got to within a yard of the ball, a strong gust of wind blew the ball off the tee. It came to rest on the 42 yard line. In doubt about what to do, I slowed down, but the other ten Ole Miss players had already taken their eyes off the ball and headed down the field to cover the kick. When I hesitated, the Navy center, lined up fifteen yards in front of me, seeing what happened, nonchalantly relaxed, apparently assuming that I would re-tee the ball.

I didn't know what to do. I had never lost a football to the wind off a kicking tee before. My teammates were headed down field to cover a kick which "graced the grass" two yards out in front of the kicking tee.

"What the heck," I thought, "I'm a kicker. When in doubt a kicker should kick, I guess." So I launched the football off the ground.

The football hit the placid Navy center in the chest and ricocheted over my head toward our own goal line. My Ole Miss teammates didn't see what happened, they were dashing down field covering a kick-off, looking up in vain for the ball. Other than the Navy center, the Navy players didn't see what happened because they were retreating to establish a protective blocking wall in front of the ball carrier. The Navy center and I knew what happened though. Twenty football players were sprinting in one direction, and the two of us were sprinting in another. I had a fifteen yard head start on the middie, which I quickly lost in my pursuit of the bouncing football. About the time I retrieved it, the Navy center tackled me from behind.

Television was brand new, so, apparently, were the cameramen.

They lost the ball. Overheard was one of the announcers asking, "What happened, what happened?"

It took the officials a while to decide what to do. Apparently kicking a ball off a tee was so new that rules had not yet been passed to cover the misfortune.

After about five minutes of intense discussion, the officials decided that the kick was illegal, since I kicked the ball beyond the forty yard line, so they penalized Ole Miss five yards and we kicked off again.

The aborted kick turned out to be a preview of things to come. Navy won the game.

CHAPTER IX

THE POOLES

I think I'm honest about it! I really don't think I'm biased, but I might be. Though you don't need it, you certainly have my permission to judge. "About what?," you might understandably ask.

The Pooles! I'm a member of the Poole family, college football's most prolific clan. Now, that's not an idle, careless, statement. The issue has been settled by numerous sport writers, and authenticated in the very first edition of Mississippi Magazine. No other family has ever placed fourteen of its members onto one college football team. The Pooles did. From the early Thirties when Buster arrived, until the early Seventies when Ray Junior graduated, fourteen of us sweated on the turf of Old Hemingway Stadium.

Buster was followed by his brothers Ray and Barney; double first cousins Philip, Fleming and Jackie; first cousins Oliver and Leslie; nephews Robbie Robertson and yours truly. Joseph Robertson and Reggie Robertson, both having Poole mothers, followed me. Buster's son Jim and Ray's son, already mentioned, concluded the run. Two Pooles made All-American, several All S.E.C., and five graduated to the National Football League, where three made All-Pro. Barney, who played eight years of college football, is a member of the College Football Hall of Fame.

I hope I can dichotomize bias from pride. I'm proud to be a member of the Poole family, but I believe my purpose for including a chapter in this book about them extends from humor, not superciliousness.

I'll explain, if I can.

My grandfather, Will Poole, the father of Buster, Ray, and Barney, had several brothers, two of whom along with him married Berryhill sisters, producing three sets of double first cousins. Two totally different genes were produced in the Poole clan: one of soft, gentle, loving compassion; and one of frivolity, fun, joking, kidding, manifested in the tendency to pull pranks — on everyone.

Beginning with the older Pooles, all of whom were tall, well-built men, every family member possessed one gene or the other. The ones with the prankish gene managed to keep all the other ones fervently amused for generations. Their acts are legendary and remembered still by the older people of Southwest Mississippi. In the common vernacular, there was nothing they wouldn't do. With absolutely no regard for the opinions of others, they relentlessly executed their hilarious and mischievous deeds.

Uncle Farley (Boss) Poole, Oliver's father, and Uncle Ira (Toad)Poole, Leslie's father were the two older Pooles. Philip, Jackie, Buster, and Ray were the younger inheritors of the gene. For brevity's sake, I plan to propound on some of the exploits of my Great Uncle Boss and my Uncle Ray, but before I do, I should explain the prevailing culture, both social and family, of that day. It deviated from other cultures around it, and it certainly differed from society today.

The Pooles of Homochitto were notoriously family oriented. My aunts and uncles, including great aunts and uncles owned spanking rights to me, as did my Mother and Dad on their nieces and nephews. We were that close, and although the word "love" may never have been mentioned outside church, which we all attended weekly, it was never - the- less, perpetually present —- I think. I have a little trouble associating love with the aggrevating antics of Buster and Ray. I had to live with them.

In our family, physical pain was never verbally recognized. Neither was emotional pain. A death brought the family together en masse, as did hospital stays. Tears flowed, but they were controlled. Heartache and the Poole mentality were antinomy. If someone asked the question, "Does it hurt?", we would of course respond "yes" or "no." Volunteer discussion about the pain though seldom occurred. It was an unwritten sign of weakness to admit suffering, which might have granted license to the one inflicting it. We would never have given another person the satisfaction of knowing he inflicted pain upon us. That attitude, of course, prevailed not only in our family but also at Ole Miss on the football field during the previously discussed years, probably one reason why the Pooles fit in so perfectly there. Or perhaps the Poole mentality influenced Ole Miss some, I don't really know.

When my Grandfather Will Poole developed appendicitis in 1924, he refused to go to the doctor, until his appendix burst. By then it was too late. He ignored the pain.

Mama Poole and her seven children buried her husband without so much as a groan. Buster, the oldest child at home, was only thirteen. Barney was the youngest at age two. In between were my mother Hilda, Ray, and Willodene. Two daughters were already married. Mama reared her family with unspoken love, discipline, and a fervent desire for them to be educated. Close relatives, all living within five miles, most inside of two, helped her.

She encouraged her children's participation in sports, if not aggressively, then certainly with silent permission. Years later that dispensary disposition would pay huge dividends for her sons and other Poole relatives.

The mind set of the Poole clan was unspoken too - - it just seemed to develop over the years - - take nothing, including yourself, seriously - neither death, nor pain, nor inconvenience, nor poverty, nor taxes - - well maybe taxes. An imperturbable culture genesised into existence and like fog rising and spreading from one of the Homochitto swamps, reached out and enveloped all of the Poole family.

From birth the Poole children knew the ones in our family who would pick on us and those who wouldn't. We grew up knowing both were accepted by everyone equally. The aggravators were never condemned by any member of the family for their irritation - - the ones who didn't annoy never received accolades for their gentleness. As Poole or Poole-related children we were as drawn to those who vexed us as we were those who didn't, sometimes more. I tagged along behind Ray, the "father of all teasers" as quickly as I did Barney, the family's most tranquil peacemaker. The two postures had existed for as long as had the family: everyone knew it, everyone expected it, everyone accepted it; and other than children who occasionally "got mad," I never saw one Poole, or Poole mate, grow angry at another Poole for teasing any of the children.

Well, some might say, I don't see anything so unusual about the Pooles from what you've said - - a lot of families have jokers, and of course, that's true. But the Pooles weren't just verbal with the humor - - they were physical. If some of the activities which occurred back then happened today, law suites would overflow from the windows of county courthouses.

The Pooles were big men, and handsome. They were tall, broad-shouldered and looked very much alike. Today they would be diagnosed as "self-confident," though that word never graced the vocabularies of any of them. A total lack of self-consciousness gave rise, I suspect, to their complete disposition of unconcern about the opinions of others.

UNCLE BOSS

Uncle Boss, my great uncle, possessed among other things, the ability to make money. Starting out as a farmer in the Homochitto Community, he graduated in the late Thirties to the lumber and oil business just in time for World War II. By the time the war ended, he was a wealthy man, certainly by Amite County standards.

He owned a flatbed truck. He owned a lot of other things too, but Uncle Boss and his truck burned an ineffaceable memory into my mind when I was only a little boy.

Uncle Boss and his flatbed truck transported the Homochitto baseball team to and from away games.

Back in the late Forties, almost every rural community fielded an adult baseball team. The Homochitto team was comprised of Pooles and was known unofficially as the Pooles of Pooletown. Our home field was a cow pasture. The Homochitto Community consisted of no more than the grammar school, Bill Robertson's country store, the Mt. Vernon Methodist Church, the baseball team and rural residences on farms.

The team had no nickname and I always wondered why! Our opponents had nicknames. The Franklin County team was the Pine Knots, an appropriate name for baseball players, I thought. Pine knots are pieces of wood. Baseballs are hit, or missed, with pieces of wood. Pine knots are hard, too. "His head is as hard as a pine knot," I grew up hearing people describe other people, parents about difficult children, wives about obstinate husbands.

Nickname or not, the Homochitto baseball team usually played two games every weekend in June, July, and August, one on Saturday afternoon and one on Sunday afternoon, after we got church changed.

For a hundred years, Mt. Vernon Methodist Church met once on Sunday, at 2:00 P.M. But when the younger Pooles, my uncles, grew old enough to form the baseball team, they wanted to move church to Sunday mornings, opening the way to play Sunday afternoon games. The older traditionalists didn't want to change and the discussion was furious. The volatile situation was finally assuaged when the older church members gave way, but not without a few closing shots declaring that the whole community might go to hell for playing baseball on Sundays. Heretofore Sunday's physical activity had been limited to cooking, milking cows and feeding chickens, tasks necessary to preserve life.

When Homochitto played away from home, Uncle Boss would crank up his flatbed truck and drive the five miles of road thoughout the Community picking up the players and anyone else brave enough to climb aboard. From the center of the community, the location of the church, the school, the store, and the ball field, one road led past Great Uncle Hillary Poole's house to Crosby; one past Great Uncle Boss's house to Meadville; and one past our house and Great Uncle Toad's house, which were only three hundred yards apart, to Gloster. The heart of the community lay near the place where Brushy Creek runs into the Homochitto River about a mile north of Mama Poole's.

The roads were gravel and bumpy. Dust boiled up behind the speeding truck like vapor trails behind a jet airplane, poking itself up our noses and sanding away at our eyeballs. By the time we got to concrete, if we ever did, ten miles toward Gloster and Crosby, fifteen toward Meadville, Uncle Boss's truck was loaded with blind baseball players. Upon arriving at our destination, we spent the first fifteen minutes clearing our lungs and eyeballs of dust.

We all disembarked gently from the good Uncle's truck when we arrived at the game site - - not so on the return trip home.

The very instant the game ended the Homochitto baseball players made a mad dash to the truck, not because we were all that anxious to go home - - we weren't. We wanted to get a grip. We knew what awaited us when Uncle Boss got to our houses and the truck offered few places where one could hold on.

Uncle Boss had a unique way of unloading us when he delivered us home. About a hundred yards from a disembarkation point, he would speed up. That was our key to tighten our grip if we could find one, or hold onto a relative who had one. Then he would move over to the side of the road. That was our key to start moaning just a little, and indicated which way to lean. Directly in front of the house, the Great Uncle would slam on the brakes and violently turn the steering wheel. The Homochitto baseball players who had no place to grip or who had not anticipated the direction of his turn became line drives off the truck, air-mailed bodies. Those who rightly anticipated the direction of the turn and whose grasp counteracted the resulting centrifugal force, stood a chance to survive, their joy, however, being temporary. The next stop would present a whole new challenge.

Uncle Boss's deep bass laughter would reverberate from the cab. Those who were propelled from the truck, would push themselves off the ground, feel all arms and legs for broken bones, dust off their clothes and with no comment, reluctantly climb back aboard the "sling-shot," shuddering at the knowledge that down the road a piece, someone else would have to get off.

But in the same way Uncle Boss had graduated from farming to lumber and oil, he matriculated from the flatbed truck to another conveyance. He moved to Gloster and bought an airplane.

Gloster had an airport. Actually it was a cow pasture on the edge of town big enough for a single engine airplane to take off and land, but it was called the airport. It had a windsock which made it official.

I never understood the purpose of that wind-sock. Years later when I got my pilot's license, I learned the wind-sock would tell a pilot the direction the wind was blowing. The pilot would, from that knowledge, determine which direction he should take-off and land his airplane, which was always into the wind in order to increase lift.

I'm not certain Uncle Boss paid any attention to the wind-sock. Everytime I saw him take off and land, he was going the same way.

It may have been that the man who sold Uncle Boss the airplane hadn't time to tell him very much. Uncle Boss wouldn't take flying lessons.

Actually he did take one lesson, on the day he bought the plane.

"Show me how to fly it," my great uncle with his beautiful, booming bass voice demanded.

An hour later, Uncle Boss was flying his new winged surrey toward Gloster.

MILKING TIME AT HOMOCHITTO

For a century, farmers at Homochitto milked their cows in the afternoon, although, the farmers' wives milked the cows. Poole men weren't allowed to milk.

When I was a young boy, learning all my chores and tasks, Mama Poole, my grandmother, explained that I wouldn't have to milk the cows. Later, I found out why. She didn't think men ought to touch a cow right there. It just wasn't decent. I agreed with her - - I didn't think I ought to have to slop the hogs, or feed the chickens, or hoe the gardens, or cut the bean poles and drag them back to where the beans were planted either. I promised myself, if I ever got off that farm, I would never cut another bean pole.

Late in the afternoon, the cows at every farmhouse would come sludging out of the pasture toward the barn, willing to give in order to get; to give their milk in order to get some special store bought feed or some shelled corn. They moved on cue, as though they could tell time, their heads bowed, their bells tinkling, one behind the other, peaceful, serene, pastoral—! That was before the Red Baron of Brushy Creek bought his airplane.

Milking cows was never the same at Homochitto.

Uncle Boss knew where everyone's cows in the community gathered to be fed and milked, which of course, was near each barn. Gates would be opened and cows would move into the barn and into their stalls where cow feed would have been placed in the feed trough. While they were eating, they were milked. The workday usually culminated with the milking of the cows.

Uncle Boss also knew what the cows would do if he buzzed them with his airplane. So he did, once or twice a week. From house to house, until he covered the entire community, Great Uncle scattered the milk cows, sending them sprinting back into the pastures, looking for places to hide. It would often be well after dark before the terrified milk progenitors sneaked back to the barn.

One day I threatened my uncle. "Uncle Boss, the next time you buzz our cows, I'm gonna hit you with a baseball."

True to his sportive nature, he was delighted, appreciating my prankish threat, ignoring the possible outcome. He then proceeded to announce the date of his next fly-by and instructed me on how to throw my missile in order to make contact.

"Now son, hitting an airplane with a baseball is a lot like shooting a quail with a shotgun. You have to lead him. I figure you've got to throw that ball about ten yards in front of the plane to hit me."

On the designated day, I was waiting, sitting on Mama Poole's front porch steps, baseball in hand, ears acute for the sound, eyes peering toward Gloster. The dust devils were cavorting in the gravel road's heat and wind. Mosquito hawks had appeared, flying their elongated circular routes across our front yard looking for their prey, being ever so careful to avoid their own predator, Ole Blue, Mama Poole's big blue and white tomcat. Ole Blue could dunk a mosquito hawk five feet off the ground. Our cows had begun their migration to the barn via the "stomp."

Sitting on Mama's front porch gazing toward the road in front, the barn lay behind the house and to the right. To the right of the house, outside the yard fence and in front of the barn, the stomp was a flat area where the cows lowed to be let into the barn lot for dinner and production.

I heard Uncle Boss coming before I saw him, the drone of the engine sounding like the plague of locust which invaded our green realm every seven years or so.

I got ready. "I'm gonna hit you, Uncle Boss. I'm gonna throw this baseball right through your windshield."

From the front porch steps, my gallery watched, Mama Poole, my mother, and my sister. Offering her final bit of advice, my mother exclaimed, "I don't think you ought to do this, Paige."

I didn't answer. I didn't have time.

The noise of the motor grew louder and louder and I searched the tops of the pine trees to the South, knowing that any moment, having passed over Uncle Toad's house, he would dip toward ours.

Suddenly, there he was, about a hundred yards away. He nosed his plane below the tops of the trees and pointed it toward the stomp and our house. I was ready, standing just outside the front gate, my glove on my left hand, the baseball in my right hand, my arm drawn back. I could easily see Uncle Boss grinning at me from the cockpit. I knew he wanted me to hit his plane with that baseball as much as I wanted to hit it. We both wondered what would happen if I did. Quickly I measured off ten yards to the front of the plane, and with all my strength, I hurled the grenade.

"I missed, d - -n it!" Gratefully the sound of the plane drowned out the profanity. I would have been in big trouble.

I caught my wayward throw. The baseball soared in front of the plane and came down behind it, the airplane actually flying under it. For several years following, I bragged, "I'll bet I'm the only person who ever threw a baseball all the way over a flying airplane and then caught it."

My great uncle flew on, to scatter other cows.

Several days later I saw Uncle Boss.

"You can throw a baseball pretty good for a thirteen year old boy, Paige. You led me just a little bit too far. But I saw that ball come up right in front of me."

"What woulda' happened if I had hit your propeller, Uncle Boss?" I asked.

"Don't know - spec' I'd a crashed!"

I didn't pursue the subject further. I suspected, true to his nature, he was teasing, although I couldn't be certain. My Great Prankster might have thought a thirteen year old boy bringing an airplane down with a baseball would be funny, even with him in it.

THE HAYSTACK

"You have him up on top of that haystack at three o'clock," Uncle Boss directed his son Oliver, and five of his nephews, Barney, Ray, Philip, Fleming, and Jackie. The haystack he was talking about was cut hay from Uncle Hillary's hundred acre hayfield, stacked on a trailer for transporting to the barn.

Every summer, farmers in Mississippi cut their hay and store it for winter feeding of their livestock. Uncle Hillary owned one of the largest farms in the Homochitto Community and the biggest hay field. Cutting and hauling a hundred acres of hay was no small task, especially in the late Forties, before the invention of modern equipment.

After cutting the hay and allowing it to fall onto the ground, farmers would rake it into piles, usually with mule-drawn equipment. The piles were loaded onto a large wagon by hand, using pitchforks. To one person fell the task of mounting the trailer in order to pull the hay up onto the center of the stack. As the pile of hay grew higher, the "puller" ascended with it. By the time the wagon was fully loaded, he would stand ten or twelve feet off the ground.

On Uncle Hillary's farm, lived sharecropper Jess (not his real name), his wife, and their several children. He was a hard working but extremely rural man who seldom left the community or even the farm. I never saw Jess in any clothes but overalls and he always seemed to need a shave. A serious-minded man, he knew little of the ways or comforts of the world - and absolutely nothing about airplanes. But he did know Uncle Boss.

No two men could be any more different. One was full of foolishness, the other completely repulsed by it. One lived in town and had money, the other a sharecropper who lived on another man's land. One had to cut, load and transport hay, the other had nothing to do with the stingy grass, that is, not directly.

The hay wagon had worked its way to the middle of the large field. Jess, with his pitchfork, was atop the haystack on the trailer, which was almost full and ready for the barn. The six young Pooles were standing around the wagon with their pitchforks in their hands, sweat cascading down their bodies, glancing toward the direction of Gloster, slight smiles on their faces.

It was three o'clock.

On a hot, still South Mississippi summer day, sounds can be heard much farther than usual. The boys, because they were listening for it heard the sound of the airplane before Jess did. Realizing the rare noise might scare him off his teetering perch, the six athletes started throwing more hay onto the trailer.

"Just a little more, Jess, one of them hollered, "and we'll take it to the barn."

From the far end of the field, the slight sonance exploded into a vibration as Uncle Boss dropped the airplane over the trees to fifteen feet above the stubbled floor of the hayfield, pointing its nose straight at the hay gatherers.

Jess heard the sound of the engine at about the time the plane leveled off above the earth. From his perch high above the ground, he maneuvered his body, facing the sound, and gripped his pitchfork. His eyes squinted from beneath his sweaty hat, his knuckles whitened from his grip, as Uncle Boss guided his projectile straight toward the haystack. Jess' eyes widened as he bent his knees, crouching in a battle stance, a soldier anticipating the arrival of the enemy.

At the last moment Uncle Boss pulled his flying machine up above Jess' head, just as the farmer sprang from his stooped position, angrily thrusting his pronged bayonet toward the adversary's underbelly. Luckily, he missed.

Like a cropduster, the elder Poole elevated his craft at the end of the field and exercised a 180 degree turn back toward the overalled opponent. Not once, not twice, not thrice, but four times the antagonists challenged each other from the most unlikely of all battlefields. Finally the skirmish ended and the flying combatant flew away, waving his wings in a salute as he climbed back above the trees and into the clouds.

The six Poole relatives were rolling on the ground.

Jess looked down at them in their glee, his eyes squinting again now, his face red from anger and the heat. Throwing his long handled weapon over their heads to the ground, he slid down off the hay, grunted an unintel-ligible sound, and without looking back, walked off the hayfield.

"What did he say?" someone asked.

"I don't know, but I'll bet that's the last time we ever get Jess back up on a haystack," came the reply.

"I'm just glad he didn't aim that pitchfork at one of us."

"He's probably saving it for Uncle Boss."

THE ENABLER

By the time I came along, Homochitto High School had consolidated with Crosby High. But the Grammar School remained, grades one through eight.

The Principal of the school was Mr. Charles Hayman, who had moved into the community several years before I was born. Although the school was very small and only about forty children or less attended, Mr. Hayman almost always dressed for work in shirt and tie. He was a lay-leader of the Mt. Vernon Methodist Church, a serious, highly respected man. He and his wife taught Sunday School, and he was bald.

But Mr. Hayman was a very slow driver. He never drove over twen-ty miles an hour.

Being a slow driver was good - for most of Homochitto's residents. Slow drivers stirred up less dust and dust invaded the front porches and open windows of the houses, most of which were built close to the roads, so folks appreciated them.

I get frustrated at slow drivers on the streets of Memphis and the highways of Mississippi. I know I shouldn't but I do. They antagonize me because they keep me from getting where I'm going on time, and they never get a ticket.

I get tickets for speeding. Back a few years ago, I got four speeding tickets in one year and almost lost my license. All my friends get tickets - for speeding. Slow drivers break the law too - - but they never get tickets.

The other day, I was driving on a stretch of road. The sign said, "Max speed 55 - Min speed 45." When my radar detector sounded, I slowed down to 55. I caught up with a senior citizen who was burning rubber at 35 miles per hour. Did the highway patrolman pull him over? No! But I'll bet if I hadn't slowed down, I would have gotten another ticket.

I've made up my mind! When I get another speeding ticket, I'm going to ask the officer how long it's been since he blue-lighted a slow driver. Depending on his answer, I just might not accept his gift, or then on the other hand, I might.

Anyway, Mr. Hayman drove his car very slowly. He stirred up little dust. Someone once said you had to line his car up with a pine tree to see if it was moving. And he drove in the middle of the road, very carefully.

Uncle Boss never got angry, but he never got serious either. And he refused to drive behind a slow driver.

One day Uncle Boss pulled up behind Mr. Hayman on the gravel road leading from Homochitto to Gloster. Mr. Hayman, meandering his way leisurely toward town some eight miles away, didn't know Uncle Boss was behind him. My great uncle thought Mr. Hayman ought to get there sooner, so very gradually, the elder Poole eased up behind the school principal, and wedded his front bumper to Mr. Hayman's rear bumper. Then he then put the pedal to the metal!

Uncle Boss took Mr. Hayman to town! Up and down steep hills, around treacherous curves, they sped, one obliging vehicle pushing a reluctant one, on an unstable gravel road reaching nefarious speeds of forty-five and fifty miles an hour. (The speeds really were wicked for that road.)

When they arrived at the edge of Gloster, Uncle Boss divorced their cars, passed the principal, and continued up the road.

Mr. Hayman never mentioned the experience, but all the Homochitto residents who, from their front porches, witnessed it did. Some wondered why Uncle Boss seemed to be chasing Mr. Hayman.

Others expressed disgust that the school principal, at his age, had suddenly decided to drive so fast and stir up all that dust.

UNCLE TOAD

Uncle Boss wasn't my only great uncle. He had brothers Hillary who, as we've already discussed, owned a large farm in the Homochitto Community; Harmon who, at the time I was young, lived in South America; my grandfather Will, the father of Buster, Ray, and Barney, who had died before I was born; and Uncle Ira (Toad).

Uncle Toad lived only three hundred yards down the road south of us, toward Gloster. He and Aunt Ida had three girls and four boys, including Leslie, one of the fourteen Pooles who played football at Ole Miss. Uncle Toad was a tall, lanky man with a kindly face and a deep resonant voice similar to his brother Boss. And like his brother, he was in the lumber business.

I don't know how he got his name because he didn't resemble a frog. Some guessed it was his voice, which sounded somewhat like a frog - a bullfrog.

Uncle Toad imbibed. That made him a little dissimilar to most residents of Homochitto who believed strongly that brew bubbled straight up from the open doors of Hell.

One night Uncle Toad came home late "under the influence." Unknowing to him, Aunt Ida had that day rearranged the furniture. He climbed upon what had been the bed, — and spent the night on top of the sewing machine.

Every Christmas Eve, knowing all of Mama Poole's clan were gathered at her home, Uncle Toad would walk over to bring his sister-in-law a Christmas present and visit. Mama's grandchildren, like me, loved him. He told funny stories, he usually had a pocket full of candy, and he let us shoot at him —- with Roman Candles.

Uncle Toad would say in his deep canorous voice, "Alright boys, get your Roman Candles, I'm leaving now."

With glee four or five of us would gather our Roman Candles, and line up on the front porch. Uncle Toad would march through the front gate and assume his customary target position in the middle of the gravel road, some thirty yards away, facing us in rural darkness.

"Now, boys, just one at a time!," he would caution. Then one by one we would light our Roman candles and fire away. Uncle Toad, with his sonorous voice, altered and slurred a little by drink, would direct the fire.

"Boys, you were just a little high," he would observe, stretching out the word "little" so that it sounded like "lleettle." The gunner would adjust his aim before the next fire-ball exploded from the barrel.

We never hit Uncle Toad - - -until - - -finally - - -one cold Christmas Eve!

Uncle Toad was wearing his finest, long wool overcoat. The projectile hit him squarely in the chest. We thought we had hit him but it was confirmed when we heard his voice, remarkably calm, "Boys, you put me on fire - - better come put me out."

With water buckets in hand, we made a mad dash to our great uncle. His coat was ablaze, as we emptied our water buckets onto the fire.

"I believe you're out, Uncle Toad," one of my fire fighting cousins exclaimed.

"I believe I am," he responded. "Ya'll have a merry Christmas."

We could hear his wet pant legs sloshing against one another as he turned to walk back home.

BADY

That Poole gene which produced the mischievous and sportive spirit in Uncle Boss and Uncle Toad somehow evaded their sons Oliver and Leslie, and darted obliquely into Ray, Buster, Phillip, and Jackie. A bottomless book could be penned on the antics of those four but limited space must confine itself to the capers of only one. Since I grew up with Ray and because he coached for the Rebels, I have restricted my stories to him. (If Ray lets me live after reading this, I may consider writing a book on all four.)

Ray was two years old when his brother Barney was born, only a baby himself. He was called, "Baby Ray," a name producing some difficulty for me. I can't imagine him ever being "Baby" Ray. When Barney reached utterance age, about two, he couldn't say "Baby Ray." It came out "Bady Ray," and from that time, Ray was known as Bady to his South Mississippi relatives. My sister still calls him that.

At this writing, Ray is seventy-six. He looks and exercises like he's fifty-six, playing golf almost every day and working long hours on his farm and in his yard-still in great shape, and he still has muscles.

That bothers me a little bit.

"Why?"

I can't sprint anymore. I have to wear a big metal knee brace when I power walk - - that's why. And I want you to know how courageous I am to write these things. I may call you for help.

My first cousins agree - - these stories need to be told for several reasons: First, they happened, and not only these stories, but hundreds more which would indeed fill a book; second, they reflect the spirit of the times, a time which we will never see again, a microcosm of life at Ole Miss during Coach Vaught's tenure as Head Coach; finally, they're funny to those of us to whom the events occurred and I hope to you.

When my cousins and I get together, we tell "Bady" stories just like former Ole Miss football players tell "Wobble" stories. It's not just coincidence that the stories are much the same. Both Ray and Wobble played football for the Rebels, roomed together for awhile, and then coached together. Like the former players who love and appreciate Wobble, all my cousins love and appreciate Ray, and we really appreciate having lived through him.

But we'd like to retaliate - so on behalf of all my cousins who lived in constant awareness that he was going to pull some prank on us soon; who love to remember and talk about them; here's to you, Ray. And I'm serious when I say, "Thank you for these hilarious memories," perhaps aggravating and exasperating at the time, and maybe just a little scary, but which are very funny now.

UNCLE RAY

My Uncle Ray was like no one I've ever met or will ever expect to meet - - Uncle Boss, Uncle Harmon, Uncle Toad all rolled up into one and then multiplied by a hundred. There was nary a moment, when Ray in the presence of his nieces and nephews, wasn't either pulling a prank, thinking up a prank; or was just finishing a prank. As soon as one ended, he immediately initiated another one. We were afraid of him, we sometimes got mad at him, and then we followed him around like an admiring puppy trails behind its young master.

THE DEER HORNS

That's what I did so much, follow him around, tag along behind him, when his devilish mind solved the problem.

Ray married later than his older brother, Buster and even his younger brother, Barney, and he was very close to his mother, Mama Poole. When football season ended, he came home to live where he grew up. That's where I lived, with my mother and sister. His being there produced a powerful dichotomy in my young, clinging spirit. On the one hand, I yearned for him to come home. After all not many twelve year old boys got to live in the same house with an All-Pro football player who was also the captain of his team -

the New York Giants. But not many, if any, faced the aggravations I did by him being there either. If those two extremes aren't grounds for an inner conflict, there are none!

The Pooles were "rich" in many ways, poor in one, at the bank. We didn't know it. We had more than enough to eat, clothes to wear, and a house which stayed warm in the winter most of the time, due primarily to its vicinage, South Mississippi. It stayed very warm in the summer, but we didn't know that either, because all our relatives were the same temperature. We cooled off by jumping into the spring-fed Brushy Creek which tumbled nervously over white sand bottoms through the Homochitto Community before escaping into the Homochitto River, only about one and one-half miles from Mama Poole's house. It ran through the heart of Mama's land before it got there.

Our farm clothes were very simple. After I reached adolescence, I wore a pair of Ole Miss athletic shorts which published its message across the rear - UMAA - signifying of course that they had been borrowed from the University of Mississippi Athletic Association equipment room by a sticky fingered relative. One day a little tow-haired non-Poole neighbor asked, "Hey Paige, what does that UMAA stand for?"

"U Made All-American."

"Oh," he responded, obviously satisfied that a riddle had been solved.

Before I reached puberty, however, I wore overalls, or as we Southerners sometimes call them "over-hauls." I rolled my pant legs up, wore no shirt and refused to enslave my two growing, bottom appendages with store bought impediments. I could run down the rockiest gravel road full speed, barefooted and never feel a thing. So could all the other boys in Homochitto.

Over-hauls had suspenders, which in my case served two purposes, an obvious one and a not so obvious one.

When my Uncle Ray grew tired of me tagging along behind him, he simply elevated me, suspenders and all, to the deer horns mounted on both sides of the hallway and impaled me there, where I stayed until female compassion, in the form of Mama Poole or my mother, freed me. I spent a measurable amount of growing-up time mounted on the wall with the deer antlers, yelling, screaming, crying, kicking, threatening to kill Ray, and waiting for my rescue, which I thought would never come in spite of the fact that it never failed to —!

I was telling about being hung on the deer horns at a party one night and a lady with a quivering voice said, "Oh no, how terrible!"

"How terrible? That was one of the nicest things he did to me!", I responded.

"Nicest things? What else did he do?"

"Well," I answered, "He would sometimes throw me up onto the roof of the house and then disappear out of my sight under the eaves. Clinging for my life, yelling at the top of my lungs, and sliding toward eternity, I could only hope that Heaven would be like my Sunday School teacher taught."

Of course he always stepped back out and caught me and I always dared to hope that he would. But I never knew for sure until he did.

Sometimes he would throw me off the Brushy Creek bridge, long before Billy Joe McAllister threw something off the Tallahatchie Bridge, creating within me an affinity with the song every time I heard it.

A half-mile from the mouth of the Brushy Creek, the gravel road split into three directions. One road ran past our house towards Gloster, one meandered down by Uncle Hillary's house toward Crosby, and one crossed the creek immediately and serpertined to Meadville.

The Homochitto swimming hole, eight feet deep, clear, cold, drinkable water lay, to pre-teenage eyes, fifty feet at least beneath the bridge. (Actually it was probably no more than ten feet.) Throwing me off the bridge and seeing who could pull me out of the water before I drowned seemed like great sport to Ray and the relatives, all of whom were football playing age.

Sometimes he would lock me up in the potato house, or the toilet.

Every family in the community had both, a potato house and an outdoor toilet. We all had barns and smoke houses too: barns for the cows, mules, horses, to house corn and hay; and smoke houses to cure the meat in hog-killing time.

The potato house was a scary, foreboding place, built partially underground, an enclosed, caliginous expanse, a perfect domicile for snakes. Everytime I was sent there my mother warned me to look out for them. I always obeyed.

Access was though a door the top of which was no more than three feet high. Before entering for my booty, I would open the door inward, stand in the entrance for several minutes until my eyes adjusted to the dark, survey the bed of potatoes which lay three feet below ground-level, for serpents, gather my loot and quickly abandon the premises, rejoicing in having escaped unscathed once again.

Being locked up in there for a while was unnerving to say the least, and much worse than being locked up in the outdoor toilet. In the toilet I always found something to read, the Sears and Roebuck catalog. It was dark in the potato house.

HAPPY BIRTHDAY

Until I reached the age of thirteen and was a starter on the Crosby High School football, basketball, and baseball teams, I hated my birthdays. Children are supposed to love birthdays. I'm told by most of my friends that they loved their pre-teen birthdays, but they didn't grow up in the Poole family in South Mississippi in the late Forties. Birthdays meant matching the number of licks across the rear to the years of your age plus "one to grow on."

I never could figure out what that meant, "one to grow on." Was that a necessary ritual releasing you to continue growth, to perpetuate life? Without that final smack and its accompanying phrase would one be locked eternally in the prison of his present age? If that's what it means, I'll take the ritual again now.

The spanking hurt. And almost all the Poole football players participated-Ray, Barney, Philip, Jackie, Fleming, sometimes Oliver. Buster was grown and gone by the time I reached hazing age, and although he came home often, he seldom came on my birthday.

The spankings stopped after my twelfth birthday.

But for my twelfth, Mother as she always did, baked a secret birthday cake for me and no one had mentioned my birthday. Almost all of the day was gone; cows had been milked, chickens had been fed, hogs slopped, and we were sitting on the front porch, Mama Poole, Mother, my sister, Ray, Barney and me. I thought I had made it, no one but Mother and Mama had remembered. It was July 12, 1947. We were trying to cool off, wishing for a breeze, hoping beyond reason for a rain.

Like an infantryman focused upon the night sounds of a hostile jungle, my ears were tuned toward the road leading from Uncle Hillary's house, where Philip, Jackie, and Fleming lived. I knew I would have indeed avoided my birthday flagellation if the three cousins had forgotten, Barney and Ray indicating no remembrance.

The maltese sky drooped to the tops of the emerald pines which lined the gravel road until it disappeared out of sight. The humid air was inert, locked into a vice-like heavenly grip, stilled beyond belief.

On late afternoons like this, we could hear sounds, small sounds, from great distances: the Church of God which met in its perennial brush arbor more than a mile to the front of the house, across Brushy Creek; the sound of voices from all the way over to Uncle Toad's house, even when the voices weren't trying to be heard; and the sound of rubber tires challenging the rocky road a half-mile away.

I heard their voices before I heard their tires, laughing, jesting, all clinging to the open bed of the pickup truck. My head snapped to the left as I stood quickly from the front porch steps, every juvenile muscle in my young maturing body growing tense.

I was big for my age, 5 feet 7 inches tall, one hundred and fifty pounds and I could run, as fast as need be, depending upon the occasion. I sensed this might be one of the occasions.

But the truck seemed not to be slowing down as it approached the little vacant house on the other side of the road, some hundred yards, or so, away. My relief was short-lived. I recognized the riders at the precise moment the driver slammed on brakes, sliding the vehicle sideways to a stop directly in front of the house.

My blood adversaries quickly disembarked yelling, "Catch him."

But I was already moving. Ray, from his sitting position on the front porch bench, reached for me as I zipped by, heading down the hall toward the back porch, and the virescent safety of the Homochitto National Forest which nudged Mama Poole's farm just one hundred yards behind the house. Ray missed but pursued.

I picked up a baseball bat as I sprinted down the hall. I was ten yards ahead of Ray, who was twenty yards ahead of the others. I needed a larger gap.

Leaping off the back porch, I turned the corner of the kitchen, stopped, and drew back my baseball bat. Two seconds later, my Uncle Ray turned the corner. I swung — from the ground — with all the strength of one hundred fifty pounds intensified by impending danger.

I caught him right across his chest - - and he fell, like a cowboy slashing into a taut rope stretched across a western trail might fall off his horse. He hit the ground with a loud two hundred twenty pound thump. I remember the satisfaction that exploded in me, as I turned to the thick vegetation of the forest. I had increased the gap and I knew, with darkness quickly approaching, my entrance into the woods would mean evasion. Nobody could find me in the Homochitto National Forest. It was my second home. Hound dog, my 410 gauge shotgun, and I spent many hours there.

My pursuers, realizing I had successfully entered my sanctuary, went back to the house, lit up the old carbide and water headlights, spread out in a hundred yard front and advanced blindly toward me.

Whether they realized it or not, they would never get close to me at night in the forest. Ten miles of deep woods lay between Mama's house and the next civilization and I knew almost every foot of it, even at night, every ridge, every hollow, every ditch.

I stayed just out in front of their anemic lights, wearing nothing except a pair of tan Ole Miss athletic shorts which screamed "UMAA" across the rear, not even shoes. I could hear them half whispering - -, "Here he is, over here."

"No, I heard him over here," would sound from the other end of the line.

Minutes turned into an hour, then two, as we slipped through the dark trees, the hunted and the hunters, until finally one of them confessed, "H - - l, we aren't gonna find him. Let's go."

And they went.

My heart raced with rapture, as much for circumventing my relatives' plans as evading the rod. I had outsmarted them and then I bested them in a physical confrontation. It was my initiation into Poole manhood, my Bar Mitzvah, my rite of blood recognition. I knew that all five of them, two uncles and three cousins, would respect me for what I did. I also knew that they would never admit it. I was satisfied.

I was twelve.

I was also smart enough not to come out of the woods until they had gone to town, which I knew they planned to do. I watched their carbide lights disappear toward the house and I sneaked behind them to within about seventy-five dark yards of the kitchen. Finally Ray's car started, and I heard the noise of it against the loose gravel move toward Gloster. Still I wasn't certain they had left. They might be drawing me into an ambush; all fears were dispelled shortly.

"Paige, they're gone," with jubilant ears I heard my mother loudly proclaim from the back porch.

I knew then I had really done it! Yes! Yes! I sprinted out of my dark hiding place to Poole respectability.

ROCK AND THE DOOR-KNOB

The preponderance of Pooles were hunters and fishermen, outdoormen, as you might imagine. It went with the territory, part of our culture, our heritage. After the crops were laid by in mid-summer, warm July and August days would find many of them sitting around a pond, fishing pole in hand or camping out on the sandbars of the Homochitto River where they had set out hooks. In the fall and winter before the years dressed them in the athletic battle pads of Rebel Red and Blue, they would hunt squirrel and quail together in the deep woods of the Homochitto National Forest, and on their farms.

That is they would, with one partial exception - Ray. Ray was a semi-hunter. He usually "went" hunting with his relatives and the hunting dogs but he and the dogs came back alone. He wouldn't stay in the woods long. Moving out of sight of his companions, he would gather up the dogs and secret them out of the woods and back home, leaving hunters who suddenly weren't hunting and didn't even know it.

By the time they discovered they had no dogs, Ray would be on the way to town, having locked the hunting animals up in the dog pen or yard. The frustrated hunters, expecting as much from Ray and appreciating his sense of humor, would then be forced to trek back home to retrieve their dogs.

Though Ray exhibited less than an absorbing interest in hunting, he did own a dog, Rock, a hound. Rock was a good squirrel dog and he could catch a biscuit no matter how high it was thrown. Taking a couple of leftover biscuits from the breakfast table, Ray would walk out into the back yard or onto the Stomp and call Rock, who with great excitement would bound to his side. With a throwing arm strong enough to pitch Triple-A professional base-ball, he would launch his bread missile into the sky. Circling like an out-fielder, Rock would open wide his mouth and snare it. He never missed.

I'm certain, to a dog, a white porcelain door knob looks exactly like a biscuit, or so it did to Rock.

Scratch one trick! Rock never even tried to catch another biscuit.

BANANA PUDDING

Not many things are desirable about growing up, shall we say, less than opulent, in the rural South. One comes quickly to mind. You remem-ber "firsts!"

I remember the first car my dad ever bought, an old Model A which stalled three-fourths the way up every hill. I remember the first squirrel I ever killed with the first gun I ever owned. I remember the first Coke I ever drank and the first Ole Miss football game I ever saw. (It was Nineteen Forty-Six against Mississippi State in Oxford. I was eleven and State won 26 to 0. My Uncle Ray was captain of the team.) I remember graduating from over-alls to long pants with a belt. I remember vividly the first time I was ever asked to pray at MYF and I remember what the teacher told mother about it.

And I remember the first time I ever saw a banana. It was also the first time I ever ate banana pudding. I was eleven years old and I ate all I could hold. It was unbelievably delicious. The Pooles were having a family reunion.

It made me violently ill, not the quality, but the quantity. My moth-er led me into Mama Pooles bedroom, took my shoes off, laid me on her feather bed and placed a slop-jar on the floor in line with my head, which I promptly began to fill.

For those who may not know, a slop-jar is neither a jar nor does it transport slop. It is a portable toilet, a metal can which enables country folk to attend to normal bodily functions without staggering to the outdoor privy in the middle of the night. During the day, it provides a way for a sick boy to vomit from a feather bed.

The slop-jar was half-full when two giant shadows filled the door-way to Mama's bedroom. It was Buster and Ray.

I grew a little nervous. I had reason to —!

One of them, I don't remember which, said to the other, "This boy looks sick."

The other one with synthetic sympathy responded, "He sure does!"

"He needs some castor oil."

"He sure does."

"Which end do you reckon we ought to put it in?"

"I don't guess it matters - - both holes go to the same place."

With that, they pulled my pants and underwear off, held my sick legs up and spread, then proceeded to pour castor oil on my bottom. I don't think any got in - but I don't really know.

My horrifying screams brought Mama Poole who quickly dispersed the medicine men and helped me re-clothe and re-position on the sick bed. Beneath the greater matter, my vomiting had stopped.

MERRY CHRISTMAS

Of all the holidays in America which people celebrate, I suppose Christmas is the greatest. At Mama Poole's, Christmas meant scurrying into the woods to cut a cedar tree which we decked with very modest decorations; all of her children and grandchildren coming; pallets on the floor; visiting in the living room with a fire burning in the fireplace; a huge Christmas dinner with "tons" of fruitcake and pies; Egg-nog with the nog (once a year Mama would allow the witches brew into her home); and Ray, who definitely deserves special mention.

Santa Claus gaveth and Uncle Ray tooketh away!

Ray was awesome at Christmas, a veritable sideshow all unto himself. He had all his nieces and nephews at one place, at one time, a captive, albeit resistant audience.

Ray and Wanda were married when I was sixteen. By then Santa had stopped bringing me presents (I held out as long as I could). Ray was single all during my pre-teen years, and seldom frequented the Christmas Eve gathering which grouped around Mama Poole's fireplace. The lure of town and attractive girls drew him away and kept him until the entire family was asleep, and Santa had deposited his loving but meager gifts around the fireplace.

Sometime between One A.M. and dawn's early light, which always brought the kids scrambling off their pallets from across the hall and dashing into the living room, Ray would come home, gather all of Santa's gifts and hide them. One year, he hid them in the potato house; another time he entombed them in the toilet; and then the barn. One year when I was fifteen and my sister was ten, he "hid" them in the back seat of his car. After wrestling the hammer out of her hand just inches short of his back window, he decided not to hide them there anymore.

Had Charles Dickens known Ray, he would have had a whole, brand new Christmas character to write about, other than Scrooge. So far as I can tell, until his conversion, the selfish old recluse never gave a gift, but he never hid the children's presents either. Ray could have provided Charles Dickens with an entirely new conspectus.

Our uncle made no effort to keep the largest separated. Since he didn't know what Santa brought whom, he just collected it all together and dumped it all in that year's designated hiding place. The parents would then be forced to re-divide the gifts, which produced an additional problem for the little kids-"How do you know, Mommy?"

DENNIS WANTED A HORSE

When my first cousin Dennis, the oldest son of Ray's elder sister Ruby, was about ten or eleven years old, he desperately wanted, if ten year olds can desire desperately, a horse. Although Santa hadn't promised him one, Dennis knew with unshakable certainty, that the old Elf would deliver. His parents tried gently to dissuade him from believing too strongly, trying to moderate his expectations so as to lesson his disappointment. Dennis would have none of that. He went to bed Christmas Eve bearing infallible faith that the light of day would reveal his pony.

Ray came home late that night and as usual, cached all the presents. Then he went out to the barnyard with a shovel and a number ten wash tub, and gathered up about a half-tub of cow manure. Stealing silently back into the house, he spread the dung carefully around the destitute fireplace where once the favors of Santa had lain. Then he went to bed.

Before the blue sky had fully repelled the gray, Dennis was standing in front of the fertilized hearth, staring quizzically down at the refuse. One by one, the other Poole children filtered into the room, conscious, of course, that the presents were once again gone, and wondering about the unsightly and smelly mess in front of the fireplace. The awakening parents had no answer.

Spreading out like we always had to do on Christmas day, we began the premature Easter Egg hunt for our "Santa Claus."

Dennis was still searching for his horse, when finally his prankish uncle, who had just gotten out of bed, found him.

"Uncle Ray," Dennis pleaded, "did you see my horse when you came in last night?'

"Dennis, Santa left your horse right by the fireplace, but when I opened the door he got out; see where he went to the bathroom?"

"Which way did he go, Uncle Ray?"

"He ran down the road."

"Daddy, Daddy," Dennis yelled running toward his dad, "Uncle Ray said my horse got out and ran down the road, let's go find him!"

For the next several days, Dennis and his dad rode up and down the gravel Homochitto road looking for his horse. Family tradition says they never did find him.

LET'S STAY IN HARMONY, BOYS!

Few Pooles are recognized for their singing abilities. I thought maybe I could sing until the invention of those cursed tape players which stripped that confidence from me, rupturing that belief. That tape player made me sing quieter in church.

One exception was Booth, one of Dennis' younger brothers. Booth sang with a deep resonant voice, reminiscent of his great uncles, Boss and Toad. He actually sounded very much like Tennessee Ernie Ford.

After I bought my tape player, I took singing lessons from a talented teacher at French Camp, Mississippi. I knew I had a problem the very first lesson. The instructor informed me that good singers sing with their diaphragms and the sound exits the body in resonance. I always thought that you sang with your vocal cords and it came out your mouth.

"No, No, No," she corrected.

I kind of gave up.

Anyway, before Booth went off to Seminary to become a Methodist minister (He recently retired.), he sang in a very famous quartette of the day, a group which traveled and performed extensively throughout the South. The singers stayed booked for months in advance, and getting them was very difficult, but because of Booth's ties to Homochitto and Mt. Vernon Methodist Church, they agreed to come on fairly short notice.

Mama and my mother fixed supper for them two hours before the program began. It was late July, Nineteen Fifty and I was fifteen. All four singers and the piano player were seated at Mama's dining room table dressed in identical blue suits. I was seated on the far end of the table listening to the conversation.

Booth had told the other fellows, most of them city boys, about Ray and warned them that not all of his words and actions were, shall we say, conventional. Words of warning, it would soon be shown, weren't sufficient to prepare sensitive young singers, who had never socialized with professional athletes, for Ray.

Suddenly my uncle stood in the dining room doorway. He had just returned from the football field in Gloster where he had been working out in preparation for his fourth year with the New York Giants. He wore only a pair of UMAA shorts and tennis shoes. His body was deep brown from the sun and sweat was still trickling down it. His shorts were soaking wet, and he filled the entrance. His legs were spread apart and both arms extended, hands grasping the doorframes. The Giant's head stopped just a couple of inches beneath the top of the opening. With a stern, uncompromising voice, my uncle roared, "What's going on here?'

I knew he was kidding; Mama Poole knew he was kidding; my mother knew he was kidding; my sister was too young to know whether or not he was kidding; and Booth knew he was kidding. But the other singers and the piano player didn't know he was kidding. They had never faced anything like this before. Their faces grew ashen, their voices silent.

"Now, fellows," Ray bellowed, "I understand you're here to sing tonight. The way I figure it, singing is a lot like beating drums. The drums all have to have the same amount of air in them to harmonize."

The singers' eyes widened, as they all gazed intently and quizzically into the speaker's face.

"So y'all need to eat the same amount. If you eat different amounts, you'll be out of tune. Now when I say 'UP,' you all eat a fork full of food and when I say 'DOWN' you take your fork back to your plate. Do it together, now!"

I was choking back a smile, grateful that my uncle's attention had swiveled in a different direction and away from me, when Mama Poole, in her soft, loving, patient voice lessened the visitor's anxiety.

"Now Bady, you be nice to our guests."

"Fellows, this is my Uncle Ray," Booth introduced. "I told you about him."

Ray smiled at them as he met each one. Then he turned briskly back toward the door and walked out of the room. No one said anything for a few seconds, when finally one of the young singers looked at Booth and cautiously asked - - "Do you think he still wants us to eat that way?"

IN CONCLUSION

You might think, "I still don't know why Paige included a chapter in this book about the Pooles." Well, that would make two of us, but it just seemed normal, I guess because the pranks, verbal quips, and ludicrous behavior which permeated Poole-life in my childhood, continued at Ole Miss, especially in Wobble. The two cultures seemed to entwine like two ivy vines wrapped around an oak tree. The stories were much the same.

Most of all, I hope you interpret this chapter as I have intended it-vast homage to the Poole spirit, particularly Ray's. As the antics of Wobble will be told and retold through the Ole Miss family for years to come, so it will be with Ray's in the Poole family.

Sometimes late at night, when I'm tossing and turning on my sleepless bed, I remember the escapades of my uncles, cousins, and great uncles. The mental impressions forge a wide grin across my face and I think, "If only Ray, Barney, and Buster, when he was alive, knew how grateful I am to them and their - well - unusual sense of humor."

So, on behalf of all your nieces and nephews, Ray, and Barney, "Thank you," Ray for the funny memories and Barney, for protecting us from Ray.

CONCLUSION

"NO WAY, COACH!"

F ear and respect for a coach often last a lifetime. Several ex-Ole Miss football players whom Wobble coached, have told me they recently discarded their cigarettes quickly when suddenly faced by Wobble. Many of us, though we may be forty, fifty, or even sixty years old, still say "Yes, sir" and "No, sir," not only to Wobble, but to the rest of the Ole Miss coaching staff. I guess some things burn into a psyche so deeply that they remain forever. We may wonder if Wobble still has the authority to put us in the stadium. If, with that same stern authoritative voice he suddenly said, even now, "Paige, you owe me twenty laps in the stadium," I'm certain, before I figured out I wouldn't really be made to run them, an impulse would tell me I have to - -! Such was the effect of all Vaught's staff upon us, especially Wobble.

Several years ago, one of my teammates' sons was playing football at Ole Miss. He and two of his friends went to a spring football game and visited Sara and Wobble.

As always, the Davidsons graciously invited the three men into their home.

After the greetings and several minutes of conversation Wobble said, "Fellows, excuse me for a just a minute or two. Make yourselves at home. There is beer in the refrigerator. Help yourselves."

He left the room.

The two friends leaped off the couch and headed to the refrigerator. My teammate didn't move.

In a few minutes Wobble re-entered the room. My teammate sat stoically on the couch empty-handed, a slight smile on his face, while the other two were enjoying their beers.

I can imagine the conflict that raged within him. I know that man well and I know how much he enjoys a beer with friends. I also know about his fear and respect for Wobble.

"Get a beer," Wobble repeated to my teammate.

"Are you crazy?," he responded nervously. "I can't drink in front of you!"

With a touch of exasperation, he declared, "Paige, I was in my mid-forties and still afraid to drink a beer in front of him!"

"Hey, I understand," I assured him. "That stadium is still there!"

A PERSONSAL WORD FROM THE AUTHOR

I admit I have derived pleasure from few earthly endeavors as much as I have enjoyed writing this book. I got to visit with Wobble and Sara, with many of my old and dearly beloved teammates, and other ex-Ole Miss football players, some of whom were my heroes when I was in high school and others who played after I was gone. I did not pick and choose ex-players to interview following any logical or even illogical pattern. I telephoned those whom I had heard were good storytellers and I wasn't disappointed.

My purposes for writing Walk Carefully Around the Dead were clear. I wanted to preserve in print, the cultural state of our great University in a twenty year period of time, a time which had never existed before and which will never exist again, for reasons already discussed- I won't bore you with them again.

Second, I wanted to honor Coach Vaught's staff of coaches, especially Wobble, for the most unusual, interesting, and humorous four years anyone could ever hope to live on this planet. I didn't want the stories to die.

Finally, I wanted to paint a clear picture of the foundation upon which football tradition is built at Ole Miss. The twenty years, about which I wrote, were Coach Vaught and his staff's glory years. Football games today certainly cannot be won by remembering the glory years, but the tradition created then provides Ole Miss Football with a target. All who love the school hope that the mark might be hit.

I hope you were not offended by the language. I softened much of it and tried to tame all of it, except when it altered the story. A genuine attempt at preserving truth was made.

Finally, from the time I started gathering information for Walk Carefully Around the Dead until the date of this sentence's penning, another wonderful member of Coach Vaught's staff has passed on - Coach Junie Hovious. At the writing only three men from the staff remain with us other than Coach Vaught; Coach Wobble, Coach Ray, and Coach Swayze. Coach Swayze is not well as I record these words.

To you four - - thank you. It's been an unbelievably great ride - playing at Ole Miss under you, knowing former players, and writing this book.

A SECOND PERSONAL WORD

After I had finished writing this manuscript but before it was actually printed, Coach J.W. "Wobble" Davidson died-in May, Nineteen Ninety-Eight. I wanted desperately to have the book published while he was alive. I failed.

Wobble was excited about the book and very appreciative that it was being produced. Although the fourth quarter of his life was very different from the first three in some ways, in many ways he was the same: his faith was deep; his love for his family was constant, and his commitment to his former players never wavered. Their love, fear, and respect for him produced clear testimony to his role in their lives.

Together, with the aid of this work, including the eulogies of two former players who remained very close to him, we *Will Preserve His Memory.*

Rodgers Brashier played guard for the Rebels in the early Fifties. Like all the rest of us, he had a deep and abiding respect for Wobble, a respect which has amplified through the years.

Several years ago, Rodgers and his wife Betty were left for dead in their home by two would-be robbers. Rodgers was shot twice and Betty beaten unmercifully in a cowardly crime, the news of which reverberated through the Ole Miss community. Both, thank God, good doctors, and innumerable friends, have fully recovered. With his uncommon courage and sense of humor, made common in him, Rodgers can even smile and joke about the horrible experience now. And he remembers the role of Wobble and Sara as he and Betty healed from their wounds.

"Wobble or Sara called us every day throughout our recovery," remembered the former star guard. "I could never express the gratitude which Betty and I have for them. He was the toughest coach I have ever known and yet the most gentle and loving man."

"People who really knew him both hated him and loved him all at the same time," Rodgers continued. "One former player told me, 'There's nothing I wouldn't do TO him or FOR him'."

Rodgers and I agree; that concise statement defines with vigor the uniqueness of Wobble.

Jon Reeves, a small halfback at Ole Miss in the mid-Fifties, and now a homebuilder in Desoto County remembers Wobble.

"You can't put the character of Wobble in a little box," Jon explained. "I respected him when I played under him, but I was scared to death of him, too."

Later Jon and Wobble became very close friends. When Wobble and Sara got ready to build their home in Oxford, the retired coach sought consultation from his former player. "I was honored when he asked me for advice," Jon declared.

"Jon, what would you like for people to remember about Wobble?" I asked.

Quickly, Jon answered, "The two sides of Wobble. He was as tough as a man could be but cared deeply about all of us."

The book on the PHYSICAL life of Wobble may now be closed but the book on his CHARACTER remains open forever.

NOTE: Many of Wobble's salty words have been changed at the request of Sara Davidson.

WOBBLE DAVIDSON ON NICKNAMES

When a coach cares enough to send the very best - - nickname - - that is, it means he is interested in the player and has invested some thought into him. Wobble certainly did that, and more. The following is his view on nicknames, taken from information printed by Ole Miss Sports Information.

The article and list of nicknames have been modified. Not all the nicknames were assigned by the coach, many were.

WOBBLE SAYS —-

"A nickname, to an athlete, is somewhat like a second christening without the pomp and circumstance or being formerly recorded on a birth certificate. These contrived monikers are often descriptive of his talents or deficiencies, peculiarities or merits, anatomical irregularities or abnormal appendages, traits, mannerisms, and even nationality."

"The nicknames may be enhancing, flattering, or derogatory. They may cause some dubious thoughts and quizzical glances from those not too well acquainted. Some athletes have acquired more than one nickname and survived them all, while others try to live down an acquired name as their lives evolve and become more sedimentary or refined."

Billy Ray "Blinky" Adams

Warner "Spider" Alford

Vaughn "Cosmetics" Alliston

James "Hoss" Anderson

J.W. "Ape" Arnette

Winkey "Hooch Belly" Autrey

Don "Bird Legs" Barkley

William Earl "Foggy" Basham

Preston "Bags" Bennett

Bob "Mr. Clean" Benton

Bernard "Mole" Blackwell

George L. "Koochy" Blair

Treva "Bookie" Bolin

A.L. "Showboat" Boykin

Kimble "Pigeon Toes" Bradley

George "Bags" Brenner

Billy "Dog" Brewer

Fred E. "Baby Butt" Brister

Oscar "Honey" Britt

W.D. "Dump" Burnett

Alan "Anheuser" Bush

Lindy T "Chief" Callahan

Lee "Poodle Dog" Castle

Hanson "Bull" Churchwell

James H. "Fats" Clark

Milton R. "Hoppy" Cole

Charles A. "Roach" Conerly

Paige "Cesspool" Cothren

Milton "Whooping" Crain

Eddie "Bullet Head" Crawford

Jimmy "Tank" Crawford

Doug "Legs" Cunningham

Roland H. "Aire" Dale

Jerry S. "Gut Foot" Daniels

J.W. "Wobble" Davidson

Curtis R. "Blinky" Davis

Herman "Eagle" Day

Luther "Curly" Dickens

Donald "Duck" Dickson

Kenneth D. "Skinny" Dill

Wilson "Wissy" Dillard

Bruce "Dillinger" Dillingham

John "Kayo" Dottley

Bob "Ace" Drewry

Doug "Snake" Elmore

Louis A. "Hap" Farber

Gordon W. "Rocky" Fleming

Ken "Dynamite" Farragut

Charles "Bear" Ferrill

Jackie "Bird Legs" Flack

Charles "Nasty Ned" Flowers

J.S. "Buntin" Frame

Bobby Ray "Waxy" Franklin

Floyd "Smiley" Franks

Frank "Jerk" Furlow

Robert M. "Rat Tails" Garrigues

Al "Band Aid" Gerrard

Charles "Chick" Gladding

Glynn "Squirrel" Griffing

Frank "Hobby Horse" Halbert

Parker "Bullet Head" Hall

Whaley "Hook" Hall

Douglas "Moose" Hamley

Leon C. "Marbles" Harbin

Everett "Hairline" Harper

Frank E. "Grumpy" Hart

Gerald "Scooter" Harvard

Willie "No Neck" Hickerson

Billy "Mama" Hitt

John A. "Puss" Hovious

Ray "White Rat" Howell, Jr.

Quinnis "Fuzzy" Huddleston

Bill "Mama" Hurst

Marvin "Turkey Buzzard" Hutson

Billy Ray "Mule" Jones

Hermit "Ice Pick" Jones

Robert "Anvil Foot" Khayat

Billy R. "Grumpy" Kinard

Frank M. "Bruiser" Kinard

George "Grumpy" Kinard

Charles "Jock" Laird

Carl "Hoppy" Langley

George "Moon" Lambert

Lewis R. "Lead Foot" Lanter

James H. "King" Lear

Harold "Monk" Lofton

Billy R. "Gold Tooth" Lott

George "Goose" Lotterhos

Jerry "Milk Toast" McKaskel

Worthy "Pillow" McClure

Robert "Slick" McCool

Rush "Jug Head" McKay

B.F. "Puny" Mann

E. William "Indian" Matthews

Charles "Trash" Montgomery

George C. "Buzz" Morrow

Roy Lee "Chucky" Mullins

Harvey A. "Ham" Murphy

Bruce "Pinky" Newell

Sam "Soupy" Owen

C.K. "Indian" Patridge

James E. "Buster" Poole

James E. "Pockets" Poole, Jr.

Leslie "Cesspool" Poole

Oliver "Hollywood" Poole

Ray S. "Teeth", "ToJo" Poole

Kenneth "Stump" Powell

J. Richard "Possum" Price

Leroy "Polio" Reed, Jr.

Jon "Mice" Reeves

Lake "Muscle Eye" Roberson, Jr.

Fred F. "Pappy" Roberts, Jr.

Joseph "Mau Mau" Robertson

Reggie "Mr. Peepers" Robertson

Bobby "Sheep Dog" Robinson

John W. "Iron Head" Robinson

Warner A. "Nubbin" Ross

C.L. "Baby" Rounsaville

Herbert "Doodle" Rushing

Michael W. "Coot" Russell

Richard H. "Stump" Russell

Farley "Fish" Salmon

Billy "Greaser" Sam

Bill "Nub", "Minus" Schneller

James L. "Boy Pig" Shows

Clyde "Wide Eyes" Simmons, Jr.

Jackie "Gorilla" Simpson

Claude M. "Tadpole" Smith

Lee J. "Stormy" Smith

Ralph A. "Catfish" Smith

Ralph G. "Bream" Smith

Robert "Thunder" Smith

Stewart E. "Preacher" Smith

Thomas Larry "Popeye" Smith

James W. "Pappy" Smith

Ed G. "Dust Blower" Stone

Charles "Chico" Taylor

Tommy "Nipple Nose" Taylor

Marvin "T-Shirt" Terrell

Ray "Spud Nose" Terrell

Dalton "Pepper" Thomas

J. Larry "Popeye" Thomas

Frank "Twinkle Toes" Thorsey

Jerry "Greek" Tiblier

Thad "Pie" Vann

Gerald "Hubby" Walker

James "Punchy" Walters

Jack "Pop" Warner

Richard "Pop" Weiss

Lloyd "Bully" White

Murray "Mule Head" Williams

Robert "Gentle Ben" Williams

Sebastian "Snake" Williams

John D. "Hot Shot" Williams

James "Cowboy" Woodruff

Lee T. "Cowboy" Woodruff

Robert "Skull" Yandell

Billy G. "Foots" Yelverton

THANK YOU SO MUCH

To those who contributed stories:

Billy Ray Adams	Charlie Flowers
Buddy Alliston	Louis Guy
Rodgers Brashier	Buddy Harbin
Jack Cavin	William Ottis Hurst
Bull Churchwell	Robert Khayat
Bobby Crespino	Gerald Morgan
Sara Davidson	Sam Owen
Wobble Davidson	Edd Tate Parker
Reed Davis	Dewey Patridge
Art Doty	Barney Poole
Bob Drewry	Ray Poole
Charles Duck	Wanda Poole
Jim Dunaway	Richard Price
Chubby Ellis	Jon Reeves
Doug Elmore	Richard Weiss
Bobby Fisher	Horace Williams

To Stan Torgeson: who had many more important things to do than dig out a long forgotten tape, first from the inner sanctum of his memory, then from the reservoir of his files.

To Lois Sawyer Jackson: my secretary for many years who recently married and moved to Houston, Texas, for typing the manuscript.

To Clay Cavett: Ole Miss M-Club Alumni Chapter

To Langston Rogers: Ole Miss Sports Information Department

To Bill Dabney: Book Layout